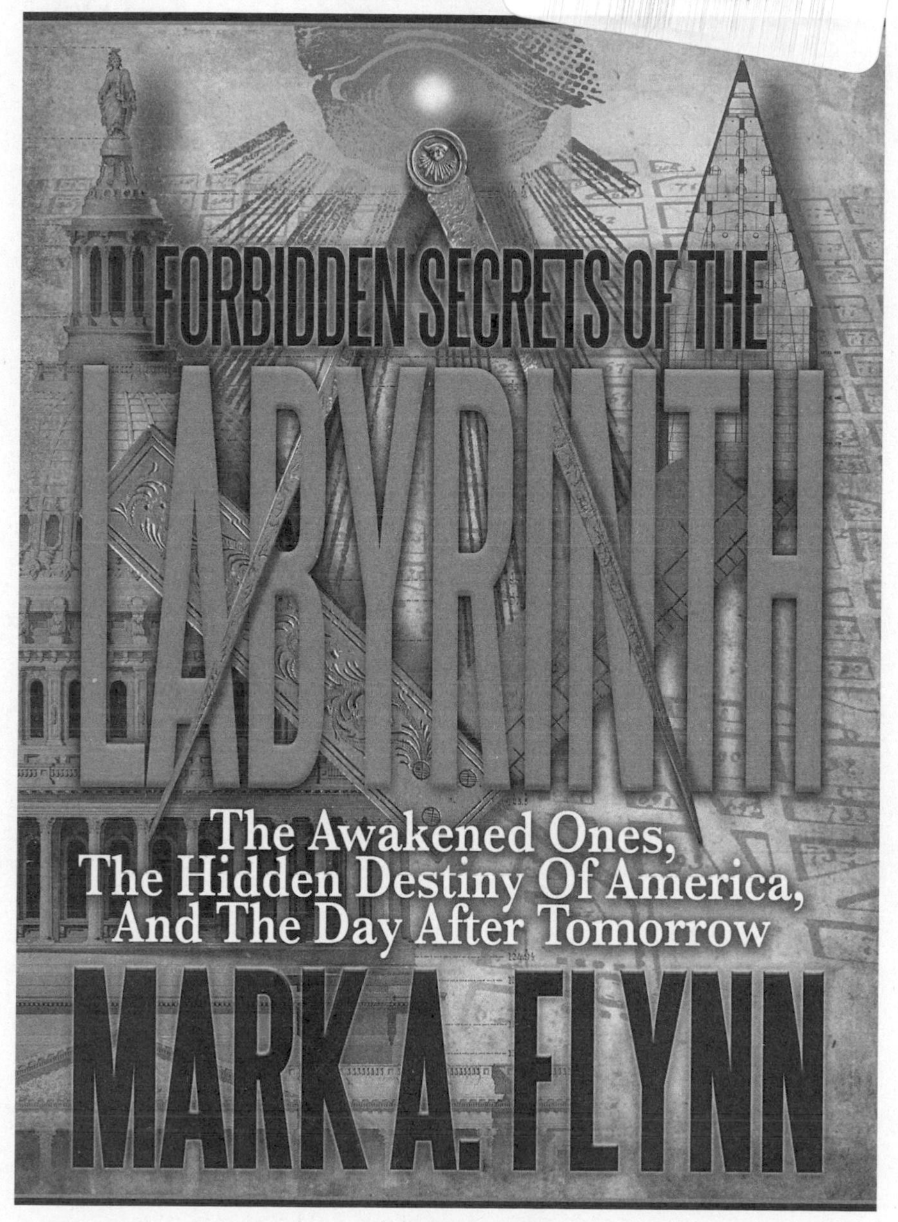

DEFENDER
CRANE, MO

FORBIDDEN SECRETS OF THE LABYRINTH:
THE AWAKENED ONES, THE HIDDEN DESTINY OF AMERICA, AND THE DAY AFTER TOMORROW

Defender
Crane, MO 65633
 Published 2014.

Printed in the United States of America.

ISBN: 978-0-9904974-0-0
A CIP catalog record of this book is available from the Library of Congress.

Cover illustration and design by Daniel Wright: www.createdwright.com.

Unless otherwise noted, Scripture quotations are from the Holy Bible, Authorized King James Version.

DEDICATION

This book is dedicated to my late twin brother,
David E. Flynn.

CONTENTS

ACKNOWLEDGMENTS

I would like to thank Daniel Noyes and Treva Abel for their excellent fellowship, support in discussion, proofreading, and literary advice without which this book would not have been possible.

INTRODUCTION

There is a religious institution whose members are the most devout and serious of any faith on earth. Those who are a part of this institution unquestionably believe in a god that directs their activities, and they look to this deity with the ultimate hope of gaining his favor. They, unlike many of the people who ascribe to the popular religions of today, have no doubt that their god lives and interacts with them. They see the favor their god bestows upon them. The riches and power gained through their piety actively demonstrate the reality of their god's existence.

This institution seeks the acquisition of wealth, the free pursuit of pleasure, and control over others. The precepts of this secretive religion are contra to that of the Judeo-Christian religion that values, above all, love for one's fellow man. The followers of this belief consider the people outside of their group inferior creatures, unworthy of their god, but necessary for manipulation towards the completion of their final objective. Through devotion, submission to the will of their god, and dedication to his secretive plan, they believe that they will achieve immortality and live in a coming golden age when their god will appear on earth and rule them in a new paradise of his design.

The truth about their secret plan is hidden in plain sight all around us—as long as we know what we're looking at. With the proper perspective, one reserved for those enlightened few who are worthy of the secrets, their god's plan is revealed. This book offers that perspective. But unlocking this understanding requires a key. The key, in this case, is ancient mythology. In the same way the Rosetta stone unlocked Egyptian hieroglyphs, mythology unlocks the secrets of the ancient mystery religion that is still being practiced.

Classical mythology has simply been considered a collection of stories designed to illustrate the nature of man or explain the natural world in a fashion in which a less-technological society would, by attributing the power of nature to human-like gods. However, the gods of myth were not merely made-up characters; they did exist, although not in the sense one might expect.

Perhaps they were beings from other worlds who visited the earth in the distant past. Perhaps they were angelic beings. Of course, this would mean that there is at least some truth in Christianity, since the God of the Christians is credited with creating angels. As it turns out, the secret religion may have the answer—an answer that has been kept hidden from the "unworthy" for thousands of years. Intriguingly, the answer begins to reveal itself in the place where the secret religion and Judeo-Christian beliefs have common ground: the place of beginning, the book of Genesis and the Garden of Eden.

Throughout this book, an unparalleled clarity of meaning behind the secrets of the mystery religion is achieved. Meaning that has been purposefully obfuscated for millennia to keep the "unworthy" in ignorance is suddenly understood by those who are willing to read and see it for themselves. Vital concepts are illustrated in a clear fashion, each one building on the one before it, until a complete understanding of the whole is realized. Using this framework and through the unique lens provided in the proper sequence, the meaning of the stories of myth are finally understood.

This god who grants wealth and power in this life requires devotion, worship, and sacrifice from his followers. To his followers, he promises a transformation of this world and a resurrection where they will be like him. To help his elect reach this goal, he has given them a symbol of his power and protection, an object that has been documented throughout history to wield enormous power.

Just as the Judeo Christian God gave his followers the Ark of the Covenant, which held great power, the god of the mystery religion has given his followers an object whose existence has been kept secret since the Middle Ages and whose power is beyond comprehension. To those who possess it, this object grants absolute hegemony as well as the ability to increase supremacy through war and conquest. Throughout history, when men failed in their discernment of its power, it was transferred to others more worthy. This object still exists and is in the possession of an elite group who will do anything to protect it. This book reveals its history, where it is hidden today, and the greatest secret of all—its ultimate purpose.

Some of the topics that will be encountered along the path of discovery include:

- The meaning behind Greek architectural form, the pillars, and pediments in light of the explanation provided by Plato.
- An explanation of the path from the goddess represented and worshipped by the illuminated ones at Washington, DC, to their mythological roots beginning with the Garden of Eden.
- The essence and function of currency in light of the Garden of Eden and the plan that the Nachash in human form, aka the Antichrist, has to replace the system in the near future.
- Why the battle of Troy is important and related to the arcane power of the Washington Monument.
- The establishment of the symbolic "pillars" at the separation of heaven and earth that occurred in the Garden of Eden.
- The concept of a circuit-based alphabet and its relationship to the symbol for the One God.
- The symbolic beginning of the false reunification of heaven and earth demonstrated by the destruction of the Twin Towers.

- The identification of the true object of worship practiced by modern Freemasonry—Athena to Mithras, to Attis and Cybele, Semiramis and Ninus, Neith and Ra, Isis and Osiris, and Eve and the Nachash.
- How the story of Samson incorporates the esoteric meaning of the mystery religion and prophesies its destruction.

The identification of the ultimate goal that has been looked forward to for thousands of years by the elite members of the mystery religion might come as a surprise to many. The truth might seem too fantastic to accept. But the fact that the common man will be made aware of this truth also points to the lateness of the hour. The final objective of the *great work* that was started by the ancient mystics will be accomplished. The true end however, won't occur as they have been expecting.

THE LOWLY INITIATE

All things are implicated with one another, and the bond is holy; and there is hardly anything unconnected with any other thing. For things have been coordinated, and they combine to form the same order. For there is one universe made up of all things, and one God who pervades all things, and one substance, and one law, one common reason in all intelligent animals, and one truth.

—Marcus Aurelius, *Meditations*, vol. VII[1]

At the end of thirty-two months of study at a college (Latin: *collegium,* "the connection of associates") or university (Latin: *universitas,* "the whole, aggregate"),[2] the degree candidate seldom thoughtfully considers the esoteric meaning of the graduation ceremony. All participants don academic-style caps and gowns. The cap, described as a "mortarboard," has a peculiar flat, square-sectioned top over an eggshell-like head cover with a tasseled string hanging over one edge. During the ritual, the graduate must ascend an elevated stage from the left to meet an individual wearing a black, five-sided, Tudor-style cap. This dean or head artisan offers a scroll or diploma (Greek: δίπλωμα, "folded paper") indicating the degree earned with his left hand, and he shakes the graduate's hand with his right. Descending the stage from the right, participants move the tassel string from one side of the mortarboard in an arc from the right to the left, mimicking the arching path of the sun from horizon to horizon, and forming the lower portion of the Masonic square and compass symbol.

What the new graduate may not know is that he or she is merely partaking in an *initiation* ceremony, and to one with understanding, the meaning of the ritual confirms the participant's *vulgar* (Latin *vulgus*, "the common people, the multitude, a crowd, the throng") status. This initiation is not to some higher intellectual class; it simply allows an offering of humble symbolic mortar to the artisans as a lowly apprentice or *hod* carrier. The priesthood of those who are able to bestow *degrees* considers the graduates as base laborers involved merely in carrying supplies to the more skilled bricklayers or stonemasons of the mystic "work."

Consider the individual symbolic components of the graduation. The hawk or *hod* that the graduation cap symbolizes is a tool used to temporarily hold mortar so that a bricklayer can apply it to a surface using a different tool. Like the cap, it consists of a board about nine inches square, but with a perpendicular handle fixed centrally on the opposite side. In a similar manner as the dean who hands the diploma to the graduate, the bricklayer artisan holds the hawk horizontally with the left hand and applies the material on the hawk with a tool (engages the "tool," who is the graduate) held in the right.

Most people today are unaware of the fortunate time in which they live. Literature, mythology, and volumes of historical research have been made available to everyone on earth. There are etymology tools available for Latin, ancient Greek, and Hebrew. The works of Plato, Aristotle, Homer, Pythagoras, Strabo, and Josephus can be rapidly searched for specific words, and the words themselves can be deciphered from their original language down to the letter. In contrast, a person fluent in Latin, Greek, and Hebrew who might have had access to all the libraries of Europe during the Renaissance would have been unable to duplicate the amount of research in a lifetime that the average person could do today from his or her computer in the course of a few months.

Imagine how much Isaac Newton would value what most people take for granted if he had lived today. Such a wealth of freely obtainable information back in the seventeenth century would have been unfathomable. While the availability of information is miraculous in the sense of its mere existence, it is unfortunate that the activities of the average person living today are centered primarily on the base pursuit of pleasure and avoidance of pain.

Since the Middle Ages, mythology has been an important part of a *classical* education, along with the required language skills in Latin, Greek, and Hebrew. Pythagoras taught that thinking skills were necessary for the serious study of philosophy and theology (i.e., mythology). A student prepared by first studying grammar, logic, and rhetoric, and then moving on to the *quadrivium,* or the "four subjects"—arithmetic, astronomy, geometry, and music.[3] The intellectual pursuit of knowledge of the highest rank or class (classical works) was the mythology of the ancient Mediterranean world. It was the highest class of knowledge and was sacred in the sense that students could approach it only after they had proven worthiness. After this stage, the student then required an equally worthy mentor.

Today, typical college graduates complete a course of study with the singular goal of becoming sufficiently enabled to do some job. They are lucky to have received anything more than just a cursory survey of ancient mythology. Today, the serious study of these subjects is left out *intentionally*. It must be this way *because* of the fact that current information available is levels of magnitude greater than it was during the last two thousand years, and learning about and understanding the meaning behind mythology, as it was once taught, is only for the chosen few. The great secret concerning the whole human race has been, at its quintessential base, required to be kept secret to all but those worthy.

Over the centuries, Freemasons have been instructed to hide their secrets from the vulgar. The "Obligation of First Degree," or oath to secrecy, from Malcolm C. Duncan's *Ritual and Monitor of Freemasonry* written in 1866, outlines this directive:

> I...do hereby and hereon most solemnly and sincerely promise and swear, that I will always hail, ever conceal, and never reveal,

> any of the arts, parts, or points of the hidden mysteries of Ancient Free Masonry, which may have been, or hereafter shall be, at this time, or any future period, communicated to me, as such, to any person or persons whomsoever, except it be to a true and lawful brother Mason, or in a regularly constituted Lodge of Masons.
>
> All this I most solemnly, sincerely promise and swear, with a firm and steadfast resolution to perform the same, without any mental reservation or secret evasion of mind whatever, binding myself under no less penalty than that of having my throat cut across, my tongue torn out by its roots, and my body buried in the rough sands of the sea, at low-water mark, where the tide ebbs and flows twice in twenty-four hours, should I ever knowingly violate this my Entered Apprentice obligation.[4]

The belief that the study of philosophy and mythology is the highest form of intellectual pursuit has never waned; the value of the quest for knowledge of the highest class has not been forgotten. A select group has had the answers to questions and concepts that the majority of people have never once considered. The keepers of the knowledge restrain it, because its nefarious source instructs them to do so.

Realizing the importance that the ancients attributed to the classics leads to the question: What can be gained through their understanding? A good way to prepare for the answer at this point is to pose the questions that this book will address:

- Is there meaning behind the various classical architectural forms used throughout the world and specifically in Washington, DC?
- Why is the Greek goddess Athena so often represented in art and architecture? When did she first appear in history?
- What is the meaning behind the triangle reference to Athena that the Pythagoreans so often used?
- Why are the characters and story of the Trojan War still remembered today even though the city of Troy had been thought fictional up to its discovery in 1868?[5]

- Why have the sacred symbols of ancient mystery religions of the Egyptian, Babylonian, and Anatolian civilizations been so readily adopted by the Greeks and Romans, and why do they remain in Freemasonry?
- What was the Roman cult of Mithras all about?
- How do the answers to these questions give insight to the meaning of the enigmatic symbols on the dollar bill, the currency of the United States?

We have the advantage of the information-rich time in which we live to help answer these questions. In addition, this exploration will begin with the unique perspective that there was a common beginning for every mythological legend and that there was a fundamental entity involved. The realization of the *who,* and the nature of the source, is extremely vital to gaining understanding of the history and destiny of our world. This source has suppressed the understanding of the highest class of knowledge, since it would be counterproductive to one of its paramount goals: to have as many as possible forget or never believe that a *creator* exists. Understanding the events of the past concerning man and the entity known as the "giver of knowledge" requires a belief in the God who created him. Conversely, learning that the giver of knowledge truly exists might well manifest into an unshakable faith in that creator God.

Like a maze, the stories in myth over the many millennia have been intentionally obfuscated in order to hide the secrets from the vulgar. Often, the paths that lead to the discovery behind the meaning of the stories, characters, and ideas in myth often come to abrupt ends where the student must retrace his steps back to alternate paths in order to gain understanding. The paths of a maze mimic the method of exploration and discovery used in this book, and are consistent with the nature of the subjects covered. In the account of Theseus and the Minotaur, Theseus was given a ball of thread known as the "clue" that led him through the Labyrinth. This book will be the thread or *clue* through the maze, where each subject explored will add to the unraveling of confusion and lay out a path so that an *escape* to understanding is possible.

In education, the practice of exposing the student to information in a global fashion but leaving out the various, meaningful relationships between concepts until enough has been surveyed to come suddenly to a more complete understanding is known as the *gestalt* (German: "essence or shape of an entity's complete form") method, from the nineteenth-century philosopher, Christian von Ehrenfels (1859–1932).[6] Through exploration, the seeker of truth will find everything needed for a gestalt moment when understanding suddenly coalesces. This is the path through the maze where each subject explored brings new choices of direction.

The Minotaur of myth, the half-man, half-bull monster, is said to have waited in the center of the Labyrinth of Knossos. We shall see that we do not need to kill the Minotaur to find our way out of the maze as Theseus did. We can do much more: We can understand what the complex maze of mythology represents, as well as the mystical identities of the characters involved and how they relate to our existence.

The information in this book offers a path showing the way that offers freedom from ignorance, and is quite different from that desired by an initiate to the mystery schools. The clues provided are meant for the nonelite and non*tapped*, as the goal is contra to those of the elite.

The *great secret* concerning the human race that has been kept hidden to all but those who are worthy concerns the process of becoming "god-like." Going farther and finding the origin of the genesis of this secret will bring us to the understanding of the true path, which leads to eternal life.

The door we must open to gain entrance to the Labyrinth is also the place of the genesis of humanity, the Garden of Eden.[7]

1

LOCUS AMOENUS—*EDEN*

Et in Arcadia ego

—Nicolas Poussin (1594–1665)

The *locus amoenus* or "place of delight" was an idyllic place of romance, comfort, and safety. The Latin term endured into medieval romance literature and typically consisted of three elements—trees, grass, and water—usually depicted within a walled enclosure.

According to the Judeo-Christian theology, God created humanity in the Garden of Eden:

> And the LORD God formed man [of] the dust of the ground, and breathed into his nostrils the breath of life; and man became a living soul.
>
> And the LORD God planted a garden eastward in Eden; and there he put the man whom he had formed. (Genesis 2:7–8)

It was in the garden (Hebrew: gan, גַּן, "enclosed garden, enclosure," from the root, *ganan,* גָּנַן, "to defend, cover, surround") where God walked with His new creation in harmony. The perfection of this state where man and God coexisted was the absolute definition of paradise. "Eden" in Hebrew means "delight."

Metamorphoses (Latin: *Metamorphoseon Libri,* "Books of Transformations") was written by the Roman poet Publius Ovidius Naso (43 BC–AD 18), or Ovid, and is considered one of the most influential works of literature in Western culture. It is made up of 250 myths that chronicle the history of the world from Creation to the glorification of Julius Caesar. The first English translation of the original Latin hexameter was by William Caxton in 1480.

In *Metamorphoses,* Ovid described various situations occurring in "pleasant gardens" (*locus amoenus*) that would change to sites of violence or calamity (*locus horridus*), accentuating the pain and loss experienced by the characters involved. The book of Genesis describes the first garden that underwent a change from perfection to calamity:

> And the LORD God planted a garden eastward in Eden; and there he put the man whom he had formed.
>
> And out of the ground made the LORD God to grow every tree that is pleasant to the sight, and good for food; the tree of life also in the midst of the garden, and the tree of knowledge of good and evil. (Genesis 2:8–9)

There was only one command from God to man concerning what he should *not* do, and that was to refrain from eating the fruit of the Tree of Knowledge of Good and Evil:

> And the LORD God commanded the man, saying, Of every tree of the garden thou mayest freely eat:
>
> But of the tree of the knowledge of good and evil, thou shalt not eat of it: for in the day that thou eatest thereof thou shalt surely die. (Genesis 2:16–17)

Adam and Eve could not have understood death, since the Tree of Life was accessible and since they had never seen, heard of, or experienced death in any way. Eating the fruit of the Tree of Knowledge of Good and Evil caused the transformation from locus amoenus to locus horridus.

> So he drove out the man; and he placed at the east of the Garden of Eden cherubim, and a flaming sword which turned every way, to keep the way of the tree of life. (Genesis 3:24)

God would not have made Adam and Eve incapable of appreciating His creation or His presence. He did not create paradise and somehow limit its inhabitants' abilities to experience joy, peace, love, vitality, the appreciation of beauty, and harmony with Him. The tree did not simply offer the knowledge of evil, but evil along with good. In other words, the fruit did not cause the earth to become a place of absolute evil or outer darkness, but a place likened to one where the *subtlety* of evil would be allowed to infect it.

According to the account in Genesis, a creature that obviously had been created before man entered the realm of heaven on earth in order to convince Eve to try the fruit of the tree. In Hebrew, the name for the creature is *Nachash*. It is important to understand that Nachash was the creature's name *before* it appeared to Eve in the garden.

The root of "Nachash" in Hebrew means to "practice divination," "to observe signs and omens," or "to learn by experience." *A Hebrew Lexicon of the Old Testament*—originally written by the theologian and master of the Hebrew language, Heinrich Friedrich Wilhelm Gesenius (1786–1842)—known as *Gesenius' Lexicon* adds that the meaning of Nachash is "hissing" or "whispering."

The creature possessed extraordinary abilities for planning and observation. It understood the intellectual and emotional nature of the *dust creatures* that God had created and knew exactly how to persuade and manipulate them.

The Nachash was unique in all of God's creation, since it was the first to presume to act contrary to the will of its Creator—the Creator of the universe. Later, the term "Nachash" would come to equal a "serpent" after it took on the value of the curse that God gave it as punishment for its act the garden.

The term "subtle" is used to describe one of the creature's essential attributes:

> Now the serpent was more subtle than any beast of the field which the LORD God had made. And he said unto the woman, Yea, hath God said, Ye shall not eat of every tree of the garden? (Genesis 3:1)

The term for "subtle" in Hebrew is *aruwm* (עָרוּם), from the root *aram* (עָרַם). In addition to meaning "subtle" or "crafty," aram can mean "to uncover" or "to be spiteful."[8]

> And the eyes of them both were opened, and they knew that they [were] naked; and they sewed fig leaves together, and made themselves aprons. (Genesis 3:7)

The consequence of obedience to the will of the Nachash was profound for Adam and Eve. It is important to recognize that in addition to the concept of the nakedness that they experienced for the first time, Adam and Eve took on an aspect of the Nachash: "subtleness." The word in Hebrew for "naked," *eyrom*, comes from the root aram, meaning "subtle."

Eden can be considered the beginning of a *circuit* where the perfection of the coexistence with humankind's Creator was interrupted and a void was created where everything was lost. A state of "lacking" replaced immortality, paradise, and communion with God. It was here in the garden that calamity occurred. Understanding what was lost, the nature of the interruption, and the creature that interjected itself into paradise are the keys to understanding the past, present, and future of mankind. The bright angel or cherub who presumed to interrupt the union of heaven on earth has left us many clues as to his intentions concerning the plans for his future and ours.

Arrows Are More than Just Arrows

In any important historical event, the sights, sounds, emotions, ramifications, aftermath, and heroes and villains involved can morph into words that describe *objects* over time. Such words bring to mind the quality of a character involved or the effects of the event. An example of a term that has undergone this type of morphing phenomenon is the word "arrow." Over a vast period of time, the word has come to represent the human senses experienced during the visit of the Nachash in the garden.

Is there a connection between the Nachash, who is described as a "bright angel" (Hebrew: *heylel*, הֵילֵל, "shining one")[9] and the concept or image of an arrow or archer? Apart from the effect of wounding or killing its target, the arrow moves too fast to avoid once it has been set on a true course. It usually doesn't kill its victim immediately, but inflicts prolonged agony until death occurs through loss of blood. A strike from a poisonous snake is similar to the effect of an arrow: sudden pain, with the victim being left to contemplate inevitable death.

Descriptions of arrows have obvious allusions to the effects of the advice the snake gave Eve. Consider the idea of separation, which occurred for the first time after the Nachash's visit, and its effects: deception, being cut off from life (death), banishment, and fear. The descriptive words illustrating the appearance and demeanor of the Nachash and the results of its interaction with Eve have also become mixed in their meaning with a physical object that has similar injurious characteristics.

The majority of words in Hebrew that describe either the physical appearance of the Nachash or the result of Adam and Eve following its advice have multiple meanings. The list of appropriate words and phrases that describe separation from God and the expulsion from paradise that forced Adam and Eve to experience terrible new states of being would be vast. Rather than investigating the meaning of Hebrew words that might relate to the event in the garden or terms for the appearance or nature of the Nachash, consider that the connection between the idea of striking weapons (such as arrows) and these terms has already been made. If this is true, then words illustrating this connection could be found by searching for three words: "arrow," "spear," and "dart."

Strong's Concordance, written by Dr. James Strong (1822–1894), is an exhaustive cross reference of all the words in the King James Version of the Bible back to the original Hebrew or Greek. The results of a search in the concordance for the Hebrew words "arrow," "dart," and "spear" support the idea of the arrow-Nachash descriptive connection. To illustrate the phenomenon more fully, the complete list of Hebrew words returned for each search is included here despite its length. The italicized terms relate to the qualities of the Nachash, and are explored in later chapters:

From *Strong's Concordance:*

Ashpah, אַשְׁפָּה—The *sense of covering* or a quiver or arrow-case:—quiver, from **Ashshaph,** אַשָּׁף—From an unused root (probably meaning *to lisp, i.e. practice enchantment*); *a conjurer:—astrologer.*

Ben, בֵּן—a son (as a builder of the family name), afflicted, arrow, bullock, calf, mighty, rebel, robber, spark, stranger, tumultuous one.

Chets, חֵץ—*A piercer,* i.e. an arrow; by implication, a wound; figuratively, (of God) thunder-bolt; the shaft of a spear:—+archer, arrow, dart, shaft, staff, wound.

Chatsats, חָצַץ—To chop into, pierce or sever; hence, to curtail, to distribute (into ranks), to shoot an arrow:—archer, *cut off in the midst.*

Chatsats, חָצָץ—Something cutting; hence, gravel (as grit); also an arrow:—arrow, gravel (stone).

Da'ah, דָּאָה—a primitive root; to dart, i.e. fly rapidly:—fly.

Lehabah, לֶהָבָה—*flame*(*-ming*), head (of a spear).

Macca, מַסָּע—the sense of projecting; a missile (spear or arrow); *also a quarry* (*whence stones are, as it were, ejected*):—before it was brought, dart.

Qesheth, קֶשֶׁת—of bending: a bow, for shooting (hence, figuratively, strength) *or the iris*:—arch(-er), + arrow, bow (-man, -shot).

Qippowz, קִפּוֹז—from an unused root meaning to contract, i.e. spring forward; an arrow-snake (as darting on its prey):—great owl.

Resheph, רֶשֶׁף—a live coal; by analogy lightning; figuratively, an arrow, (*as flashing through the air*); specifically, fever:—arrow, (*burning*) *coal, burning heat,* + *spark, hot thunderbolt.*

Shebet, שֵׁבֶט—from an unused root probably meaning *to branch off;* a scion, i.e. (literally) a stick (for punishing, writing, fighting, ruling, walking, etc.) or (figuratively) a clan:—correction, dart, rod, scepter, staff, tribe.

Shelach, שֶׁלַח—a missile of attack, i.e. spear; also (figuratively) a shoot of growth; i.e. branch:—dart, plant, put off, sword, weapon.

Tslatsal, צְלָצַל—a clatter, i.e. (abstractly) *whirring* (*of wings*); (concretely) a cricket; also a harpoon (as rattling), a cymbal (as clanging):—cymbal, locust, shadowing, spear.

Taqa, תָּקַע—a primitive root; to clatter, i.e. slap (the hands together), clang (an instrument); by analogy, to drive (a nail or tent-pin, a dart, etc.); by implication, to become bondsman by handclasping):—blow (a trumpet), cast, clap, fasten, pitch (tent), *smite, sound, strike*, X suretiship, thrust.

Yadah, יָדָה—a primitive root, literally, to use (i.e., hold out) the hand; physically, to throw (a stone, an arrow) at or away; especially to revere or worship (with extended hands); intensively, to bemoan (by wringing the hands):—*cast* (*out*), (make) confess(-ion), praise, shoot, (give) thank(-ful, -s, -sgiving).

Yarah, יָרָה—a primitive root; properly, to flow as water (i.e. to rain); transitively, to lay or throw (especially an arrow, i.e. to shoot); figuratively, to point out (as if by aiming the finger), to *teach*:—(+) archer, cast, direct, *inform, instruct*, lay, shew, shoot, *teach*(*-er,-ing*), through.

Zanaq, זָנַק—a primitive root; properly, to draw together the feet (as an animal about to dart upon its prey), i.e. *to spring forward:—leap.*

Ziyqah, זיקות—*what leaps forth, i.e. flash of fire*, or a burning arrow; also (from the original sense of the root) a bond:—chain, fetter, firebrand, spark.

The clashing noises made by cymbals as shown in the words *tslatsal* and *taqa* are notable, since the same type of cymbal-clattering noise making often occurs in ancient rituals and in the dances of gods and goddesses associated with the serpent. (Explained in chapter 5.)

The Hebrew prophet Ezekiel described the Nachash as being a member of the angelic class known as the *cherubim* (singular form, *cherub*):

> *Thou hast been in Eden the garden of God;* every precious stone [was] thy covering, the sardius, topaz, and the diamond, the beryl, the onyx, and the jasper, the sapphire, the emerald, and the carbuncle, and gold: the workmanship of thy tabrets and of thy pipes was prepared in thee in the day that thou wast created.
>
> Thou [art] the anointed cherub that *covereth*; and I have set thee [so]: thou wast upon the holy mountain of God; thou hast walked up and down in the midst *of the stones of fire*. (Ezekiel 28:13–14, emphasis added)

The word "covereth" stands out as a unique quality of the cherub and deserves further study. The Hebrew for "cover" in Ezekiel 28:14 is *cakak:* "Cakak סָכַךְ saw-kak' or sakak. A primitive root; properly, to entwine as a screen; by implication, to fence in, cover over, (figuratively) protect:—cover, defense, defend, hedge in, join together, set, shut up."[10]

The similarly sounding but unrelated Hebrew word, *chakam*, adds a further description to the nature of the Nachash. "*Chakam* חָכַם khaw-kam', a primitive root, to be wise (in mind, word or act): exceeding, teach wisdom, be (make self, shew self) wise, deal (never so) wisely, make wiser."[11]

Chakam is an appropriate description of the clever Nachash, who knew exactly how to persuade and manipulate the *dust creatures* in the garden.

Ezekiel described the appearance of the cherubim:

> And every one had four faces: the first face [was] the face of a cherub, and the second face [was] the face of a man, and the third the face of a lion, and the fourth the face of an eagle....
>
> Every one had four faces apiece, and every one four wings; and the likeness of the hands of a man [was] under their wings. (Ezekiel 10:14, 21)

The cherubim's four faces are linked to the arrangement of the constellations that encircle the earth. In *Cydonia: The Secret Chronicles of Mars*, David Flynn writes:

> The cardinal points of the Zodiac are the constellations Taurus, Leo Scorpio and Aquarius. They correspond to the bull, lion eagle which was an ancient form of Ophiuchus, the serpent holder that stands above Scorpio, and the man.[12]

The Fiery Nachash

The majority of Greek words having something to do with fire, burning, flame, or the color red have three letters appearing in the beginning: The word for "fire" is *pyr* (πυρ [*pi-upsilon-rho*]) or *pyros* (πυρος [*pi-upsion-rho-omicron-sigma*]). Other words that happen to begin with *pi-upsilon-rho* in Greek are "pear," "stone," and "wheat."

While it is not such a stretch to say that the color red would be a near equivalent to the word "fire," the link between "fire" and "pear" can be understood in light of the story in the garden. The word for "fruit" in Hebrew is *peri* (פרי, *pe,* פ—"mouth," *resh,* ר—"head," *yod,* י,—"hand"). The letters reveal a very famous moment when Eve moved an object with her hand toward her head and mouth.

While wheat kernels or stones look like little pears, the "fire" prefix for stone and wheat would come after the "fire"-"pear" link, as it alludes to the creature that "walked up and down in the midst of the *stones of fire*" (Ezekiel 28:14, emphasis added).

Looking at the Phoenician root meaning of the individual Greek letters in the word "pyros" reveals more layers of significance:

- *PI* (Ππ), from the Phoenician *pey* or Hebrew *pe* (ף), meaning "mouth." The upper-case *Π* is used as a symbol for a *plaintiff.* In the lower case, it represents the ratio of a circle's circumference to its diameter in Euclidean geometry.
- *Upsion* (Υυ), from *waw* or *vav* meaning "hook, peg or spear." Pythagoras wrote about the path of virtue or vice and likened it to the letter *upsilon.*
- *Rho* (Ρρ), from Phoenician *rosh* or Hebrew *resh* (ר), meaning "head," is used as a symbol for the radius in cylindrical or spherical coordinate systems.
- *Omicron* (Οο) is derived from the Phoenician letter *eyn,* meaning "eye."
- *Sigma* (Σσς), from the Phoenician *shin,* means "tooth or weapon."

> It has been theorized that *sigma* was a Greek letter for "hissing," based on the verb σίζω ("sízō"), meaning, "I hiss."[13] The lowercase in word-final position of the *sigma* (ς) is distinctly snakelike.

Based on this information, the interpretation of the esoteric letter meaning of the Greek word "pyros" ("fire") is this: "A highly intelligent, far-seeing, hissing, snake-like creature with the appearance of a bright, burning red flame encouraged a choice that caused pain."

Later, we will explore the ideas of a circuit (*pi*) and plaintiff as they relate to the pyros creature.

Who Is the Phoenix?

The bright, four-winged cherub that filled the garden with its red, fiery light was an impressive sight while it rested in the Tree of Knowledge of Good and Evil. The image of the tree with the angel overwhelming its branches has a name: phoenix, a word related to the Greek *phoinos* (φοῖνιξ) or *phonos,* meaning "blood red or purple," the color of royalty. "Phonos" also means "to murder" or "to strike."[14]

The Nachash in the Tree of the Knowledge of Good and Evil[15]

The description of the phoenix as a legendary bird of fire fits the image of the cherub in the tree. Ovid describes the mythical bird in his *Metamorphoses:*

> There is one, a bird, which renews itself, and reproduces from itself. The Assyrians call it the phoenix. It does not live on seeds and herbs, but on drops of incense, and the sap of the cardamom plant. When it has lived for five centuries, it then builds a nest for itself in the topmost branches of a swaying palm tree, using only its beak and talons. As soon as it has lined it with cassia bark, and smooth spikes of nard, cinnamon fragments and yellow myrrh, it settles on top, and ends its life among the perfumes.
>
> They say that, from the father's body, a young phoenix is reborn, destined to live the same number of years. When age has given it strength, and it can carry burdens, it lightens the branches of the tall palm of the heavy nest, and piously carries its own cradle, that was its father's tomb, and, reaching the city of Hyperion, the sun-god, through the clear air, lays it down in front of the sacred doors of Hyperion's temple.[16]

The Phoenix by Friedrich Johann Justin Bertuch (1747–1822)[17]

Like the phoenix, the Nachash "dies" from the curse imposed on him by God:

> And the LORD God said unto the serpent, Because thou hast done this, thou [art] cursed above all cattle, and above every beast of the field; upon thy belly shalt thou go, and dust shalt thou eat all the days of thy life. (Genesis 3:14)

As we shall see, the Nachash plans to raise himself up from the ashes of his demise and throw off the image of the lowly snake, ultimately to rule the earth as the god of light. The Nachash caused paradise to become a desert and introduced death, which can be thought of as the first act of murder done to humanity. Indeed, in His response to the Pharisees who were questioning Him, Jesus referred to the cherub specifically as a murderer:

> Ye are of [your] father the devil, and the lusts of your father ye will do. He was a murderer from the beginning, and abode not in the truth, because there is no truth in him. When he speaketh a lie, he speaketh of his own: for he is a liar, and the father of it. (John 8:44)

The palm tree is often seen in Masonic art. The *pinnate* or "feather-like" leaves of the palm mimic the appearance of the cherub in the tree. In a typical reversal to the true nature of the Nachash, a person wandering in a desert might find an oasis. In the place surrounded by the "death lands" of the desert, the water of the oasis and the life-giving fruit of the *Phoenix dactylifera* (date palm) would provide restoration.

Jesus not only points out the fact that Satan was the original murderer, but indicates that he imitates the truth by taking the symbol of the cherub of light in the tree symbolized by the phoenix:

> Jesus said unto them, If God were your Father, ye would love me: for I proceeded forth and came from God; neither came I of myself, but he sent me. (John 8:42)

The Nachash has always tried to mimic Christ and replace Him as the "light" of the world. Just as Ovid describes the cycle of the phoenix, the Nachash comes from himself and for himself. Those who intentionally reject God to follow the cherub's false light, the "way of desolation," epitomize what it means to break the Second Commandment:

> Thou shalt not take the name of the LORD thy God in vain; for the LORD will not hold him guiltless that taketh his name in vain. (Exodus 20:7)

The Hebrew word for "vain" is *shav* (שָׁוְא), meaning "emptiness," "nothingness," "falsehood," or "desolation."

THE ARCH-ARCHERY

The arrow concept that mirrors the quality of the creature in the garden can be extended to the centaur, the mythological bowman whose skill makes the investigation of the etymology behind the word "archer" significant. In Greek, the *archi* or *arch* means "the chief or principal leader, the first in rank." The Nachash was known as the most beautiful of the cherubim.[18] The Latin *arche* from the Greek "archi" also means "to begin, to lead, rule or govern." In architecture, the structure known as the "arch" used extensively in stonemasonry actually comes from the Proto-Indo-European word for the bow and arrow. "Archery," from the Latin *arcus,* is "the art, practice, or skill of propelling arrows with the use of a bow." Anyone known in mythology as a skilled archer was also an effective hunter or warrior.

The Greek "arche" has the primary meaning of a beginning or an origin of first cause. The meaning of arche or *archai* during the eighth century BC always meant the beginning foundation of an idea or principle, or something with a solid foundation.

The Greek philosopher Anaximander (610–546 BC) was the first to use the term "arche," later termed the "substratum" by Greek philosopher Aristotle (384–322 BC) to ascribe something as having divine attributes. The substratum is the divine, eternal substance that encompasses all things and gives them value.[19]

Aristotle used "substratum" to define an element or principle not easily understood but described in such a way as to make its existence possible. To him, the arche was the element or first principle of all that exists.

He considered it as a permanent substance in nature *physis*, and asserted that all things first come to be from it until they are resolved into a final state.[20]

The "illuminated" stonemasons who utilize the structure of the arch symbolically honor and represent their god continually in the form and names of the structures they skillfully produce. The classical Greek philosopher Plato's (428–347 BC) "unmoved mover," or "demiurge," as described later by the Neoplatonists, had three ordering principles:

1. Arche: "Beginning"—the source of all things
2. Logos: "Word"—the underlying order that is hidden beneath appearances
3. Harmonia: "Harmony"—numerical ratios in mathematics

The idea of the arche, logos, and importantly, special ratios, combine to make a distinctive building style known today as Palladian architecture, which has been used in all of the ancient temples. The Greek poet Hesiod (750—650 BC) wrote that the arche or origin of the world started with nothingness (chaos) and that the earth and heaven came forth out of chaos.

PILLARS

A wedge or obstruction was set in place at the time when the union of God and men, heaven and earth, was interrupted. An appropriate illustration of this new state would be the symbol of the pillars. The most rigid and graceful of architectural edifices were set in place after Eden and now symbolically separate heaven from earth. They were partly removed at the reconciliation between God and man that occurred through the death and resurrection of Jesus Christ. Pillars that represent the physical separation of heaven and earth still exist. In later chapters, we will see how these will be "removed" in the future, first in a counterfeit fashion by the Nachash and then by God Himself.

The Story of Atlas

Mythology has been interpreted as allegory to explain or personify natural phenomena or approached as an ancient evolution of science. Usually, comparative mythology interprets the narratives as simply "stories," fashioned perhaps to teach, entertain, or explain the origin of man. It is not common to look at the characters in myth and make associations with them to ones found in story of the Garden of Eden. However, by using and extending this unique approach, the characters that might not directly display any similarities to the characters in Eden can be understood to represent antitypes or ones gaining symbolic forms or attributes through the point of view of the Nachash.

The personification of the pillars in Greek myth is the Titan Atlas. In his *Theogony*, Greek for "origin of the gods," Hesiod wrote that the first of all the gods was Chaos. He reigned as the "personification of nothingness."

Magnum Chaos represented at the Basilica di Santa Maria Maggiore in Rome[21]

The next primordial god from Chaos was the Earth (Greek: *Gaia*), who brought forth Heaven (Greek: *Ouranos*; Latin: *Uranus*). The first-born of Earth and Heaven was Chronos (Time). He was the first of the Titans ("Strainers"), as Heaven called them. Time was said to have hated his father, Heaven:

> But these sons whom be begot himself great Heaven used to call Titans (Strainers) in reproach, for he said that they strained and did presumptuously a fearful deed, and that vengeance for it would come afterwards.[22]

Earth and Heaven made many children as well as terrible monsters. Some of these were the Cyclopes, Cottus, Briareos and the fifty-headed, one-hundred-armed Gyes. Heaven knew that he would eventually be dethroned by one of his children and decided to force all of his newly born back into Gaia to a place called Tartarus, the "horrid or terrible region":

> And he used to hide them all away in a secret place of Earth so soon as each was born, and would not suffer them to come up into the light: and Heaven rejoiced in his evil doing.[23]

Gaia and her son, Chronos, were so angered by Heaven's actions that they made plans to punish him. Hesiod writes:

> And Heaven came, bringing on night and longing for love, and he lay about Earth spreading himself full upon her.
>
> Then the son from his ambush stretched forth his left hand and in his right took the great long sickle with jagged teeth, and swiftly lopped off his own father's members and cast them away to fall behind him. And not vainly did they fall from his hand; for all the bloody drops that gushed forth Earth received, and as the seasons moved round she bare the strong Erinyes and the great Giants with gleaming armour, holding long spears in their hands and the Nymphs whom they call Meliae all over the boundless earth.[24]

After Chronos took his father's throne, he decided to reimprison his siblings, turning to the same unjust rule as his father. He began swallowing his own children from his sister-wife Rhea.

Rhea and the Goddess Cybele

Rhea is related to the important goddess Cybele (described in chapter 5) since she is identical in many ways. Both have been represented in ancient art as a woman seated on a throne flanked by lions.[25]

Rhea or Cybele[26]

Birth of Zeus

Rhea hid her youngest child, Zeus, from Chronos by substituting him with a stone wrapped in a blanket. She then brought Zeus to a cave, where he was raised by Amalthea or Adrasteia, meaning "the inescapable," and the goat god, Pan. Amalthea has also been referred to as Ide or the Nymph of Mt. Ida, which is located in Anatolia (modern-day Turkey), and is said to be the origin of the Trojans and the mountain of the goddess Cybele. Adrasteia was also known as the remorseless Greek goddess of revenge, Nemesis.

Infancy of Zeus by Jacob Jordaens, early 1630s (Louvre Museum). Notice the goat god Pan to the right.[27]

In order to keep Cronus from hearing the infant, Amalthea had the dancing male youths known as the Kuretes or Korybantes yell and clash their spears against their shields to drown out his cries. This is an example of how the myth/garden comparative technique is applied. The stone substitute can be thought of as a trick that Satan orchestrated against the one God, the idea being that the will of God was subverted by the Nachash and that "God-Zeus" now *needed to be nurtured by the actions of the Nachash and Eve.* Using this unorthodox technique, the image of Zeus (God), Amalthea

(Eve), and Pan (Nachash) together in the cave hiding away from Chronos is perversely similar to the situation in the Garden of Eden.

Earth and Chronos

The Nachash was present when God made the earth. The oldest book of the Old Testament, Job, mentions the establishment of the earth:

> Where wast thou when I laid the foundations of the earth? declare, if thou hast understanding.
>
> Who hath laid the measures thereof, if thou knowest? or who hath stretched the line upon it?
>
> Whereupon are the foundations thereof fastened? or who laid the corner stone thereof;
>
> When the morning stars sang together, and *all the sons of God shouted for joy?* (Job 38:4–7, emphasis added)

A passage earlier in the book of Job identifies Satan as having the moniker "son of God":

> Now there was a day when the sons of God came to present themselves before the LORD, and Satan came also among them. (Job 1:6)

The account of how Earth and Heaven became separated in Ovid's *Theogony*, the "castration of paradise" as mirrored in the garden story, was, according to the view of Satan, a twisted representation of the act he orchestrated against God—his Creator, the God of the Universe. It was the ultimate disrespectful and undignified "emasculation" of God Himself.

The "Zeus-God" helped by Rhea-Cybele and later Amalthea (Eve) in the *Theogony* can be viewed as another outrageous insult, as if the act of Satan in the garden was for God's sake or that God didn't realize the greatness of what Satan had done for Him. "God" was "nurtured," *allowed,* to participate in this "plan of the subtle."

Chronos takes on a new identity at this point in the *Theogony* and represents the "unjust" God. The act of bringing Eve to the knowledge of good and evil is symbolically reversed with Rhea protecting Zeus as a saving, helpful act to God Himself, who now is represented by Zeus.

The Titanomachy

Upon reaching adulthood, Zeus became the cupbearer of Cronus and tricked him into drinking a mixture of mustard and wine, causing him to vomit up his swallowed children. After freeing his siblings, Zeus led them in rebellion against the Titans, known as the "Titanomachy," or "War of the Titans."

Atlas entered the story along with his brother, Menoetius, as enemies of Zeus fighting on the side of the Titans. When they were eventually defeated, all of them except Atlas were confined to Tartarus. Zeus condemned Atlas to stand at the western edge of Gaia (Earth) to hold up Ouranos (Heaven) on his shoulders, *and prevent the two from ever resuming their primordial embrace.*

Hesiod writes about the birth of Atlas:

> Now Iapetus took to wife the neat-ankled maid Clymene, daughter of Ocean, and went up with her into one bed. And she bare him a stout-hearted son, Atlas: also she bare very glorious Menoetius and clever Prometheus, full of various wiles, and scatter-brained Epimetheus.[28]

The name "Atlas" comes from the Proto-Indo-European root *tel,* "to uphold or support."[29] Two Atlases are mentioned in ancient myth. The Atlas involved in the Titanomachy was the son of the Titan Iapetus and the Oceanid Asia or Klyménē (Κλυμένη). The other is known as the son of Poseidon and Cleito, the daughter of Evenor, king of Atlantis.[30] The term "Atlantic Ocean" refers to the "sea of Atlas," and "Atlantis" refers to the "island of Atlas."

The Hidden Meaning of Myth

The ancients believed that the gods of myth had power over nature and the lives of men, and it is reasonable to start the exploration of the highest class of knowledge with their origin. The study of mythology in this regard would not seem to present such a difficult task. While some of the stories passed down over the centuries might have been lost, we can still gain a good understanding of the quality, personality, and power of each mythological deity. We still have the works of many ancient writers who describe them at great length. Why, then, was theology considered to be the highest form of knowledge? We must consider that there must be more to mythology than simply understanding the attributes and origins of the ancient gods. An underlying secret woven into the stories of myth can only be discerned by the wise. Approaching this learning from the point of reference of the Garden of Eden is an essential part of our unique path of exploration. Continuing in this fashion but stepping back for a moment to the study of a portion of the quadrivium (i.e., geometry) will add the wisdom necessary to continue.

The Greek philosopher Plato understood the importance of geometry, writing:

> The knowledge at which geometry aims is knowledge of the eternal, and not of aught perishing and transient.... geometry will draw the soul towards truth, and create the spirit of philosophy, and raise up that which is now unhappily allowed to fall down.[31]

2

THE SUN

> Geometry, the first and noblest of sciences, is the basis on which the superstructure of Masonry is erected. By geometry, we may curiously trace nature, through her various windings, to her most concealed recesses. By it, we discover the power, the wisdom, and the goodness of the Grand Artificer of the Universe, and view with delight the proportions which connect this vast machine.
>
> —Thomas Smith Webb, *Freemason's Monitor,* 1863[32]

In *The Republic*, Plato uses the sun, the cave, and the segmented line as a metaphor for the source of intellectual illumination. He writes:

> The eye is unique in that it requires the medium of light to operate. The best source of this light is the sun and with it all objects can be clearly discerned. The same can be said for the understanding of intelligible objects or philosophical concepts.... When [the soul] is firmly fixed on the domain where truth and reality shine resplendent it apprehends and knows them and appears to possess reason, but when it inclines to that region which is mingled with darkness, the world of becoming and passing away, it opines only and its edge is blunted, and it shifts its opinions hither and thither, and again seems as if it lacked reason.[33]

Plato also says the sun and the *good* ("the object of knowledge") are both sources of "generation":

> The sun…not only furnishes to those that see the power of visibility but it also provides for their generation and growth and nurture though it is not itself generation.… In like manner, then…the objects of knowledge not only receive from the presence of the good their being known, but their very existence and essence is derived to them from it, though the good itself is not essence but still transcends essence in dignity and surpassing power.[34]

The Cave

The dialogue between Socrates and Glaucon, whose name means the same as Glaucus (his story is related in chapter 9), "wide-shining," continues to the idea of *the cave*. Socrates asks Glaucon to imagine a cave inhabited by prisoners who have had their legs chained since birth and their heads fixed in one direction so that they could only see a single wall in front of them. Behind them is light from a fire that is partly blocked by a raised ramp where free people walk while carrying various objects. The prisoners never see the ramp or the people walking behind them, but can only watch the shadows, unaware of the fact that they are shadows. They can hear echoes off the wall from the noise produced behind them.

Socrates suggests that the prisoners would believe that the *shadows* were the most real. The philosophers among them would be ones who could explain the forms on the wall and predict their movements.

The Escape

Socrates then asks what would happen if one of the cave dwellers was released and shown all the things that had cast shadows. He would not recognize or be able to name anything, and would insist that the shadows on the wall were "real."

Plato's Allegory of the Cave by Jan Saenredam, according to Cornelis van Haarlem, 1604, Albertina, Vienna[35]

Socrates asks:

What if the man was compelled to look at the fire: wouldn't he be struck blind and try to turn his gaze back toward the shadows, as toward what he can see clearly and hold to be real? What if someone forcibly dragged such a man upward, out of the cave: would not the man be angry with the one doing this to him? And if dragged all the way out into the sunlight, wouldn't he be distressed and unable to see "even one of the things now said to be true" because he was "blinded by the light?"

The freed prisoner's senses would change after some time on the surface. Soon he would see more of things around him, until he could finally look towards the sun.

He would learn that sun was the "source of the seasons and the years, and is the steward of all things in the visible place, and is in a certain way the cause of all those things he and his companions had been seeing."[36]

The Masonic fraternities venerate Apollo, who slayed the dragon Python, as well as St. George, who saved the Selenite king's daughter.

To the illuminated, the idea of "slaying the dragon" would represent that moment when the initiate "left the cave."

Return to the Cave

Socrates next asks Glaucon to consider the condition of this same man returning to the cave:

> Wouldn't he remember his first home, what passed for wisdom there, and his fellow prisoners, and consider himself happy and them pitiable? And wouldn't he disdain whatever honors, praises, and prizes were awarded there to the ones who guessed best which shadows followed which? Moreover, were he to return there, wouldn't he be rather bad at their game, no longer being accustomed to the darkness? Wouldn't it be said of him that he went up and came back with his eyes corrupted, and that it's not even worth trying to go up? And if they were somehow able to get their hands on and kill the man who attempts to release and lead them up, wouldn't they kill him?[37]

The prisoners, still ignorant of the world behind them, would be afraid of anything outside of what they already knew and would consider the intellectually *free* man corrupted or stupid.

The Line Segment

Plato used the allegory of the Divided Line to further illustrate the path to knowledge:

> Now take a line which has been cut into *two unequal parts*, and divide each of them again in the same proportion, and suppose the two main divisions to answer, one to the visible and the other to the intelligible, and then compare the subdivisions in respect of their clearness and want of clearness, and you will find that the

first section in the sphere of the visible consists of images. And by images I mean, in the first place, shadows, and in the second place, reflections in water and in solid, smooth and polished bodies and the like:

Do you understand?

Yes, I understand. Imagine, now, the other section, of which this is only the resemblance, to include the animals which we see, and everything that grows or is made.[38] (emphasis added)

The Divided Line illustrates levels of man's understanding from illusion to belief, to reason, and finally then to philosophical understanding or *illumination.* So to Plato, the sun represented the highest form of philosophical understanding or *noesis* and was ultimately expressed in his "Ideas" or "Forms of the Good."

The second-highest form of understanding consisted of mathematical reasoning, or *dianoia,* which includes theoretical science and abstract mathematical objects such as numbers and lines. Beliefs about physical things were a step up from the lowest level of understanding, or *pistis,* which included empirical science and physical objects. The lowest form was opinion and illusion, *eikasia,* the shadows and reflections of physical objects.

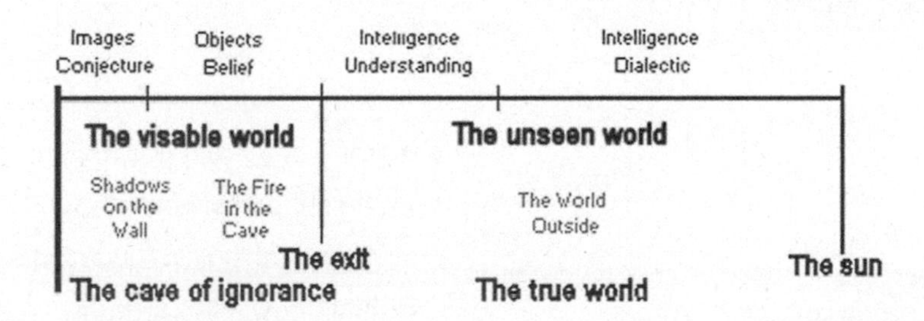

The Allegory of the Divided Line[39]

The highest level of understanding that Plato called noesis describes a true perception of all that is hidden. This has sometimes been referred to the understanding gained though the *mind's eye* in contemporary philosophy.

The symbolism of the bright sun representing the highest attainable, yet hidden, knowledge is also referred to as "gnosis," a word whose origin was from the same area as the Minoan cult of the Minotaur: the island of Knossos.

Plato did not describe just a random bisection of the line into "two unequal parts." He was referring to the "golden section" described by Greek philosopher and mathematician Pythagoras (570–495 BC). The "golden section" or "golden mean" is a divine ratio based on the irrational number expressed as *phi* Φφ (1.6180339887…), which comes from the Phoenician letter *qof* (needle head) or the Hebrew letter *qoph* ק. *Phi* can be understood and easily calculated by first taking the numbers 0 and 1 and making a list of the sum of the previous two numbers:

0,1 (0+1 = 1) 1, (1+ 1 = 2) 2, (1+ 2 = 3) 3, (2 + 3 = 5) 5, (3 + 5 = 8) 8, …

This is known as the Fibonacci Series, after the Italian mathematician Leonardo Fibonacci (1170–1250), who introduced it. *Phi* then can be estimated by dividing any two numbers in the series. By using numbers that have been calculated farther down the series, a more accurate value can be attained.

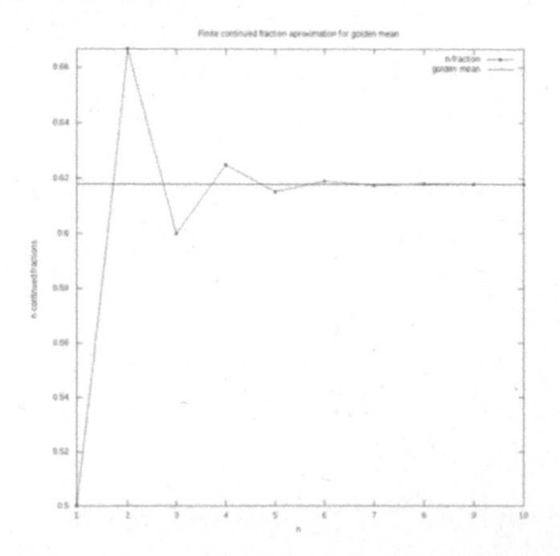

A graph of the approximations to the reciprocal golden ratio by ratios of Fibonacci numbers. Notice the values become closer and closer to *phi* as the sequence progresses.[40]

Example:
8/5 = 1.6
233/144 = 1.61805

Alternatively, the formula $(1+\sqrt{5})/2$ can be used to find the true value for *phi* Φ (1.6180339887…).

The golden section, then, is any line or area divided into sections that have the *phi* ratio. To do this, first draw a horizontal line of any length (A) and then draw a line exactly half the first length and connect it on one end at 90 degrees (B). Draw an arc from the center point (C) starting at the 90-degree corner to the hypotenuse and call that point (D). Continue with one more arc from the center point E starting at D back down to the horizontal line. This point (X) is where the line must be divided to be "golden."

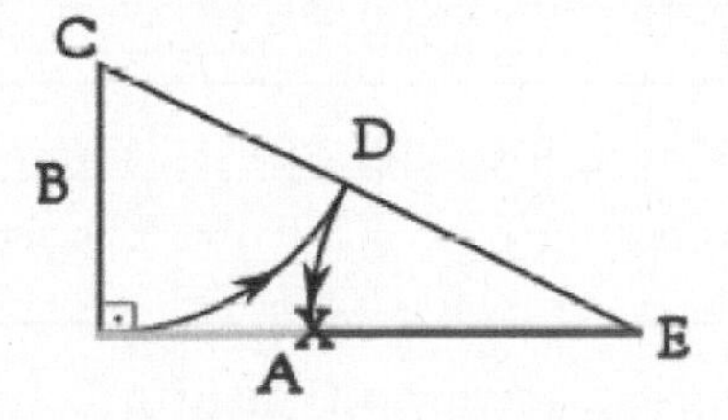

The line A divided into a golden section.

A triangle constructed in this manner has the vertical (B) and horizontal (A) line lengths of 1 and 2. Using the Pythagorean theorem, the hypotenuse (D) then equals $\sqrt{5}$. ($c = \sqrt{a^2 + b^2}$.)

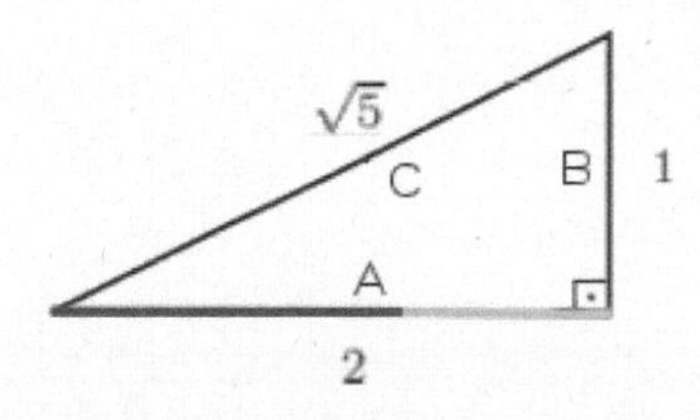

When the values for the length of each side are arranged in this manner, $(1 + \sqrt{5}) / 2$, it is the equation for finding the value of the golden ratio known as *phi* Φ.

$\Phi = (1 + \sqrt{5}) / 2 = 1.6180339887\ldots$

Triangles with the longest and shortest side lengths equaling Fibonacci numbers (Pythagorean triples) are known as Fibonacci triangles. The triangle described above is not considered golden, per se, but Fibonacci.

A regular pentagram has five golden triangles at each corner. The ratio of the longest and shortest sides (a:b) equal *phi*.

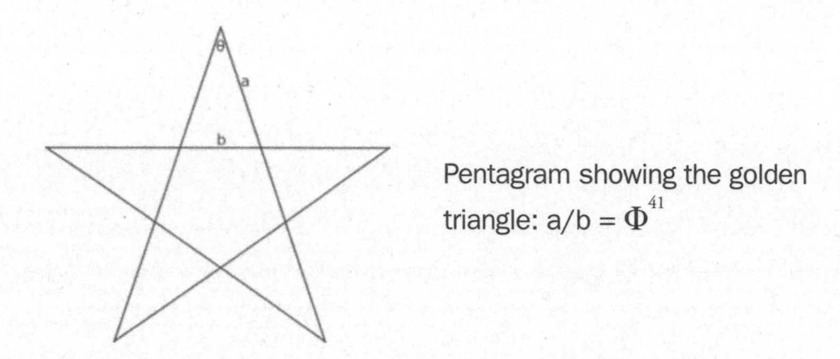

Pentagram showing the golden triangle: $a/b = \Phi$[41]

These triangles are used frequently in Palladian architecture and are commonly seen above entranceways always supported below by two or more pillars. Although the Palladian style was used far back in the construction of ancient temples, the term "Palladian" architecture came from the work of Venetian architect Andrea Palladio, also known as Andrea Di Pietro della Gondola (1508–1580).

Palladio was influenced by the work of the Roman architect Vitruvius (80–15 BC) and employed by the Italian scholar Gian Giorgio Trissino from 1538 to 1539. Trissino took an interest in Palladio's work and helped him study ancient architecture in Rome. Later he gave Gondola the name "Palladio" based on the goddess of wisdom, Pallas Athena.[42]

The Pediment

The Palladian structure that uses the golden triangle is known in classical architecture as the pediment and is supported by columns or pillars. Pediments most commonly either have the two halves of a golden triangle set side by side or consist of two Fibonacci triangles. The area inside the structure is known as the tympanum. The pediment was used in ancient Greek temples and earlier by the Phrygians in Anatolia.

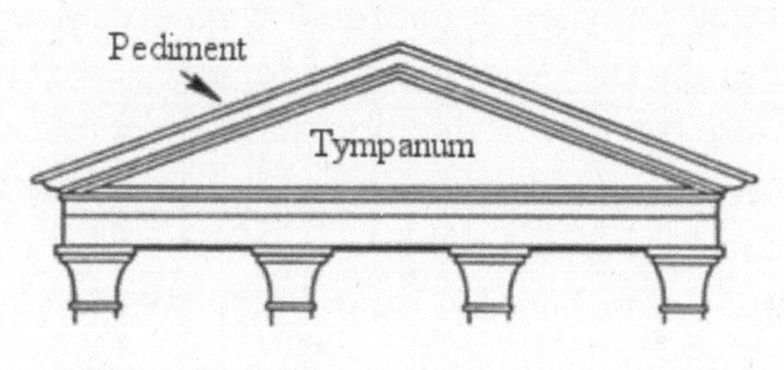

Pediment and tympanum[43]

The word "pediment" comes from the Latin *pedis*, meaning "foot." The Latin suffix *ment* relates to "a means of a place, state, instrument, or agent of action." The related form, *menti*, from the Latin *mens* or *mentalis*, is the intellectual faculty of the mind or memory.[44] Combined, "pedi" and "ment" would make the meaning of "pediment" literally "the action at the foot." The words for doing something quickly (ex*ped*itious) or being restrained (im*ped*iment) use the idea of either freeing or restraining the feet.

The meaning and identity of who does the "action at the foot" is described in the Genesis account of God cursing the Nachash:

> And I will put enmity between thee and the woman, and between thy seed and her seed; it shall bruise thy head, *and thou shalt bruise his heel.*" (Genesis 3:15, emphasis added)

In ancient Greek temples, the area inside the triangle of the pediment, the tympanum (from the Greek: *typtein*, "to beat or strike"), which can be related to the idea of the noisy Korybantes mentioned in the *Theogony* present at the cave of Amalthea, often contained elaborate depictions of the god or gods to whom the temple was dedicated. In modern Palladian architecture, various symbols or scenes are used. Masonic temples commonly use the compass and square, or simply the letter *G*, which is said to stand for "geometry under the Great Architect of the Universe,"[45] or the third letter in the Hebrew alphabet, *gimel* (ג).

The symbolism behind this architecture is obvious when one examines the meaning of the form of the structure and the words used to describe it. The nature of the knowledge or institution represented by the building or the temple is related to the curse that God gave the Nachash in the garden. It is a rejection of the curse and a reversal of the idea that the serpent would strike at the foot of Man-God. He would now strike at His head. This reversal is contained in the institution or the religious system the structure represents. It is from where the "strike" referred to in Genesis 3:15 will manifest itself. It is the literal representation of rebellion to God's will and symbolizes both the separation brought about by the interjection of evil via the "light bringer" in the garden and the illuminated concept of where to look for the reconciliation of that separation, the symbol that commonly resides above or in the middle of the triangular pediment or through its entrance. Buildings with Palladian architecture represent the institution and power of the kingdom of the Nachash.

The quintessential example of Palladian architecture, the Parthenon of Athena, is the expression of the parthenogenesis of Eve (explained in chapter 3). Eve became the first to know good *and* evil though her own act of willful disobedience. The golden-ratio geometry of the pediment expresses the genealogical, numeric progression of parthenogenesis. The descriptive terms used in the structure depict the esoteric symbols representing the plans of the Nachash after his interruption of paradise as well as his hatred for God.

Notice that the entry in Genesis in which God curses the subtle, bright angel happens to be in chapter 3, verse 14:

> And the LORD God said unto the serpent, Because thou hast done this, thou [art] cursed above all cattle, and above every beast of the field; upon thy belly shalt thou go, and dust shalt thou eat all the days of thy life. (Genesis 3:14)

It is not a coincidence that 3:14 stands out as related to ratio of the radius and circumference of a circle, *pi* (π), for here is where everything changed. Earth and heaven were united; God walked with man. After the parthenogenesis of Eve, the pillars separating heaven and earth were set in place. God left the presence of humanity, and the kingdom of the Nachash was established. The columns separating the pediment from the ground represent the separation of heaven and earth. In Palladian architecture, a path is shown to the location of the knowledge that will eventually eliminate the separating columns, as one entering the structure must first pass between the pillars to the inner sanctum, where the knowledge is kept. God will join heaven and earth once more, completing the *circuit* or circle that began in Eden. Before this occurs however, the Nachash plans a counterfeit joining.

THE BIBLIOTHECA

The *Bibliotheca,* which means in ancient Greek "library" or "collection," was a summary collection from 279 volumes of classic works said to have been written by Apollodorus of Athens, who lived around 180 BC. Many of the references in this book are taken from it. Scholars have argued that Apollodorus could not have been its author, since it cites individuals who were born many years after his death, and so the term "pseudo" was added to the name as the writer of the *Library*. Today, no complete versions exist.

The patriarch Photius I of Constantinople (AD 810–893)[46] was known to have been in possession of the complete work and used it in his writings. He understood its value concerning the tales in ancient myth:

> Draw your knowledge of the past from me and read the ancient tales of learned lore. Look neither at the page of Homer, nor of elegy, nor tragic muse, nor epic strain. Seek not the vaunted verse of the cycle; but look in me and you will find in me all that the world contains.[47]

LIBRARY

The word "library" is an appropriate term for such a collection since it is related to the idea of giving one "freedom from ignorance." The 1913 edition of *Webster's Revised Unabridged Dictionary* defines *libellus* as "a little book, from liber, a book, from the sense of bark, and this from stripping separating. Hence liber, a book, and liber, free, are the same word."[48]

Connected with the Latin suffix *ary,* meaning "a person a place or a thing which, or pertaining to; connected with; having the character of; apparatus," the word "library" is "that which gives freedom." The Latin *libra*, *liber,* and *libri* can also mean "balance, to be balanced, level, to make even or a Roman pound."[49] The *Library* mentions the story of Oedipus Rex, an important character in light of the "pediment" concept.

OEDIPUS REX

Oedipus Rex (Latin: "king") was left to die as an infant by his father Laius, king of Thebes. Laius (Greek λαιός, "left") had received a prophecy from the Oracle at Delphi that he must never father a child with his wife Jocasta (Greek "shining moon"), because a son would be born who would kill him and marry her. The child born to them despite the advice of the oracle was Oedipus, which means in Greek, "swollen foot."

Apollodorus writes about the birth of Oedipus:

> And when the babe was born he pierced the child's ankles with brooches and gave it to a herdsman to expose. But the herdsman exposed it on Cithaeron; and the neatherds [cow herders] of Polybus, king of Corinth, found the infant and brought it to his wife Periboea [Greek: *peri*, περί, "round about," and *boea*, βόειος, "of an ox"[50]]. She adopted him and passed him off as her own, and after she had healed his ankles she called him Oedipus, giving him that name on account of his swollen feet.[51]

Oedipus wished to discover who his true parents were and did as his father before him, went the Oracle at Delphi for an answer. He was given the same warning: He would kill his father and marry his mother, and he should never go to his "native land." Believing the Oracle meant that his adopted parents were his true parents, he left Corinth. While driving his chariot on a narrow road, he killed his real father in a dispute on who should "make way."

After the death of King Laius, the goddess Hera sent the Sphinx (Greek: "to bind") to the kingdom of Thebes, which means "city of light." Apollodorus continues:

> For Hera sent the Sphinx, whose mother was Echidna and her father Typhon; and she had the face of a woman, the breast and feet and tail of a lion, and the wings of a bird. And having learned a riddle from the Muses, she sat on Mount Phicium, and propounded it to the Thebans. And the riddle was this:—What is that which has one voice and yet becomes four-footed and two-footed and three-footed? Now the Thebans were in possession of an oracle which declared that they should be rid of the Sphinx whenever they had read her riddle; so they often met and discussed the answer, and when they could not find it the Sphinx used to snatch away one of them and gobble him up. When many had perished, and last of all Creon's son Haemon, Creon made proclamation that to him who should read the riddle he would give both the kingdom and the wife of Laius. On hearing that, Oedipus found the solution, declaring that the riddle of the Sphinx referred to man; for as a babe he is four-footed, going on four limbs, as an adult he is two-footed, and as an old man he gets besides a third support in a staff. So the Sphinx threw herself from the citadel, and Oedipus both succeeded to the kingdom and unwittingly married his mother, and begat sons by her.[52]

The mountain where the Sphinx sat, the *Phicium,* is related to the word *phoenicium,* which is the possessive plural of the word "phoenix."[53]

The story of Oedipus is one of truth within corruption. The plan of God is well understood by Satan. The truth can be sifted from the obfuscation in ancient myth that is sometimes mixed with *mockery* that manifests the essence of the fruit of the Tree of the Knowledge of Good and Evil known by its scientific name, *pyrus cydonia*.

David Flynn relates the truth of the story:

> The real question couched ingeniously in the riddle was this, who will redeem man?
>
> The earliest prophecy in the Bible concerning the Messiah who will defeat the serpent, or the rebel cherub is in Genesis 3:15. Oedipus the Wounded Foot is symbolic of the coming Messiah, who would be born of the lineage of Adam and Eve. The defeater of the Greek Sphinx—the defeater of death—would speak the answer and the cherub would be destroyed. That is, The Word is Wounded Foot's weapon, and the means by which the bride, and all of the land, would be redeemed.[54]

Like Zeus, Oedipus was saved from an early death, raised by adopted parents, and protected until he grew strong enough to avenge the wrongs done to him. Zeus started the Titanomachy, in which he and his siblings fought against his father, Chronos. Oedipus killed the father who blocked his way to his native land, his "rightful" kingdom, just as the Oracle of Apollo at Delphi had prophesied. He went on to marry his "shining moon," an example of the amalgamation of the cherub Nachash and the woman who has been recapitulated in the many versions of the ancient goddess worship (which will be explained in depth in later chapters).

Through the lens of the subverting intent of the Nachash, the story is prophetic of his future plans. The God-Man personified in Jesus and symbolized in the story of Oedipus is replaced with an Oedipus who represents the serpent joining with Eve in victory over his unrighteous father and the establishment of his kingdom of "illumination." This is a much different answer to the question of who will redeem man.

Oedipus killed the Sphinx, the monster whose name means "to bind," while it sat on the Phicium, the "mountain of the phoenixes." The Sphinx represents the completion of the circuit that started when God cursed the snake; he rises again as the victorious Oedipus to enter his city of light.

Assigning still another twisted layer to the tale by first establishing that Oedipus is an allegory for the Redeemer by assigning the identity of Christ to Oedipus, Eve to his mother, Jocasta, and God to his father, Laius, the story is corrupted in a way that would make Oedipus a very unsuccessful savior of man since it mixes in murder, incest, and divination—all of which are expressly forbidden by God. Adding insult, Oedipus leaves Thebes after blinding himself:

> When the secret afterwards came to light, Jocasta hanged herself in a noose, and Oedipus was driven from Thebes, after he had put out his eyes and cursed his sons, who saw him cast out of the city without lifting a hand to help him. And having come with Antigone to Colonus in Attica, where is the precinct of the Eumenides, he sat down there as a suppliant, was kindly received by Theseus, and died not long afterwards.[55]

The God-man, blinded along with his daughter Antigone (Greek: "anti-man"), would leave the place of light and go to the place of Attica named for the god "Attis" (described in chapter 6) at Colonus (Latin: "tiller of the ground, husbandman, farmer"). Like Cain, the first "tiller of the ground" who was banished by God after killing his brother, Abel, he was exiled to wander in darkness. Later, Oedipus died a peaceful death and was taken by the gods.[56]

"Iluminated" illustration from the eighteenth century shows aspects of the cave, pillars, and "Eve" in front of the sun.[57]

The number-2 card of the Rider-Waite tarot card deck co created by Pamela Colman Smith (1878–1951), a British-American artist, and A. E. Waite (1857–1942), the British-American author and Freemason, both members of the Hermetic Order of the Golden Dawn, shows a "woman" between the pillars of the Temple of Solomon.

The High Priestess or the *Popess* (II) in the Rider-Waite-Smith deck[58]

The English occultist, magician, writer, founder of the religion of Thelema, and member of the Hermetic Order of the Golden Dawn, Aleister Crowley (1875–1947), demonstrated his understanding of the meaning behind the "Pediment and Pillars" as he posed for this peculiar portrait at left.[59]

Atlas supporting the pillars of heaven from a literal position on the earth, the Alas Mountains of Algeria. The prime meridian is anchored at the star Sirius in Canis Major above Gemini, symbolized by the pillars.[60]

3

ATHENA

> I begin to sing of Pallas Athene, the glorious goddess, bright-eyed, inventive, unbending of heart, pure virgin, saviour of cities, courageous, Tritogeneia. From his awful head wise Zeus himself bare her arrayed in warlike arms of flashing gold, and awe seized all the gods as they gazed.
>
> —HOMERIC HYMN XXVIII. TO ATHENA[61]

Athena was the Greek patron goddess of the city of Athens. She was the goddess of wisdom, civilization, warfare, mathematics, strength, art, law, justice, and weaving. Throughout ancient mythology, she was the companion of heroes and the nemesis of Zeus, Jupiter, Poseidon, and Neptune.

Athena has been called the *Atrytone* (Ἀτρυτώνη), "the unwearying," and the *arche*, "the first." Plato said that her name means "the mind of god," or *theou noesis*.[62] St. Justin (AD 100–165), the Christian apologist, said that "when Zeus had the idea of making a world through a word (logos) his first thought was Athena."[63]

She was the self-engendered daughter who sprang from the head of Zeus when Prometheus, the god who had given men fire, cleaved his head with a double-bladed axe known as the *labrys*. The labrys is associated with the lightning bolt. Seal stones have been found from the Greek island of

Tenedos bearing the impression of the double-bladed axe placed together with a zigzag line representing lightning.[64]

One of the most common epitaphs for Athena is the Greek *glaukopis* (γλαυκώπις), which means "bright or gleaming eyes."[65] Eve was the first human to experience the "opening of the eyes," and, like the bright-eyed Athena, she was the first to "see." Athena was the *promachos* (Πρόμαχος), the "first fighter," or "she who fights in front," and the *parthénos* (Παρθένος), born "singularly from her will." As far as the Nachash was concerned, Eve was not only the firstborn, but was so different that she could be considered a new creature altogether, as she had been created by her own act of disobedience to God. She was formed through parthenogenesis via the Nachish's strike against God with the labrys, the double-bladed lightning axe, the weapon with the two sides: the knowledge of good and evil.

The Latin version of the Bible translated by St. Jerome (AD 347–420) used the word "Lucifer" for the Hebrew *heylel* (הֵילֵל), meaning "shining one." Jesus made the comparison of Lucifer with lightning after some of His followers joyfully marveled that they had power over "demons" in His name:

> And he said unto them, I beheld Satan as lightning fall from heaven. (Luke 18:10)

Lucifer corrupted the state of mankind by striking at God Himself via Eve. The same story is related in myth. Zeus, the greatest of the Greek gods, suffered a blow from Prometheus, who gave fire (light, knowledge) to man.

The labrys-Prometheus combination *is* Lucifer, the lightning bolt striking the head of God Himself in an insolent, symbolic reversal of the curse that God gave him after Adam and Eve ate from the fruit of the Tree of Knowledge of Good and Evil. It was the beginning of the terrible new world establishing the mighty pillars separating heaven from earth.

Athena-Eve, Prometheus-Nachash, and Zeus-God together define the enigmatic Athenian epitaph, *Tritogeneia,* meaning "the third that was generated," and the Pythagoreans used the equilateral triangle to symbolize the mythological trinity, calling it Athena (Ἀθηνᾶ).[66]

PARTHENOGENESIS

A modern term for a type of reproduction not requiring fertilization is "parthenogenesis," from the Greek *parthenos* ("virgin") and *genesis* ("source or origin").

THE PARTHENON

Athena's temple on the Greek Acropolis in Athens was known as the Parthenon (Greek: Παρθενών), or "temple of the self-born virgin." The building that still stands today began construction in 447 BC when the Athenian empire was at the height of its power and was a replacement for an older version that was destroyed by the Persian invasion of 480 BC *thirty-three* years earlier. The Parthenon is considered the most important surviving building of classical Greece and the quintessential example of Doric[67] order architecture. Her temple is astronomically aligned to the Hyades star cluster in Taurus,[68] and, like most Greek temples, it was used as a treasury.

From the perspective of observers on earth, the Hyades Cluster appears in the constellation Taurus, where its brightest stars, along with the bright-red, giant Aldebaran, form a *lambda* (Λ) or triangle. The *lambda* (Λλ), the eleventh letter in the Greek alphabet, evolved from the Phoenician *lamda* or Hebrew *lamed* (ל), meaning an "ox goad."

Strong's entry for the Hebrew *lamad* (לָמַד—*Strong's* 3925) means "to goad, to teach, act diligently, expert, instruct, learn or skillful."

The word for the British unit of money, or pound (£), comes from the Latin unit of currency, the libra, represented by the capital letter *L* symbolizing the libra (scales). Again, the Latin *L* was from the Greek *Λ* and earlier Phoenician *lemda*.

The Spartans were known to have used a capital letter *lamba* (Λ) or

Pan, the Goat God[70]

chevron on their shields. The word "chevron" comes from the from old French for "rafter," since it looks like the rafter of a shallow roof, which is from the Vulgar Latin *caprione*, or the Latin *caper*, meaning "goat." It is believed that the resemblance of the rafter to the shape of the goat's angular hind legs linked the word meaning over time.[69]

In *Cydonia: The Secret Chronicles of Mars*, David Flynn further describes the significance of *lamba-libra* symbol:

> Sitting on the constellation Libra "the scales" is a small child with his finger to his lips. This is the symbol of the young Horus, which was called Heru-pa-khart, Horus the Younger, Harpocrates in the Greek, the god of silence and secrets. The portrayal of this symbol on the Dendera zodiac from 700 BC demonstrates the understanding shared by the initiates of Isis, that Libra was a sign of Horus himself.... The significance of Libra for the mystery schools is apparent in the short-hand glyph for the sign. The "rising sun" of Libra, called Hardetcher "Horus on the Horizon" indicates that those initiated into the mysteries understand Libra as representing both dualism and an esoteric symbol for "the son of Mars."[71]

Aldebaran means "follower," since it seems to chase after the Pleiades, or Seven Sisters star cluster in the night sky.

The Hyades triangle in the face of Taurus[72]

The names that identify the celestial objects that make up the Hyades triangle are all related to the core Nachash mystery religion that has gone through many subtle twists throughout the millennia. Their whole significance will be presented in forthcoming chapters. At this point, it is important to mention them in order to provide a base structure of the mystery religion that can be linked together though later revelation.

According to the English astronomer John Flamsteed (1646–1719), Aegipan, who was in the cave with Amalthea and the infant Zeus, was associated with the Hyades star cluster in Taurus. He called the cluster *Parilicium,* from the Roman *Palilia*, the feast of Pales. Pales was the shepherd's god and a feminine form of Pan. The feast of Pales occurred on April 21 and was the date of Rome's founding.[73] According to legend, the monster Typhon attacked Aegipan, or the goat Pan, and he dove into the Nile to escape. His body above water remained a goat, but the lower parts changed into a fish.[74] It was Aegipan and Hermes who secretly restored the sinews of Zeus' hand and feet during his battle with the Titans.[75]

Hyas (Greek: ἅπτω, "to fasten or bind" or "set on fire"), the brother of the Hyades, was a great archer and the son of Atlas and the Oceanid Aethra (Greek: Αἴθρα, "bright sky"). In some stories, a serpent killed him, but more commonly, he was said to have been gored by a wild boar. His sisters, the Hyades, mourned his death until they, too, died from grief and were placed among the stars. The Greek god Adonis, also killed by a wild boar, has many similarities to Hyas.

In mythology, the Hyades (Greek: Ὑάδες), meaning "the rainy ones" or "weeping ones," were daughters of the personification of the separation event, Atlas. The Pleiades (ancient Greek: Πλειάδες) were the seven sisters of the Hyades by Atlas and companions of Artemis. Their name means either "sail," since the name can be derived from the Greek *pleo* (πλέω), which means "sail" or "go by sea," or the word *peleias* (πελειάς), meaning "doves." They and the seven Hyades were also called the Atlantides, who taught and cared for the infant Dionysus, also known to the Romans as Bacchus, the androgynous god of wine and ritual madness. Bacchus is usually depicted holding the pinecone-tipped fennel staff or goad known as the *thyrsus*, the same that Prometheus used to hide the fire he stole from Zeus and gave to man.

After Atlas was forced to carry the heavens on his shoulders, the giant hunter Orion (called "Nephilia" or "Nephilim" by the ancient Arameans of Canaan),[76] was free to pursue all of the Pleiades. Zeus, in order to protect them and comfort Atlas, transformed them first into doves, and then into stars, where the constellations of Orion and Taurus still pursue them across the sky. In one version of the story, the seven sisters were so saddened by the fate of their father that they committed suicide before Zeus made them stars.

Calypso, although not a part of the Hyades cluster, was another daughter of Atlas. She enchanted Odysseus with her singing and weaving using a golden shuttle. Calypso's name means "to cover," "to conceal," "to hide," or "to deceive."[77] In *The Odyssey*, Homer describes her as the "subtle concealer of knowledge." Odysseus remained on her island for seven years and would have stayed longer if it were not for Athena asking Zeus to order his release.

4

BEES

The bee-hive is the emblem of industry, and recommends the practice of that virtue to all created beings, from the *highest seraph in heaven*, to the *lowest reptile of the dust.*

—THOMAS SMITH WEBB, *FREEMASON'S MONITOR* 1863[78]

And the Lord God said unto the serpent, Because thou hast done this, thou art cursed above all cattle, and above every beast of the field; upon thy belly shalt thou go, and dust shalt thou eat all the days of thy life.

—GENESIS 3:14

In ancient times, the honeybee was considered sacred. The Egyptians believed that bees had been created from the tears of Ra falling on the desert sand and were a symbol of kingship, associated particularly with Lower Egypt.

The exquisite, geometrically perfect beehive chambers were seemingly built by miracle and attributed to the actions of the gods. Honey was also considered sacred, not only because of its healing power and longevity, but because it was produced by the mystical insects. The miraculously generated bees symbolized human souls flying toward life from the hive at birth and returning at death. In this aspect, the bee was also a symbol of *resurrection.*

The *Apis mellifera,* or common European honeybee, was said to have first been domesticated by the Egyptians more than five thousand years ago. Depictions of humans collecting honey have been found in ancient cave art from as far back as fifteen thousand years. The Egyptian manner of creating an enclosure for bees was to coil glued rope into a conical shape, making a hole on one side. Hives, smoking pots, and honey extractors have been found at ancient sites on the island of Knossos. Aristotle wrote at length about the activities and lives of bees and proper ways to go about the art of beekeeping.[79] The Greeks believed that honey gave the gift of eloquent speech.[80]

The belief that the ancients held, that honey bestowed the powers of eloquence, leads to the story of Deborah, whose name in Hebrew (dĕbowrah) means "bee," and its root, *dabar,* means "to speak." Deborah first appears in Scripture in Genesis 35:8, where she is mentioned as the nurse of Rebekah ("ensnarer"), the mother of Jacob. She was at Bethel after Jacob left the city of Shechem after a conflict with the Canaanites. While at Shechem, Jacob asked his family to rid themselves of their foreign gods and bury their idols under an oak tree. When they arrived at Bethel ("house of God"), Deborah died and was buried under an oak tree at Allonbachuth ("the oak of weeping"). Bethel was the area where Jacob set up a stone pillar at the place where God had given him his new name, "Israel."

Interestingly, in the same way that the two oak trees bring up the idea of pillars, one in the land of evil conflict and the other in the land that God brought the family guidance, the number occurances of the name "Deborah" mimics pillars, appearing in the Old Testament eleven times.

The second person identified as Deborah was Israel's leader during the time when the nation relied on judges rather than kings to reveal the will of God. Deborah, whose court was held between Ramah, meaning a "high place of illicit worship," and Bethel, the place of Jacob's stone pillar, led the Israelites to defeat the Canaanites, resulting in forty years of peace.

In light of the soul aspect of the bee meaning, the foreign gods ended their influence at the oak (first pillar) in Shechem that was under their influence. The much-loved first Deborah "bee" who cared for Jacob's mother met death at the second pillar. Symbolically, the judge Deborah at Jacob's second state, where he was known as Israel, replaced the bee associated with the Eve-snake religion from the former state of Jacob.

The place where God began His plan for redemption was at the pillar established by Jacob, from whose descendants came the Redeemer of all humanity. The second Deborah was a *type* of the coming Redeemer. The religion of the priestesses speaking (dabar) the lies of the serpent was replaced by the woman judge acting under God's will. Routing the Canaanites was an act that freed the souls of men from the midst of the region that was the heart of the worship of the Nachash.

In one of the accounts of the raising of Zeus, Melissa (Greek: "bee"), the sister of Amalthea, was said to have fed him honey. The Oracle of Delphi was referred to as the "Delphic bee" and the second temple at Delphi was said to be built by bees.[81]

Gold plaques of the goddess Artemis as a bee, from Camiros Rhodes, from the seventh century BC[82]

The reason the bee was associated with the priestesses of Artemis and the Oracle of Delphi was that, in addition to the fact that females worked for a "queen," the esoteric symbolism of the bees as parthenogenic creatures made them holy. Like Athena springing from the head of Zeus and Eve becoming the first "new" creature, the queen bee recapitulates the pathenogenic act when it forms a drone.

The list on the next page is an illustration of the lineage of a drone bee going back five generations. Each male is a product of parthenogenesis. The queen requires two parents.

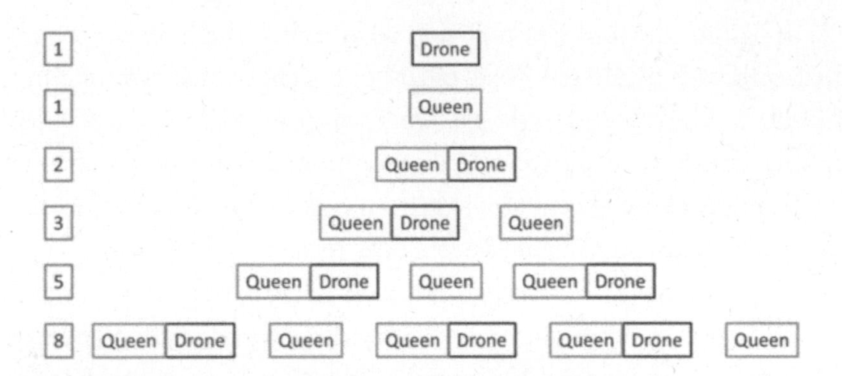

The lineage of a drone bee going back five generations[83]

The genealogy progresses in this fashion:

0, 1, 1, 2, 3, 5, 8, 13, 21, 34, 55, 89, 144, 233, 377, 610, 987…

This sequence of numbers is the same divine sequence described by Plato, the basis for the golden ratio, and of course *the* vital component in Palladian architecture.

Each queen has the power to reenact the power of Eve. The Fibonacci series that describes this power and the magic in the golden segment represent Athena-Eve. The Parthenon has been used as the quintessential example of architecture that exhibits the use of the golden ratio.

Cupid the Honey Thief (1514)
by Albrecht Dürer[84]

Cupid, the god of love, is often pictured with bees or being stung. For example, Venus tells her son Cupid, as he runs to her for comfort, that, "Thou too art like a bee, for although a tiny child, yet how terrible are the wounds thou dost inflict!"[85]

Creatures that are known to be parthenogenic are often depicted in ancient and modern "illuminated" art. One of the Founding Fathers of the United States and Grand Master Freemason, Benjamin Franklin

(1706–1790), wrote a letter to his daughter in which he mentioned that he would prefer the turkey over the bald eagle as the national symbol:

> For my own part I wish the Bald Eagle had not been chosen the Representative of our Country. He is a Bird of bad moral Character. He does not get his Living honestly....
>
> I am on this account not displeased that the Figure is not known as a Bald Eagle, but looks more like a Turkey. For in Truth the Turkey is in Comparison a much more respectable Bird, and withal a true original Native of America.[86]

The turkey is one of the two warm-blooded animals known to occasionally produce offspring through parthenogenesis.[87] The other is the chicken.

THOLOI BEEHIVE CHAMBERS

In Ancient Egyptian and Aegean cultures, the bee was believed to be the sacred insect that bridged the natural world to the underworld, and it often appeared in tomb decorations. Mycenaean *tholos* (Greek: θόλος, "domed tombs") were shaped as beehives. Tholoi chambers have been used for burial from the early Minoan period and before.[88] In Greece, nine such chambers have been discovered. One, known as the Treasury of Atreus, was built into the side of a mountain with a 131-foot entryway and lined with heavy masonry. The mammoth blocks fit together perfectly using no cement. The eighteen-foot-tall door at the entrance was topped by a giant monolith estimated to weigh 120 tons.[89]

NEITH

A weaver needs a loom—along with skill, patience, and a well-thought-out plan—in order to create a tapestry. The woman with the knowledge of the Nachash will ultimately weave men into "gods." Athena, known as the goddess of weaving, has as her Egyptian equivalent Neith, the goddess of the loom—the goddess of war, hunting and weaving—whose symbols are two arrows crossed on a shield or a loom. As the goddess responsible for weaving the cosmos into existence, Neith has been depicted with a line of stars across her back, supporting the vault of heaven. She was often shown holding an ox goad or a bow and arrows. The crossed-arrow symbol, or sometimes the weaver's shuttle, was typically displayed on top of her head in Egyptian art. She was depicted with the head of a lion, a snake, or a cow—or sometimes with all three.

The "snake" loom hieroglyph of Neith[90]

As the goddess of war, Neith was said to have invented weapons and guarded warriors' bodies after death. Part of her hieroglyph bears a resemblance to a loom, but more specifically, it resembles a loom with two snakes.

Neith holding the goad with the weaver's shuttle on her head[92]

Neith is described as being a creator god from the primordial waters who wove all of existence into being. She was the mother of Ra, sometimes described as the great cow who gave him birth. Neith was also the partner of Seth and the mother of Sobek, the crocodile god. Neith was also known as the nurse of the crocodile, but was represented as a deity that had no specific gender. In Hebrew, "Neith," "nath," is written "נת" (*nun*, נ, "serpent" or "whale," *tav*, ת, "mark").[91]

Like Athena, Neith was self born via the god Thoth. Neith was the one who sent "sparks" or "rays" into the primordial waters of Nun to create life.[93] According to Raymond O. Faulkner's *Concise Dictionary of Middle Egyptian*, the word for "rays," such as the rays of light from the sun or moon, is *stwt*. The hieroglyph for stwt can also represent an arrow or dart, and is used in words for targets and shooting.[94]

The god Mehet-Weret mentioned in the Pyramid Texts carved on the walls and sarcophagi of the pyramids at Saqqara is associated with Neith. "Mehet-Weret" means "great flood," "the one who belongs to the floods," or "cow goddess of the great flood." As Mehet-Weret, Neith emerged from the waters of Nun carrying the sun disk of Ra between her horns. Mehet-Weret is associated with the goddesses Hathor and Isis as well as Neith, all of whom have similar characteristics and were referred to as the "Eye of Ra."[95]

The Deshret

Neith was often shown wearing a red crown or Deshret, which symbolized the wearer's authority over Lower Egypt, the domain of the goddess Wadjet.

A Deshret[96]

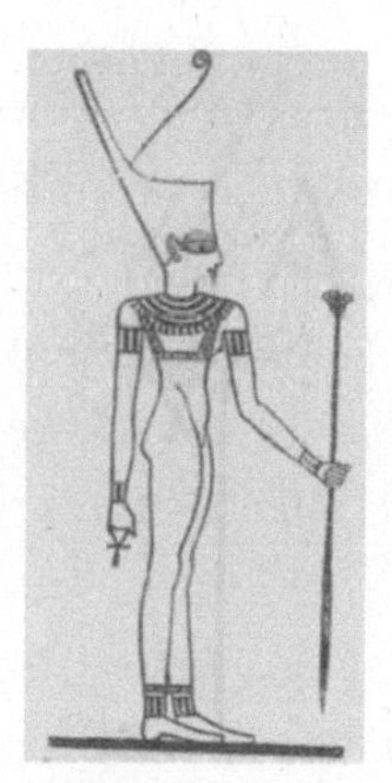

Neith wearing the Deshret[97]

The hieroglyph for Wedjat or Eye of Ra[98]

The Deshret represented the red desert lands on either sides of the crop-bearing Kemet bordering the Nile or "dark lands." The red lands were ruled by Set, where chaos was said to reign. The crown is characterized by a curly, wire-like prominence that represents a honeybee proboscis. Other deities that wore the Deshret included the serpent goddess Wadjet, mentioned above. Her hieroglyph was called the Wedjat or "Eye of Ra."

THE AEGIS OF ATHENA AND NEITH

Athena and Neith have both been depicted wearing a peculiar, shield-like covering around their neck and shoulders known as an "aegis." The Greek word *aegis* (αιγίς), in addition to the shield garment worn by Athena and Neith, can also mean "a rushing storm," from the verb *aessah* (αΐσσω), which means to "to move with a quick shooting motion, to shoot, dart or glance" or a "goatskin shield," from *aigh* (αἰγ), meaning "goat," and the suffix *es* (ίς), meaning "strength."[99]

The Romans adopted the wearing of the aegis as a symbol indicating that protection was provided to the wearer from a higher authority or power. In ancient art, the aegis worn by Athena appears to have come from the skin of a giant serpent, the Titan Pallas. Pallas (Greek: *pallō*) means "brandisher of the spear"[100] and has many descriptions in antiquity. The common thread amongst all of them was that she had come into some type of conflict with Athena either in battle or by accident, and had been killed. In one of the accounts of the identity of Pallas, she was a snake-like giant born from the blood of her father Uranus spilled onto the earth (Gaia).[101] After the Titanomachy, in a conflict also led by Zeus known as the Gigantomachy (Greek: "Battle of Giants"), Athena killed her. Pallas was also known as the son of the king Lycaon of Arcadia, the teacher of Athena,[102] and the Titan son of Crius, again killed by Athena in a contest over Zeus.

In yet another version of Pallas' story, Apollodorus writes that a blow from Zeus stunned Pallas, who was the daughter of Triton and foster parent to Athena, during a friendly fight. Athena, taking advantage of Pallas' momentary helplessness, accidently killed her. In remorse, Athena took on the name as well as the protective skin of her fallen companion, and made the holy Palladium in her likeness.[103] (The vital importance of the Palladium will be illustrated in chapter 14.)

The dragon Ladon (Greek: Λάδων) also appears in mythology to resemble Pallas. He was the serpent that guarded the golden apples of the Garden of the Hesperides (from the name of the Greek god, Hesperus, "the evening star"). Like Pallas, Ladon has been attributed to various sets of parents, including the sea monsters Keto and Phorcys,[104] or Typhon and Echidna,[105] the father and mother of all monsters who came after them. Ladon was also the brother of the invulnerable Nemean lion, who, in a story similar to the dragon of St. George, took women into its cave to lure warriors from nearby towns. Anyone entering the cave would be eaten and the bones would be left for Hades, the god of the underworld.[106]

Ajax the Lesser dragging Cassandra of Troy from the Palladium[107]

Eve-Athena consorted with the snake that, in the "benevolent" act of helping her become a new creature, was struck down and cursed by God. Eve-Athena was sorry for his misfortune and took on his protection, help, knowledge, and "way showing" power that was symbolized by her aegis. The aegis is both the protective skin of the giant snake and the skin of the goat god Pan, whose identity is the same as the protector of Zeus in the cave and the serpent in Genesis.

Athena's aegis made from the serpent Pallas, with the image of Medusa. The serpent who guards the Golden Fleece is shown holding Jason in its mouth.[108]

Plato drew a parallel between Athena and the Egyptian goddess Neith:

> In the Egyptian Delta, at the head of which the river Nile divides, there is a certain district which is called the district

of Sais, and the great city of the district is also called Sais, and is the city from which King Amasis came. The citizens have a deity for their foundress; she is called in the Egyptian tongue Neith, and is asserted by them to be the same whom the Hellenes call Athene; they are great lovers of the Athenians, and say that they are in some way related to them.[109]

Aegis of Neith from the twenty-sixth dynasty of Egypt[110]

5

CYBELE

> Sing of the mother of all gods and men. She is well-pleased with the sound of rattles and of timbrels, with the voice of flutes and the outcry of wolves and bright-eyed lions, with echoing hills and wooded coombes.
>
> —Homeric Hymn XVI, To Mother of Gods.[111]

Going back to Hesiod's *Theogony*, before the war of the Titans and the genesis of Atlas, the characters responsible for raising the infant Zeus were said to have been the inescapable surrogate mother, Amalthea, and the goat god. It is important to note that the worship of a "mother god" is common to *every* ancient civilization. Throughout the ancient land of Anatolia, which means, "where the sun rises," numerous and very ancient archeological sites have been found where such mother goddesses were worshipped. Curiously, the worship of the bull or ox is often included.

Catal Hüyük

One Anatolian civilization that worshipped the bull and mother goddess existed as far back in history as 7500 BC and occupied the area known today as Katal Huyuk (Turkish: "forked mounds").[112]

The Cybele goddess on a throne with lions. From Katal Huyuk.[113]

Statues of this civilization's Stone-Age-looking goddess known as Cybele (Phrygian for "mother") are always depicted sitting with lions. Many clay figures of the goddess have been found in Katal Huyuk, as have the stylized heads of the aurochs, the now-extinct ancestors of modern cattle. Auroch bulls grew to an estimated 3,300 pounds and stood almost six feet at the shoulder.

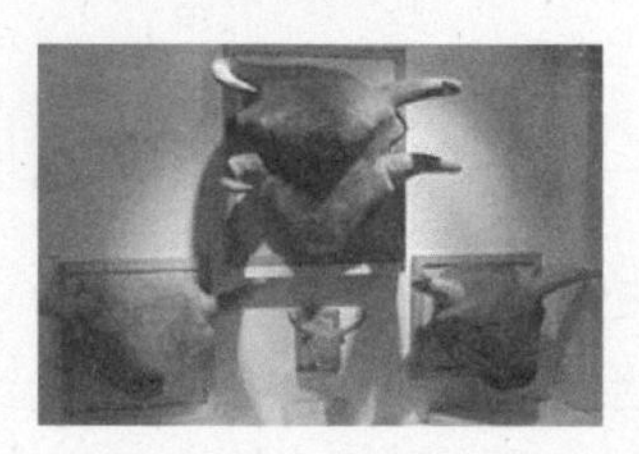

Auroch heads from Katal Huyuk in the Angora Museum[114]

The practice of worshipping bulls and the goddess Cybele has been proven to have existed in Anatolia long before even the beginnings of ancient Egypt, which developed sometime around 3150 BC. The Anatolian Cybele-worshipping cults developed around the same time as the Proto-Babylonian cultures of Mesopotamia (Greek: *meso,* "between," and *potamia*, "rivers," or "the land between two rivers" between the Tigris and Euphrates), which started around 10,000–8700 BC, according to the dating of archeological remains from the region.

Armenian has recently been theorized to be a subgroup of Balkan-Indo-European languages that shared attributes of the Albanian, Greek, and Phrygian languages that originated in Anatolia.[115] The Armenian word for the Mesopotamian river "Euphrates" is *diademata,* which alludes to the Cybele and means "she of the crown."[116]

Archeological evidence from Katal Huyuk has also shown that the labrys or double-bladed axe existed in art long before even the Lydian civilization or the Minoan in Crete. This demonstrates the extreme antiquity and religious importance of the dual-natured labrys. The labrys is likened to the "weapon" of the fruit of the Tree of Knowledge of Good and Evil that the Nachash used against God, in effect creating the prototype of the "mother goddess" in the fallen Eve.

Gobekli Tepe

According to the artifacts and monument inscriptions found at the newly discovered site in Turkey, this system of religion appears to have been around much earlier. The southeastern Turkey archeological site known as Gobekli Tepe (Turkish: "Potbelly Hill") was discovered in the 1960s by University of Chicago and Istanbul University anthropologists, but was dismissed as nothing more than an abandoned, medieval cemetery.[117] The German archeologist Klaus Schmidt reexamined the site in 1994 and realized that it was a temple complex. It has since been estimated to be more than 11,500 years old, making it the oldest temple structure ever found.

The areas that have been excavated so far have concentric-ring-shaped areas ranging from thirty-two to one hundred feet in diameter with T-shaped or ax-like limestone pillars that weigh ten to sixty metric tons and are evenly set within thick, interior walls of unworked stone. There are two taller pillars at the center of each circle, and many feature pictograms of animals and other unknown symbols. Some of the pillars have human arms, along with loincloths, carved on their lower halves.[118] The pillars were transported from bedrock quarries located 330 feet from the hilltop that still has a remaining unfinished pillar estimated to weigh fifty tons. So far, only a tiny portion of the complex—around 5 percent—has been excavated.[119] As of 2013, four of the circular structures have been excavated, and geophysical surveys show sixteen more, with each containing up to eight pillars—amounting to nearly two hundred pillars in all.[120]

Pillar number 2 from Enclosure A (Layer III) with bull, fox, and crane. Notice the "sun" between the horns of the bull.[121]

According to modern-day archeologists, humans living even twelve thousand years ago lacked metal tools and pottery, and they had not yet domesticated animals or invented the wheel. Consistent with this belief, researchers have wondered how the complex was constructed, since the rock would have had to been quarried and shaped using stone tools.

One of the most amazing discoveries made at the site was that it had been deliberately buried after its completion approximately one thousand years later. After more than twelve thousand years of erosion, the area wouldn't have been distinguishable today if this hadn't occurred. Archeologists have no clear ideas about why it might have been backfilled, but they conjecture that it might have been because of some religious dictate.

The people who built Gobekli Tepe might have sought to preserve the complex from destruction. The area today has extensively eroded, as if a great amount of water inundated the area. Although it is now a desert wasteland, the types of animals and plant life depicted on the pillars show that the area was much different when it was built. Foreknowledge of a coming, great flood would have been a possible reason to bury the complex in order to preserve it.

The plateau where the site is located lies 337 miles southwest of Mt. Ararat, where legend says that Noah's Ark rested, and which mimics the shape of a bull lying on its side, facing west. The temple area, viewed from above, is situated in a space with raised areas appearing to be ancient walls outlining the shape of a bull's head and horns. The circular, maze-like structures are laid out in a pattern corresponding to where the Hyades star cluster resides in the head of the constellation Taurus.

The belief that the builders of the temple lacked the technology to use wheels and relied on stone tools is not consistent with its sophisticated design, its construction, or the enormity of the site. It is amusing to see representations of the how the area might have looked eleven thousand years ago in illustrations in which artists stubbornly depict the builders as cave dwellers dressed in the height of animal-skin fashion.

Gobekli Tepe is approximately twenty-five miles north of the area known as Haran (Hebrew: *charan*, from *charar*, "to be scorched or burned, angry"). Abraham lived in the area for several years during his family's migration from Ur of the Chaldeans to the land of Canaan (Genesis 11:31), and it is the land from which Isaac and Jacob both obtained their wives.

The rounded temple structures of Gobleki Tepe are similar to the very stylized, classical Labyrinth drawings found in caves of the Minoan cults. To find a path to the center of the circular structures at the Gobekli Tepe complex, a person entering from the outside to the first "hallway" would have a choice of other possible doors or dead ends to get to the next circular path.

Gobekli Tepe is in the historical region of Cappadocia, where at least thirty-six underground cities have been found. The Cappadocian civilization is thought to have occupied the area from Mt. Taurus to the Black Sea.[122]

Derinkuyu, the deepest known city, at approximately two hundred feet, was large enough to shelter around twenty thousand people together with their livestock and food stores. It is the largest excavated, underground city in Turkey, and is thought to have been built by the Phrygians in around 800 BC.

The Greek historian Herodotus (484–425 BC) said that the name "Cappadocian" was applied by the Persians, while the people were termed "Syrians" (*Leucosyri,* "white Syrians") by the Greeks.[123] The Romano-Jewish historian Flavius Josephus (AD 37–100) relates the Cappadocians to the biblical figure Meshech, son of Japheth who was the progenitor of peoples to the north of Israel.[124]

PHRYGIAN

An important Anatolian culture was the Phrygian kingdom, which existed from around 1200 to 700 BC and was a close ally of the Trojans, who were said to have come from Mt. Ida in the northwest.[125] According to Herodotus, the pharaoh Psammetichus wanted to know which language was the oldest, Phrygian or Egyptian,[126] so he ordered that two newly born children were to be reared by a shepherd, who was never to speak to them. After two years, the shepherd reported that the children would ask for *bekos* as they extended their hands out for food. The pharaoh discovered that "bekos" was the Phrygian word for "wheat bread," so he declared that the Phrygian nation was older than Egypt's.

Part (about 70 percent) of Phrygian inscription in Midas City[127]

Legend says that the first mythological king of the Phrygians, Annacus, lived for three hundred years. His people had much love for him, and decided to ask their oracle how long he would live. The oracle's unexpected reply was that he would die with all of them at the time of the destruction of the whole world. The Phrygians lamented the prophecy, which became known as the "Lamentation of Annacus." The event that destroyed their world was known as the "Great Flood of Deucalion."

Deucalion's father, Prometheus, knew that Zeus was about to destroy humanity and instructed his son to build a chest so that Deucalion and his wife, Pyrrha (Greek: "flaming") might escape. Once the flood was over, Deucalion and Pyrrha touched solid ground on the mountain that towered above the Oracle of Delphi, Mount Parnassus, the mountain of Apollo.[128]

Deucalion consulted the oracle (who apparently survived the flood) about what he should do to repopulate the earth. He was instructed to "leave the temple and with veiled heads and loosened clothes throw behind you the bones of your great mother!"

Understanding that his "mother" was Gaia, Deucalion and Pyrrha picked up rocks. The ones thrown by Deucalion became men and the ones from Pyrrha became women.[129]

From antiquity to the present day, spilling wine at the dinner table has been considered a sign of good fortune, but spilling salt has been regarded as ominous. Throwing spilled salt over one's shoulder to "escape the bad luck" is related to the story of Deucalion and Pyrrha repopulating the earth. One would not wish to mock the gods by wasting the seeds of Gaia. The error is rectified by commemorating the act of Deucalion (Greek: *deucos*, "sweet wine," and *halieus*, a "seaman or sailor").[130] In the same way, spilling wine, especially wine unmixed with water, honors the "wine sailor" who escaped the flood.

The Cybele of Mt. Ida

Cybele was the goddess of ancient Anatolians, most notably the only known goddess of the Phrygians.[131] Known as the "self-created,"[132] the goddess "born from stone," and "the goddess who hangs in the air," she was associated with mountains and especially lions. As the goddess born from rock, bees and beehives were said to be sacred to Cybele, since they were often found near cave entrances. Cybele is commemorated today by the term "alma mater," meaning "the college or university from which one has graduated." The literal meaning of "alma mater" in Latin is "nourishing mother" and was the title the Romans gave to Cybele.[133]

According to the Greek geographer Pausanias (AD 110–180), the androgynous god Agdistis was castrated by the Olympian gods who feared him. After this, he became known as Cybele. To the Minoans and later the Greeks, Cybele was associated with Rhea, "Mother of all Gods." The Greeks worshipped her as the mystery goddess of the lion-drawn chariot. Her eunuch priests worshipped her accompanied by chaotic music, wine, and revelry. She was known to the Romans as the Trojan goddess, and was partly assimilated into to the cult of grain goddess, Demeter.

The Phrygian Korybantes (also, Corybantes), worshippers of the goddess, were known for their loud tympanum music with clashing cymbals and flutes and frenzied "Phrygian dancing,"[134] mirroring the story of the Korybantes protecting the infant Zeus while he was hidden in the cave with his adopted mother, Amalthea.

A highly eroded statue of Cybele carved out of the side of the Mt. Sipylus, east of Manisa, Turkey, was said to have been created by Broteas, the son of the Phrygian king, Tantalus. Tantalus was the son of Zeus who was thrown into Tartarus by his father after offending Zeus by offering his son, Pelops, as a meal to the gods. The story of Tantalus' punishment gives us the modern word "tantalize,"[135] since Tantalus would forever reach for food that was just out of reach.

The Cybele of Mt. Sipylus[136]

The rock carving mentioned by Pausanias was rediscovered in 1881 by W. M. Ramsay.[137] The sitting goddess has a *polos* (Greek: πόλος) crown and holds her breasts with her hands.

In addition to the rock-hewed Cybele statue, Mt. Sipylus features a natural rock formation that has the appearance of a woman's face. This is known as the "weeping rock" that has been associated with the legend of Niobe. Immediately before the story of Oedipus, Pseudo-Apollodorus relates the story of Niobe, daughter of Tantalus:

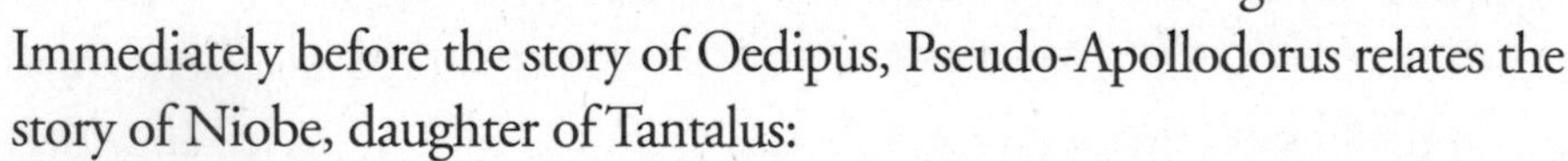

> Zethus married Thebe, after whom the city of Thebes is named; and Amphion married Niobe, daughter of Tantalus.... Being blessed with children, Niobe said that she was more blessed with children than Latona. Stung by the taunt, Latona incited Artemis and Apollo against them, and Artemis shot down the females in the house, and Apollo killed all the males together as they were hunting on Cithaeron.... Niobe herself quitted Thebes and went to her father Tantalus at Sipylus, and there, on praying to Zeus, she was transformed into a stone, and tears flow night and day from the stone.[138]

The spiteful Latona mentioned in the story of Niobe is an earlier name for the goddess Diana, the Roman goddess of light and the "shining moon."

The Greeks made small statues in Cybele's likeness, copying the many rock-hewed images that they found in the highlands of Phrygia. These were often crowned with peculiar, high, cylindrical hats knowns as "polos," or *polio* in Greek, which means an "axis or pivot." The English word "pole" comes from the Greek *polio*. The polos is the crown worn by "she of the crown" or *diademata*.

Seated Cybele within a Greek *naiskos* ("temple"). Naiskos always have columns or pillars and a pediment.[139]

Cybele was usually depicted wearing the *chiton,* which consisted of a single rectangle of woolen or linen fabric, and a *tympanon,* or hand drum. "Tympanon" is an alternate spelling of the same word in Latin that describes the center area of the pediment structure in Greek architecture, the *tympanum*.

Cybele drawn in her chariot by lions. The Sol Invictus like Sun God is similar to the one depicted in the later Roman Mithraian cults.[140]

The center of Phrygian Cybele worship in Anatolia was the ancient town of Pessinus or Pessinos under the rulership of King Midas.[141] It was discovered in 1834 by the French explorer Charles Texier. Pessinus is approximately thirty-three miles from the town of Gordium. Cybele was worshipped there as a shapeless, black, ironstone meteorite.[142]

The Romans adopted the cult of Cybele or the Great Mother of Mt. Ida after becoming concerned with the large number of meteor showers occurring at the time of the second Punic wars, around 219 BC. After looking to the Sibylline Books, the Romans went to Pessinus and retrieved the goddess' black stone image that was said to have fallen from heaven and brought it to Rome.[143]

The Sibylline Books, or *Libri Sibyllini,* were a collection of mystical instructional and prophetic utterances of a priestess from the temple of Cybele known as the Hellespontine Sibyl, who was born on Mt. Ida. The Sibyl offered her collection of nine books to the last king of Rome, Tarquinius Superbus (535–495 BC), who rejected her offer because the price was too high. Sibyl immediately burned three of the books and offered the king the remaining books for the same price. Again, he refused, causing the Sibyl to burn three more. Finally, the king capitulated and bought the remaining books to save them from destruction. He placed them in the temple of Jupiter. The keepers of the Sibylline Books in Rome later worshipped Apollo and the "Great Mother" Cybele under the instruction that the books provided.

Pessinos was near Mount Adgistis, named after the prior androgynous aspect of the Cybele. In the form of Adgistis, she-he had many similarities to the god Chronos. The mountain was considered the personification of Cybele-Adgistis, and was also known as a *daemon* to the Greeks.

6

ATTIS

How compact your bodies are. And what a variety of senses you have. This thing you call language though, most remarkable. You depend on it for so very much. But is any one of you really its master?

—The Medusian Kollos[144, 145]

The consort of Cybele was Attis. He was born from the pre-Cybele-aspect, multi-gendered god, Agdistis. The story of his birth is similar to that of Chronos, Rhea, Amalthea, and Zeus. Like Chronos, his father Agdistis had also undergone castration by other gods who either hated him or feared his power. The goddess Nana (similar to Rhea) picked an almond (or pomegranate) from the tree spawned from his male organ and laid it in her bosom, which resulted in the birth of Attis. Like Zeus, Attis was later abandoned and raised by the he-goat, Pan.

As Attis was preparing to marry the daughter of King Midas, Cybele appeared in a jealous rage, driving everyone at the wedding feast mad and causing an orgy of bloody self-destruction in which Attis followed the fate of his father-mother by castrating himself. Unlike his mother, the half-mortal Attis died from loss of blood.

Cybele repented of her jealousy and implored Zeus to resurrect her son. To punish Cybele, Zeus didn't fully resurrect Attis, but turned him into a pine tree, dooming him to exist as the ever-enduring god who waits in hope of becoming complete once again.[146, 147]

In some accounts, a wild boar killed Attis in similarity to the story of the Greek gods Hyas and Adonis. The young Attis is always depicted in ancient art with a distinctive Phrygian cap and peculiar trousers open at the front. His Phrygian cap is a stylized, red, bee-proboscis Deshret crown worn by the Egyptian goddess Neith. The Deshret cap and wings represent the bee-like aspect of the god. In ancient art, the youthful Attis is depicted as a bee. He wears the Phrygian version of the bee proboscis crown of Neith and flies as one directed by the light. The bee-like Attis shows the way, having the power of resurrection.

The *Encyclopedia Britannica* mentions that the "beehive-shaped" triple crown or tiara worn by Roman Catholic popes probably developed from the Phrygian cap, or *frigium.* It is interesting in light of the understanding that a Phrygian cap is representative of the bee that a beehive-shaped crown would naturally follow as a replacement to the original.[148]

In another version of Attis' death, he was killed by a wild boar, which is similar to the story of Hyas and also to that of Adonis, who died after Artemis, jealous of his hunting skills, sent a vicious boar.[149]

Sir James George Frazer (1854–1941), known for his comprehensive research in mythology, wrote *The Golden Bough: A Study in Magic and Religion,* in which he described the activities of the Roman cult of Cybele and Attis that involved taking a pine tree from the forest, decorating it, and worshipping it in the temple of Cybele:

> A further step was taken by the Emperor Claudius when he incorporated the Phrygian worship of the sacred tree, and with it probably the orgiastic rites of Attis, in the established religion of Rome. The great spring festival of Cybele and Attis is best known to us in the form in which it was celebrated at Rome; but as we are informed that the Roman ceremonies were also Phrygian, we may

> assume that they differed hardly, if at all, from their Asiatic original. The order of the festival seems to have been as follows.
>
> On the twenty-second day of March, a pine-tree was cut in the woods and brought into the sanctuary of Cybele, where it was treated as a great divinity. The duty of carrying the sacred tree was entrusted to a guild of Tree-bearers. The trunk was swathed like a corpse with woollen bands and decked with wreaths of violets, for violets were said to have sprung from the blood of Attis, as roses and anemones from the blood of Adonis; and the effigy of a young man, doubtless Attis himself, was tied to the middle of the stem. On the second day of the festival, the twenty-third of March, the chief ceremony seems to have been a blowing of trumpets.[150]

The Phrygian worship of the "sacred tree" cannot be overlooked when examining the origins of the modern-day practice of Christmas tree decoration.

The priests of Cybele and Attis were known as Galli, so called because of their raving madness[151] (and likely the origin of the English word "giddy"). While in Rome, the cult practiced its peculiar form of worship with self-castration during the ecstatic ceremonial mourning for Attis known as *Dies Sanguinis*, the "Day of Blood," which took place on March 24. Participants would dress as women with heavy makeup and tell fortunes in return for charity. On the day of mourning for Attis, they would wildly dance to pipes and tambourines and flog themselves until they bled.[152]

Frazer describes the Day of Blood:

> [The] high priest drew blood from his arms and presented it as an offering. Nor was he alone in making this bloody sacrifice. Stirred by the wild barbaric music of clashing cymbals, rumbling drums, droning horns, and screaming flutes, the inferior clergy whirled about in the dance with waggling heads

> and streaming hair, until, rapt into a frenzy of excitement and insensible to pain, they gashed their bodies with potsherds or slashed them with knives in order to bespatter the altar and the sacred tree with their flowing blood.[153]

The Romans called the next day the *hilaria* ("days of merriment"), which is the origin of the English word "hilarious." The hilaria was a *feria stativa,* or "fixed or stationary day of freedom," and fell on March 25, the day of the vernal equinox, according to the Julian calendar established by Julius Caesar in 45 BC.[154] On this day, slaves could do as they pleased and citizens masqueraded imitating whomever they liked.[155]

The Romans made Attis a solar deity in the second century AD, when he became known as Sol Invictus, the "Invincible Sun."[156]

The symbol of the Cybele-Attis cult was the pinecone, and shrines to Attis have been found with depictions of him gathering pinecones under the sacred pine tree.[157] In his *Metamorphoses*, Ovid mentioned that the pinecone was sacred to Cybele:

> And Pynapple [pinecone] with tufted top and harsh and prickling heare, The tree to Cybele, mother of the Goddes, most deere. For why? Her minion Atys [Attis] putting off the shape of man, did dye, And hardened into this same tree.[158]

The reclining Attis, after his self-emasculation. He holds a shepherd's crook in his left hand and a pomegranate in his right. His head is crowned with bronze rays of the sun and on his Phrygian cap is the crescent moon.[159]

The male aspect of Attis, becoming the non-gendered "enduring one," strangely recapitulates the evolution of his father *and* mother god, Agdistis, as the multi-gendered, proto-Cybele.

Although the legend of the founding of Troy includes the intercession of Athena (explained in chapter 14), it is more likely that it was not the Greek goddess who sent Palladium to Ilus, but the Attis aspect of Anatolian Cybele. The cult of Cybele and Attis existed long before the early Bronze Age (c. 3000 BC), the time of the early Minoan civilization.[160] The city of Troy has been excavated down to a level that shows that it was established as early as 3000 BC.

"Attis," also written "Atthis" or "Atys," is related to the word "attic," meaning "Athenian."[161] Today, the English word "attic" is a general term for the area located under the roof of a structure. More specifically, it is the area behind the part of the peaked exterior known as the pediment in Palladian architecture—literally, "the place of Attis."

The killing of Pallas by Athena and the death of Attis are similar in that both Athena and Attis were greatly loved and then greatly mourned by their killers after their unintentional deaths. Attis was said to have been tended by the "he-goat" in infancy. Athena's companion, Pallas, was said to have been a he-goat, and is also ambiguously described as teacher, Titan serpent, stepsister, or stepson. Athena took on her consort's name and skin as a shield, which established her authority to act in place of or under the power and authority of Pallas.

Cybele's jealousy resulted in the madness and death of her son, the unintentionally born, abandoned son, her most desired and greatest love. She forever associated herself with his-her symbols, taking on the power of the indistinct god, the god who was once alive and beautiful, who was male turned female, mortal turned immortal, the enduring pine.

The Colossus of Rhodes

Cybele, Attis, Helios, and Apollo are all aspects of the same god. The Colossus of Rhodes (Greek: Κολοσσός της Ρόδου) was a statue of the Titan Helios, constructed in the city of Rhodes by Chares of Lindos between 292 and 280 BC after their successful resistance to the siege of Antigonus the "one-eyed" known as Antigonus I Monophthalmu after their patron god. The statue was one of the Seven Wonders of the Ancient

World and stood over ninety-eight feet high. Helios is the Titan equivalent to the Olympian god Apollo. To the Romans, he was Sol Invictus, also known as Attis. The dedication text for the Colossus has been preserved in the *Anthologia Graeca* or *Greek Anthology,* a collection of poems spanning the Classical and Byzantine periods of Greek literature:

> To you, o Sun, the people of Dorian Rhodes set up this bronze statue reaching to Olympus, when they had pacified the waves of war and crowned their city with the spoils taken from the enemy. Not only over the seas but also on land did they kindle the lovely torch of freedom and independence. For to the descendants of Herakles belongs dominion over sea and land.[162]

Nineteenth-century engraving of the Colossus of Rhodes[163]

The ambiguously gendered face of the Statue of Liberty is also a representation of this multi-aspect god. The essence of the overlapping Eve-Nachash symbolic gods, the stories of how they came to be and how they "reinvent" themselves over time, reveal the essential mysteries kept by the elite to this day.

ARTEMIS

Artemis was the goddess associated with mountains (Greek: *oread*), specifically Mt. Ida in northwest Anatolia. She was the same goddess as the Cybele, who was worshipped in the region as far back as 7000 BC. At her great temple in Ephesus in Ionia, Anatolia, Artemis was depicted with multiple protuberances on her chest that have been described as breasts, garlands of pomegranates, or bull testes. Associated with the bull-sacrificial aspect of the Cybele, it would make sense that devotees would honor her with tokens of sacrificed bulls (more on this in chapter 7). However, the nature of myth does not always attribute singular interpretations to the nature of the gods. *Each* possibility as to the identification of what the objects represent may be correct. The pomegranates and bull testes are similar in that they indicate the regenerative-power aspect of the goddess. The many breasts allude to this idea as well.

Although Mt. Ida has often been referred to by the ancients as the "many fountained,"[164] today it does not have any water, much less fountains, near its surface. It has been theorized that before the Flood, there was a vast but fairly uniform layer of water trapped under the surface of the earth's crust. The water layer was under tremendous pressure, and found its way to the surface in many places, creating artesian springs. At the time of the Flood, this subterranean water system catastrophically failed, along with the massive firmament (*raqiya*, רָקִיעַ, "the vault of heaven supporting waters above").[165]

> In the six hundredth year of Noah's life, in the second month, the seventeenth day of the month, the same day were all the fountains of the great deep broken up, and the windows of heaven were opened. (Genesis 7:11)

The Artemis of Ephesus[167]

Homer called Artemis *Agrotera, Potnia Theron,* which meant, "Artemis of the wild land, mistress of animals."[166] The Romans associated her with the goddess Diana, and the Greeks linked her with Demeter. The priestesses of Artemis and Demeter were known as bee mistresses. Artistic representations of Artemis typically show her with multiple "breasts," alluding to the many-fountained mountain that she personified before the Flood.

The Artemis Fountain of Villa de Este in Trivoli "in action." Notice the polos or "tower" on her head and the tiny lions clinging to her upper arms.[168]

The statue of the Artemis of Ephesus (of which a Roman marble copy of the Greek original exists in the Vatican museum) has a peculiar progression of animal figures carved around her legs. At the bottom are two bulls. Progressing upwards are two griffon-like creatures, followed by three lions, three deer, and, finally, three strange, horned lions. On the sides of the statue's leg, images alternate between a single rose and a bee, topped by an angel. The upper arms each feature lions. The progression of animals in the statue mimics the description of a particular cherub known as the Nachash. In effect, Artemis and the Nachash have become superimposed.

Fountains

A word for "fountain" in Hebrew is *ayin* (עַיִן), which also means "eye or spiritual faculties, knowledge, conceit, sight or furrow."[169] A word in Hebrew for "heaven" or "astrologer" is *shamayim* (שָׁמַיִם). *Gesenius' Lexicon* describes the word as deriving from the root *shamayie* (שָׁמַיִה), meaning "firmament, which seems to be spread out like a vault over the globe, as supported on foundations and columns."[170]

The Pigna at the Vatican

Pigna, meaning "pinecone" in Italian (Latin: *pinus*, "pine," and *pyramidis*, "pyramid") was the symbol and name for the ninth region of ancient Rome. The Pigna was originally a fountain next to the Temple of Isis. It was set in the center of many smaller fountains, and water flowed copiously from its top and sides. The Pigna region was set on the Campus Martius (the Field of Mars). Today, it stands at the upper end of the Belvedere (Italian: "beautiful sight") Courtyard at the Vatican.[171]

The Pigna at the Vatican Belvedere Courtyard[172]

The male peacocks, also from the fountain at the Temple of Isis, are stylized Wedjat snakes. Their "many-eyed" courtship display mimics the "all-seeing" Egyptian goddess, Wedjat.

Male peacock displaying "eyes"[173]

Kemetian Rod of Osiris with the two Wedjat snake goddesses wearing the Deshret crowns[174]

Eye of Horus

Wedjat's hieroglyph was the eye, also known as the "Eye of Horus." The Pigna fountain not only had a large hole at the top, but many smaller holes at each of the prominences or "scales" (the technical term for the layered sections of a pinecone) on the sides, mimicking the ancient representation of the goddess

Artemis, the "many breasted" who was the same goddess worshipped by the Lydians at the Temple of Artemis at Ephesus in Ionia, Anatolia, one of the Seven Wonders of the Ancient World.

A word for "breast" in Hebrew is *shad* (*shin, dalet*, שַׁד; pronounced the same way as the river herring, "shad"), and the word for "demon" is spelled the same (שֵׁד), but pronounced "shade," as in "the shade of the tree." It is only used in the plural (*shad*, שֵׁד, "demons, idols"). Still another "shin, dalet" word means "violence or devastation": *shod* (שׁד, "violence, devastation").

Adding various letters to the root letters, "shin" and "dalet" make up interesting words related to the idea of the earth mother goddess:

- *Sadad* (*shin, dalet, dalet;* שָׂדַד, "to harrow, break up clods of dirt")
- *Sadeh* (*shin, dalet, he;* שָׂדֶה, "a cultivated field")
- *Shadday* (*shin, dalet, yod;* שַׁדַּי, "almighty, most powerful")
- *Shedeur* (*shin, dalet, yod, alef, vav, rosh;* שְׁדֵיאוּר, "darter of light")
- Another word for "breast" in Hebrew is *dad* (*dalet, dalet;* דַּד).

Notice the *dalet, gimel* letter-based words and their relations:

- *Dag* (*dalet, gimel;* דָּג, "a fish")
- *Dagah* (*dalet, gimel, he;* דָּגָה, "to multiply, to cover, to grow dark")
- *Dagal* (*dalet, gimel, lamed;* דָּגַל, "to look, behold")
- *Dagown* (*dalet, gimel, vav, nun;* דָּגוֹן, "the philistine fish god Dagon")

The word for "scale" of a fish, *qasqeseth* (קַשְׂקֶשֶׂת), is a duplication of an unused root meaning "to scale off as bark from a tree."

The Pineal, "Pinecone-Shaped" Gland or Third Eye

The life-giving seed cone of the undying pine has become associated with the goddess whose eyes were opened. The goddess of the Knossos' sacred symbol, the pinecone as a fountain with a column of water spreading out like the firmament of heaven as it falls back to the earth, accentuates the idea of where the Knossos was centered. Not only did the water from the Pigna fountain create a pillar and a firmament, but, like Artemis, it leaked from her many "scales" or breasts.

The Pope Symmachus, whose papacy endured from AD 498–514, had a "cantharus" built at his "place of paradise" at St Peter's. A cantharus is a large, wide-bellied, drinking vessel with handles used by the follower of the god Bacchus. It is also a name for the black spot under the tongue of the Egyptian Apis bull.[175]

Symmachus' cantharus was a large version of the vessel converted to a fountain. A portion from *Le Miracole De Roma* (*Rome's Wonders*), written sometime in the thirteenth century by an unknown author, describes Symmachus' Place of Paradise:

> In St. Peter's paradise is the Cantharus, built by pope Symmachus. And it was adorned with columns of porphyry (Greek "purple"). And it was faced with marble all around. And above were four golden griffons. And the ceiling was made of copper, and adorned with golden flowers and four copper dolphins above spouted water from their mouths. And in the middle of the Cantharus was a golden pine-cone, which once covered Santa Maria Rotonda's church. Above the pine-cone was the statue of goddess Cybele, mother of all gods. The pine-cone, through a lead pipe, poured water for all who wanted it. And by means of a duct that water reached the spire, by the baths of emperor Nero.[176]

The symbolism further identifying the Cybele at the court of the Pinecone at the Vatican are the two Egyptian lions from the fourth century BC at the base of the terrace supporting the pinecone. Cybele is especially associated with lions, and is usually depicted with two reclining at her feet. The Babylonian goddess Ishtar also was depicted in the same fashion.

Queen of the Night Ishtar relief from the British museum. She holds two Egyptian *ankh*-like symbols that signify her control over eternal life. This image combines all the Nachash-endowed symbolism of angelic wings and feet along with the owls associated with Athena and the lions at her feet like that of Anatolian goddess, Cybele.[177]

The common practice of throwing coins into fountains for good luck is not a just a quaint tradition. Since the coin is the symbol of human life (explained in chapter 10), it is the gesture sacrifice of a piece of that life to the goddess whose fountain forms a sacred pillar reaching out to heaven from earth, spreading out above as the firmament of heaven.

Head of the Hindu Shiva, the transgendered destroyer god. Notice the third eye, the *polos* crown, and crescent moon.[178]

As the exploration into the specific qualities and traits of the ancient goddesses continues in this book, we shall see that *every* goddess can be linked to the others worshipped throughout history, from Egyptian to Babylonian to Anatolian to Greek and Roman. (See *The Links of All the Goddesses after Cybele* in the appendix.)

ELAGABALUS

A male aspect of the Cybele was known as Elagabalus, who was worshipped in Syria during the time of the Roman Empire. Like Cybele, he was said to have been born from rock. The name comes from the Syrian *Ilāh hag-Gabal,* which means "god" (*Ilāh*) and "of the mountain" (*hag-Gabal*).[179]

Emperor Marcus Aurelius Antoninus (AD 203–222) brought the cult of Elagabalus to Rome from Emesa, Syria. Antonius served as hereditary high priest to the god Elagabalus during his youth in Emesa, where his mother and family lived. After his death, Antoninus himself was referred to as Elagabalus or Heliogabalus (*helios,* "sun"), since the god was associated with the Invincible Sun, Sol Invictus—the same that was worshipped in the cult of Mithras.

The emperor built a new temple on the eastern side of Palatine Hill known as the Elagabalium and put in it the image of his god—a black, conical, meteorite "heaven stone" that he had removed from the temple in Syria at the start of his reign in AD 218.

The Roman historian Herodian (AD 170–240) wrote concerning the stone of Elagabalus:

> This stone is worshipped as though it were sent from heaven; on it there are some small projecting pieces and markings that are pointed out, which the people would like to believe are a rough picture of the sun, because this is how they see them.[180]

Antoninus forced the Roman senate to watch as he danced around the altar of his god to loud clashes of cymbals and drums. During the summer solstice, the holy stone was removed from the temple, set on an ornate chariot, and paraded throughout Rome.

Herodian continues:

> A six horse chariot carried the divinity, the horses huge and flawlessly white, with expensive gold fittings and rich ornaments. No one held the reins, and no one rode in the chariot; the vehicle was escorted as if the god himself were the charioteer. Elagabalus ran backward in front of the chariot, facing the god and holding the horses [sic] reins. He made the whole journey in this reverse fashion, looking up into the face of his god.

Antoninus removed the most sacred objects from all the various temples on Palatine Hill and placed them in the Elagabalium. Among these was the emblem of the great Cybele, the Palladium, and the shields of the Salii. He required that Jews and Christians worship only in the new temple.[181] After his death in AD 222, the stone was returned to Emesa and his cult disbanded.[182]

Roman aureus depicting Elagabalus. The reverse reads "Sanct Deo Soli Elagabal" ("To the Holy Sun God Elagabal"), and depicts a four-horse, gold chariot carrying the holy stone of the Emesa temple.[183]

Biblical scholars have identified Emesa (now called Homs) with the kingdom of Zobah mentioned in 1 Chronicles.[184] Zobah is significant because it was the place of origin of the brass that was used to cast the two great pillars placed at the Temple of Solomon. King David had defeated the entire army of Hadarezer, king of Zobah:

> And David smote Hadarezer king of Zobah unto Hamath, as he went to stablish his dominion by the river Euphrates.
>
> And David took from him a thousand chariots, and seven thousand horsemen, and twenty thousand footmen: David also houghed all the chariot [horses], but reserved of them an hundred chariots.
>
> And when the Syrians of Damascus came to help Hadarezer king of Zobah, David slew of the Syrians two and twenty thousand men.
>
> Then David put [garrisons] in Syriadamascus; and the Syrians became David's servants, [and] brought gifts. Thus the Lord preserved David whithersoever he went.

> And David took the shields of gold that were on the servants of Hadarezer, and brought them to Jerusalem.
>
> Likewise from Tibhath, and from Chun, cities of Hadarezer, brought David very much brass, wherewith Solomon made the brasen sea, and the pillars, and the vessels of brass. (1 Chronicles 18:3–8)

The towns of the defeated king had their brass implements taken and made into the two pillars in the Temple and the bronze sea. Both of these symbolize the state of the earth after the Fall in the garden. Bronze specifically symbolizes judgment. The root word in Hebrew for brass, *nĕchosheth,* is "Nachash."

David Flynn, in his book, *Cydonia: The Secret Chronicles of Mars,* describes the shattering of the planet Rahab that occupied the region known today as the asteroid belt and the escape of its leaping "war god":

> Biblical sources confirm that Rahab was a planet, a kingdom on a planet, which was shattered; the planet Rahab exploded and the glittering remains exist as comets, asteroids and the detritus between the orbits of Jupiter and Mars.[185]

Concerning the Hindu mythology referencing the event that also mentions the identity of the "leaper," he continues:

> Appropriately, the war god of Mars is also called Skanda, which means "leaper." Another Hindu legend, found in the *Bhagavad Gita* and the *Skanda Puranas,* linked the God of Mars, the war god Karttikeya, to "shards" or "sparks" which fell from the heavenly eye of Shiva.[186]

At the time of the cataclysmic destruction of Mars and the escape of the bright "leapers," portions of the planet that were blasted out into space fell to earth in fiery streaks. At same time that the glorious civilization was destroyed, its habitants were sent fleeing, where they, too, fell to earth. Like the phoenix, the angel of light was taken down from his high place. He *leapt* to earth, where he waits until the time when he can rise to his former position. He corrupted the *Adam* creatures that God created to spite the God that banished him and destroyed his former domain.

Over time, legend later substituted the meteorites that fell at the time of the destruction of Mars and Rahab with the "powers of the air" that escaped. They were after all, similar looking to the "fiery ones" as they entered the earth's atmosphere. It is fitting then that the bronze implements of war taken from the defeated worshippers of the "meteorite gods" were made into the two pillars that showed the separation of heaven and earth, but between them, rather than the blasphemous path signified by the image of god-stone was the Holy of Holies. At the time of Solomon's Temple, the veil between the outer court and the Holy of Holies represented the separation between God and man initiated in the garden. The pillars (named Boaz and Jachin) symbolized the separation, but also gave a picture of the future reunification of heaven and earth. Here the Temple shows the *true* path to reconciliation. In the same way, the leaping god's former glory faded and cooled like the stone pieces of Mars and Rahab that fell to earth, the worshippers of the meteorites "dia-morphed," or attributed the stones themselves as gods.

Legend has it that the heavenly meteorite Kaaba stone worshipped at Mecca was a piece of Mars and that it once had eyes, ears, and a tongue to confirm to men that Allah was their creator.[187]

Stone deity in temple. Coin from Emesa, Syria, showing the temple at Emesa, containing the holy stone, on the reverse of this bronze coin by Roman usurper Uranius.[188]

7

THE BULL

> The heavens declare the glory of God; and the firmament sheweth his handywork. Day unto day uttereth speech, and night unto night sheweth knowledge. There is no speech nor language, where their voice is not heard. Their line is gone out through all the earth, and their words to the end of the world. In them hath he set a tabernacle for the sun, Which is as a bridegroom coming out of his chamber, and rejoiceth as a strong man to run a race. His going forth is from the end of the heaven, and his circuit unto the ends of it: and there is nothing hid from the heat thereof.
>
> —Psalms 19:1–6

Zeus appears commonly in Greek and Roman myth disguised as a bull. As the Cretan bull, he abducts Europa and later sires the half-man, half-bull Minotaur. It is reasonable that the greatest god of the Greek pantheon would take on the form of such a powerful creature or that ancient cultures would worship an animal they depended on so thoroughly for survival, one represented by the most impressive constellation in the darkness of the ancient world, Taurus.

The theme of the woman goddess, snake, or star and the bull is recapitulated in ancient myth, with the bull playing a central part. Many

Egyptian goddesses illustrate a *combination* theme aspect in which they are woman, bull, star, or all three at once. For example, Hathor is both bovine and woman, and is usually depicted with a light between her horns or with a star above her head.

A critical and very unorthodox concept must be put forth in order to gain understanding of the ancient gods and their mythology as the "illuminated" understand. When the bull appears in myth, it doesn't necessarily symbolize Zeus or some other powerful god specifically, but is a corrupt representation for the *One God*, the God who cursed the serpent in the garden.

There is much more to the idea that a bull should symbolize the One God. The word in Hebrew for "ox" or "bullock" is *showr* (שׁוֹר, *shin*, *vav*, *resh*), and means simply "an ox." But the root for showr is *shuwr* (שׁוּר), which means "to go round, to go about, to journey."[189]

Differences in Hebrew word pronunciation are represented by a system of dots or points known as *niqqud.* The example of bull (showr, שׁוֹר) compared to the root (shuwr, שׁוּר) involves the same letters but different pronunciations indicated by the niqqud dots and bars. Niqqud is used in dictionaries, poetry, and other special circumstances, but not in modern Hebrew.

The threshing floor in ancient times was a flat, circular area of smooth rock where an ox or a team of oxen would loosen wheat grain from the hard, outer chaff. The method is still used today in places where modern machinery is not available.

A threshing circle[190]

The idea of "going round" would apply to the ox in the light of the constellation Taurus passing through the heavens. Of course, the ox was an essential part of the threshing, processing at grain harvest, and the image of the animal traveling around the center post of a threshing circle as well as the constellation Taurus revolving overhead come to mind. Still, there is another aspect of the circuit quality to the idea of the ox. For this, we look to the alphabet of the language of the Pentateuch and the genesis of this writing system, Phoenician to the Aramaic.

In his *Temple at the Center of Time*, David Flynn writes:

> The Semitic (Hebrew and Phoenician) and Egyptian cultures were in contact with each other from greatest antiquity.... Renaissance theologians believed that Moses was the inventor of the first "sound based" script in the ancient world. They derived this understanding from the writings of Eupolemus ca. 158 BC that states: "Moses was the first wise man to teach the alphabet to the Jews who transferred them to the Phoenicians and the Phoenicians passed to the Greeks."[191, 192]

CIRCUIT OF TRUTH

The word in Hebrew for "truth" is emeth (אֱמֶת, *aleph*, *mem*, *tav*)—the first, middle, and last letters in the alphabet. The letter meaning for each, respectively, is: "ox," "water," and "mark." Each of these letters in Phoenician, Aramaic, and Hebrew has the same letter meaning, and the pronunciations are very similar.

In the *Sefer Yetzirah* (*The Book of Formation or Creation*, of unknown origin), the letter *aleph* is described as meaning "king over breath" or "life," and the letter *mem* is "king over water."

> And the earth was without form, and void; and darkness [was] upon the face of the deep. And the Spirit of God moved upon the face of the waters. (Genesis 1:2)

The letter *tav,* meaning, "mark," is the same as the sign used in Ezekiel's vision to mark the foreheads of the righteous:

> And the LORD said unto him, Go through the midst of the city, through the midst of Jerusalem, and set a mark upon the foreheads of the men that sigh and that cry for all the abominations that be done in the midst thereof. (Ezekiel 9:4)

The lamb's blood was similarly marked on the sides and top of the doorposts during the Exodus from Egypt in a motion forming a *tau:*

> And they shall take of the blood, and strike [it] on the two side posts and on the upper door post of the houses, wherein they shall eat it.... And the blood shall be to you for a token upon the houses where ye [are]: and when I see the blood, I will pass over you, and the plague shall not be upon you to destroy [you], when I smite the land of Egypt. (Exodus 12:7, 13)

The Imperial Aramaic (chronologically later than Phoenician, but before Hebrew) *tau* has no correlation in form with the Phoenician, but its *alaph* looks like the *last* letter in the Phoenician alphabet, *tau.*

Alaph *Tau*

A better representation of a letter system that would be considered holy to the God of the Universe, who has no beginning or end, would be appropriately depicted in the form of a *circuit.* Consider that the "top" letter in the circuit would be the "mark" or (X) and that the other letters would proceed from left to right just as the constellations pass overhead in the night sky. This one letter, if known to "mark" the start *and* the end of the circular arrangement, would later evolve into separate forms over a vast period of time. The aggregation of the *taus*, when thought of as two separate ideas, could also be represented as the same mark *combined*, forming a new letter.

The combination of the *taus* would indeed appear as the Phoenician *alf*, mimicking the image of a bull or ox head turned to the side.

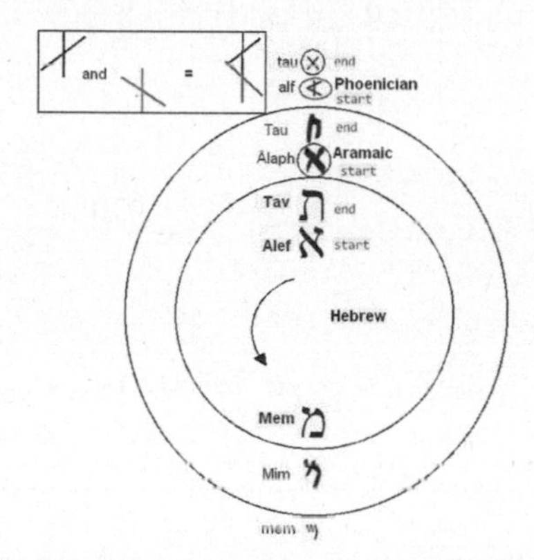

The combination of the *taus* mimic the image of a bull or ox head turned to the side.[193]

The representation of the first "sound-based" script as a circuit with the same sign, the sign of the cross, becomes separate letters when represented in a list. The limited or linear list has a beginning and an end and is unlike the nature of God, whereas a circuit has neither. The beginning and the end are both separate and yet are one, man as God—starting and ending with the cross.

Christ refers to Himself:

> I am Alpha and Omega, the beginning and the end, the first and the last. (Revelation 22:13)

Yet, there is always an effort by the Nachash to invert or substitute himself with any symbolic references to the truth.

Notice the similarity between the Masonic compass and square and the Phoenician *alf*.

Masonic compass and square

Phoenician *alf*

The compass and square are often depicted with the "joined hands" directly above or below to illustrate the unity of the society of the Masonic brotherhood. When the hands are shown joined inside the symbol, the union of the *taus* is most apparent.

A more revealing rendition of the compass and square with the hands "joining" the *taus*.[194]

The Phoenician letter *shin* is described as meaning "tooth," "sharp," or, interestingly, "a bow." Apart from this, in Hebrew, the shin is the *Tetragrammaton* (the proper name of the God of Israel) shorthand (so to speak) symbol that the high priest would make when reciting the blessing over the people after the morning sacrifice at the Temple in Jerusalem.[195] The *shem* (שֵׁם), or acquiring of the "name" that was the goal of the people building the tower of Babel, alludes to the same idea, but as a replacement of God by the people in their effort to be gods.

> And they said, Go to, let us build us a city and a tower, whose top [may reach] unto heaven; and let us make us a name, lest we be scattered abroad upon the face of the whole earth. (Genesis 11:4)

Perhaps it is not a stretch to interpret the Hebrew word for "circuit" (*shuwr*, שׁוּר) as: "The 'name' (*shem*) is hooked or attached (*vav*) to the beginning, the first, at the top, at the head (*resh*)."

In Plato's dialogue, *Timaeus*, Plato describes how the Demiurge formed the universe out of two circles joined in the "center like the letter X":

> This entire compound he divided lengthways into two parts, which he joined to one another at the center like the letter X, and bent them into a circular form, connecting them with themselves and each other at the point opposite to their original meeting-point; and, comprehending them in a uniform revolution upon the same axis, he made the one the outer and the other the inner circle.[196]

Richard Amiel McGough has proposed that the structure of the Bible was patterned after a wheel-like circuit in which the order of the Hebrew alphabet presented a structured pattern that is consistent with the theme of each book, from *aleph* to *tav*.

He explains the "Bible Wheel" phenomenon:

> The Bible Wheel is a circular presentation of the Bible that I discovered by rolling up the traditional list of the sixty-six books like a scroll on a spindle wheel of twenty-two spokes, corresponding to the twenty-two letters of the Hebrew alphabet.[197]

McGough mentions that the first ("spoke") of the wheel represented by the letter *aleph* is a "symbol of God."[198] In the ending *tav* or twenty-second spoke of his Bible Wheel, he illustrates the literal and esoteric meaning of the letter by listing key words. These have been reproduced here via *Strong's Hebrew Lexicon:*

> Tav—8420, a mark; by implication, a signature:—desire, mark.

> Tahm—8535, complete; usually (morally) pious; specifically, gentle, dear:—coupled together, perfect, plain, undefiled, upright.

Tom—8552, completeness; figuratively, prosperity; usually (morally). innocence:—full, integrity, perfect(-ion), simplicity, upright(-ly, -ness), at a venture.

Tamam—8552, to complete, in a good or a bad sense, literal, or figurative, transitive or intransitive (as follows):—accomplish, cease, be clean (pass-)ed, consume, have done, (come to an, have an, make an) end, fail, come to the full, be all gone, X be all here, be (make) perfect, be spent, sum, be (shew self) upright, be wasted, whole.

Tamim—8549, entire (literally, figuratively or morally); also (as noun) integrity, truth:—without blemish, complete, full, perfect, sincerely (-ity), sound, without spot, undefiled, upright(-ly), whole.

Tiklah—8502, completeness:—perfection.

Talah—8518, to suspend (especially to gibbet):—hang (up) [Author's note: This is *an obvious meaning towards crucifixion*]

McGough explains that the *tav* spoke completes and seals the Bible since the cross (*tav*) is the "central theme of all scripture."[199]

On a side note, it interesting that after all his revelatory discoveries, McGough later rejected his Christian faith, but to this day, he maintains that the phenomenon of the Bible Wheel is intelligently designed and real.[200] He writes, "The evidence of some sort of 'supernatural design' seems as solid and incontrovertible to me now as it did when I was a Christian."

Strong's Hebrew Lexicon reveals two more words beginning with the letter *tav* that have a very important relationship to the idea of the superimposition or joining of the same letter on itself to form a circuit, *tawam* and *taom*:

8380—ta'owm taw-ome' or taom: a twin (in plural only), literally or figuratively:—twins.

8382—ta'am taw-am' to be complete; but used only as denominative from 8380, to be (causatively, make) twinned, i.e. (figuratively) duplicate or (arch) jointed:—coupled (together), bear twins.

The twin aspect in myth is one that turns up repeatedly. Some examples are the stories of Castor and Pollux, Helen of Troy and Clytemnestra, and Romulus and Remus.

Begonia—Bees from the Ox

The son of Apollo, known as Aristaeus, meaning in Greek, "ever-close follower of the flocks," was the god of beekeeping. The Greek poet Pindar (522–443 BC) said that Aristaeus was an epithet for Apollo himself. It was through his cult that the method and care of bees was taught, as well as the idea that new beehives could be generated from *killing and burying oxen.*

Antigonus of Carystus (third century BC) wrote that in ancient Egypt, an ox would be completely buried, with just the horns projecting above the ground. Later, when the head was struck with an axe, bees would emerge.[201]

The bull, being the symbol of the creator of mankind, would thus be the obvious place where "souls" were created, and the crescent moon, with its bull-horn-like appearance, would signify a holy time when the power of this generation was more abundant. The Neoplatonists believed that souls (the many) descend into incarnation on earth and ascend back to the heaven or the monad ("the one").[202] The ancient belief that bees would spontaneously generate from the body of a bull was called *begonia,* from the Greek *boos* meaning "ox" and *onia*, "genesis."[203]

The book of instruction on agricultural pursuits, *The Geoponica*, attributed to the Roman philosopher Pliny the Elder (AD 23–79), had a peculiar set of macabre instructions on how to generate bees:

> Build a house, ten cubits high, with all the sides of equal dimensions, with one door, and four windows, one on each side; put an ox into it, thirty months old, very fat and fleshy; let a number of young men kill him by beating him violently with clubs, so as to mangle both flesh and bones, but taking care not to shed any blood; let all the orifices, mouth, eyes, nose etc. be stopped up with clean and fine linen, impregnated with pitch; let a quantity of thyme be strewed under the reclining animal, and then let windows and doors be closed and covered with a thick coating of clay, to prevent the access of air or wind. Three weeks latter [sic] let the house be opened, and let light and fresh air get access to it, except from the side from which the wind blows strongest. After eleven days you will find the house full of bees, hanging together in clusters, and nothing left of the ox but horns, bones and hair.[204]

The idea of the bull carcass generating bees is explained by the Neoplatonic philosopher Porphyry (AD 234–305) in his *On the Cave of the Nymphs in the Thirteenth Book of the Odyssey.* He writes:

> The priestesses of Ceres, also, as being initiated into the mysteries of the terrene Goddess, were called by the ancients bees; and Proserpine herself was denominated by them honied. The moon, likewise, who presides over generation, was called by them a bee, and also a bull. And Taurus is the exaltation of the moon. But bees are ox-begotten. And this application is also given to souls proceeding into generation. The God, likewise, who is occultly connected with generation, is a stealer of oxen. To which may be added, that honey is considered as a symbol of death, and on this account it is usual to offer libations of honey to the terrestrial Gods.... All souls, however, proceeding into generation, are not simply called bees, but those who will live in it justly and who, after having performed such things as are acceptable to the Gods, will again return (to

> their kindred stars). For this insect loves to return to the place from whence it first came, and is eminently just and sober.[205]

Why would the carcass of an ox do something as incredible as spontaneously generate bees? A better question: Why is such violence to the animal necessary? Stepping back and looking at the practice of begonia in the light of the ox being a symbol for the *oppressor* God, and of the bees as symbolizing human souls, the answer can be described in simple terms: God must be subdued with violent prejudice before the souls of all humanity can be made "free." This is precisely what the Nachash sought to do in Eden.

Porphyry adds to the understanding of begonia, mentioning fountains and *Mithras*:

> For water co-operates in the work of generation. On this account the bees are said, by the poet, to deposit their honey in bowls and amphorae; the bowls being a symbol of fountains, and therefore a bowl is placed near to Mithra, instead of a fountain; but the amphorae are symbols of the vessels with which we draw water from fountains. And fountains and streams are adapted to aquatic Nymphs, and still more so to the Nymphs that are souls, which the ancient peculiarly called bees, as the efficient causes of sweetness. Hence Sophocles does not speak unappropriately when he says of souls:—
>
> "In swarms while wandering, from the dead,
> A humming sound is heard."[206]

MEDUSA AND ATHENA

Medusa did not start out as a monster, but as a ravishing beauty. Athena caught her with Poseidon in her temple and, in a rage, transformed Medusa's beautiful, golden hair into serpents and changed her face to one so hideous that the mere sight of it would turn onlookers into pillars of stone.

Ovid writes:

Medusa once had charms; to gain her love
A rival crowd of envious lovers strove.
They, who have seen her, own, they ne'er did trace
More moving features in a sweeter face.
Yet above all, her length of hair, they own,
In golden ringlets wav'd, and graceful shone.
Her Neptune [Poseidon] saw, and with such beauties fir'd,
Resolv'd to compass, what his soul desir'd.
In chaste Minerva's fane, he, lustful, stay'd,
And seiz'd, and rifled the young, blushing maid.
The bashful Goddess turn'd her eyes away.[207]
Ovid continues, describing Athena's vengeance:
But on the ravish'd virgin vengeance takes,
Her shining hair is chang'd to hissing snakes.
These in her Aegis Pallas joys to bear,
The hissing snakes her foes more sure ensnare,
Than they did lovers once, when shining hair.

Medusa consorted with *God*. Poseidon is Zeus' (symbol for God—the bull) brother. Athena would naturally find this a most blasphemous and insulting act in her own temple. As an example of the Nachash's attitude toward any human who would presume to look to God, she is transformed into something that accentuates his opposition. Just as she is desired by and looks to Poseidon, she becomes a monster, a lying example to all who would follow God. The beautiful Medusa opposed what the snake would have men believe, and was punished as a warning to men. The image of her snake-haired head is worn by Athena at the center of her aegis as a warning to all.

WHO IS THE LION?

The lions seen with Egyptian Neith, Babylonian Ishtar, Greek Artemis, and Phrygian Cybele are particularly enigmatic. Thirteen different words refer to "lion" in the Old Testament. Four examples can be found in the book of Job:

> The roaring [*shĕagah,* שאגה, "to roar, lion, the wicked"] of the lion, [*'ariy,* ארי, "lion"] and the voice [*qowl,* קול] of the fierce lion [*shachal,* שחל, "lion, wicked men"], and the teeth [*shen,* שן] of the young lions [*kĕphiyr,* כפיר, "young lion," from *kaphar,* כָּפַר, "to coat or cover with pitch"], are broken [*natha,* נתע]. (Job 4:10)

The words for "sharp teeth," "fierceness," and "roaring" all begin with the letter *shin* (ש), which, by itself, is the image of teeth or a bow. It is the Nachash who injures by piercing. The arrow that strikes via the bow and teeth is consistent with this idea.

The word *ariy* lacks the letter *shin,* and it was the word for "lion" that was given to the tribe of Judah in Genesis 49:9. It is Jesus who will return as the Lion of Judah, since He was from the tribe of Judah, as depicted in Revelation 5:5. The "covering over" meaning of the root word for "young lion" (*kĕphiyr*) reflects the description for the Nachash used in Ezekiel 28:14, "the anointed cherub that covereth."

As explored previously, the shin is used as a reference to the name of God, El Shaddai, and this especially points to the desire of the Nachash to be worshipped as God or in place of God. The goddess who would subdue the lion and always have lions protecting her is the quintessential aspect of the ancient Eve-Nachash-bull mystery religion.

Gesenius adds this interesting notation in his *Lexicon* at the end of the definition of the word for "lion" (*shachal, Strong's* H7826): "Compare שָׁחַל, the letters ל and ר being interchanged." He doesn't continue his explanation, but alludes that the difference between the Hebrew word for "lion" (שָׁחַל) and "dawn" (שַׁחַר) is the *resh* ("head") and the *lamed* ("ox goad").

Continuing farther along the thread of the shin-lion idea, one of the names used in reference to the shining angel in the book of Isaiah is "son of the morning [dawn]":

> How art thou fallen from heaven, O Lucifer, son of the morning! [how] art thou cut down to the ground, which didst weaken the nations! (Isaiah 14:12)

The Hebrew word used for "morning" or "dawn" is the masculine noun *shachar* (שַׁחַר). Thinking through this in the esoteric light of understanding, the origin and meaning of the *aleph* or ox head as the symbol for God, the head of the cherubim, the one who was the greatest, the "dawn," became an antagonist to God—as symbolized by the replacement of the ox goad (ל) for the head (ר).

In contrast, the verb *shachar* (שָׁחַר) that uses the same letters as the word for "dawn" means "to become black." Substituting the middle letter *heth* in *shachar* with the letter *qoph* forms the word *sheqer* (שקר), "to lie" with letters meaning: *bow, needle,* and *head.* Still another word for "lion" in Hebrew is *mĕriy* (מְרִי), which also means "bitter" or "rebellious." Its root is *marah* (מָרָה), meaning "to be rebellious towards God."[208]

The Cult of Mithras

The wearing of a distinctive red Phrygian cap, the hat of Attis, Cybele, Neith, and Athena, identified the members of the mysterious cult of Mithras. One enigmatic symbol of the cult was a naked, lion-headed (Greek: *leontocephaline*) man. Depicted with four cherubim-like wings and entwined by a snake, he stands on the cosmic sphere or earth inscribed with the *tav* or cross, and holds a key in his right hand. The figure combines all the symbols of the Nachash in one image: the lion head, the serpent, and the four cherubim wings in possession of the "keys" to the knowledge he has given and yet controls. At the same time, he is the man intertwined in the angel's symbols, signifying beyond a doubt the essence of the nature of the power behind the cult. "Mithras" comes from the Proto-Indo-Iranian word *mitra,* "to bind," and *tra,* meaning, "causing to." He is the power that binds itself with the worshipers of Mithras.

Stone carving from India of the Leontocephaline standing on the earth with the inscribed tav.[209]

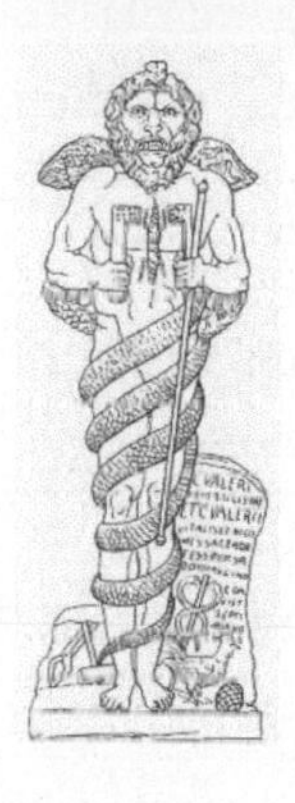

A drawing of the figure found at the mithraeum of C. Valerius Heracles and sons (dedicated AD 190) at Ostia Antica, Italy, 1896. Notice the chicken, a creature capable of parthenogenesis, and the "Cybeline" pinecone at his feet.[210]

Mithras was worshipped openly until the later period of Roman history, when Christianity overshadowed the practice. Mithras was a Persian god said to have "come from the East." The name "Mithra" was adapted into Greek as Mithras. The Roman military was said to favor the cult.[211]

The word *mitra* is the same root used for the modern word "mitre."[212] The mitre is the ceremonial hat used by Catholic bishops and was known by the Romans as the headdress worn by the Asiatics (Anatolians). They regarded it as a mark of effeminacy consistent with the predominance of the eunuch priests who were related to the Cybele-Attis cults. When rendering the Hebrew *micnepheth* in the late fourth-century Latin translation of the Bible known as the Vulgate, the word came to signify any headdress of a priest.[213] An earlier meaning of "mitre" was a belt of woolen clothing worn under armor about the waist similar to the *zonus* girdle used by St. George to control the dragon and the military girdle or the *labicus* introduced by the resurrected Glaucus (explained in chapter 9).

Numerous archeological artifacts have contributed to the modern knowledge of Mithraism. Depictions of Mithras show him being born from the rock, slaughtering a bull, and sharing a banquet with the sun god known to the Romans as Sol Invictus. Worshippers of Mithras had a complex system of seven grades of initiation and ritual meals. Initiates, who called themselves *syndexioi*, those "united by the handshake,"[214] met in natural or manmade cave temples called Mithraeum, which can still be found today.[215] Mithraeum are usually small and unremarkable in their construction and located near streams or springs. Typically, the archways of the constructed varieties are made to imitate the arched appearance of cave entrances. Archeologists theorize that water must have been essential for some of the Mithraic rituals, since most have been found near ancient springs or streams. The Mithraeum represented the cave where Mithras was said to have taken and killed the bull. Many such structures have been found throughout the reaches of the Roman Empire as far north as Britain and in Greece, Syria, and Egypt.

A Mithraeum from the ruins of Ostia Antica, Italy, with the typical, arched-brick entranceway and the likeness of Mithras with the bull in the center.[216]

A Mithraeum is located at the grounds of the United States Capitol just to the northwest of the building next to Northwest Drive. It is exactly 666 feet from the center west entrance of the Capitol building.[217] Known as the "grotto" (a word that comes from the Italian *grotta* [Latin: *cryypta*, "crypt"]) or "cave," it is the Summerhouse originally designed by Frederick Law Olmsted in 1874 that provided a place of "quiet rest." It contains a fountain at the center that provides visitors with fresh drinking water.

Olmsted was going to build another Mithraeum in the south portion of the grounds, but it was never constructed.

Entrance to the "Grotto" at the US Capitol grounds[218]

The Phrygian cap of the cult of Mithras embodied the idea of the initiate's journey from death to life, darkness to illumination, and the path of freedom from the will of God toward the pursuit of the god-forming knowledge given in the garden. The binding of the serpent with men as well as the amalgamation of Attis and Cybele is also a part of the mystery of the cult. One might gain a better understanding of the secretive method of religious worship that the Mithras cult practiced in their caves and underground shrines by reading the Socratic dialogue in Plato's Republic. Plato was recognized as a source of revelation in respect to the knowledge that had been steadfastly hidden throughout the ages by the elite mystery schools by the 33rd-degree Freemason, mystic, and historian Manly P. Hall (1901–1990). He writes:

> In all cities of the ancient world were temples for public worship and offering. In every community also were philosophers and mystics, deeply versed in Nature's lore. These individuals were usually banded together, forming seclusive philosophic and religious schools. The more important of these groups were known as

> the Mysteries. Many of the great minds of antiquity were initiated into these secret fraternities by strange and mysterious rites, some of which were extremely cruel. Alexander Wilder defines the Mysteries as "Sacred dramas performed at stated periods. The most celebrated were those of Isis, Sabazius, Cybele, and Eleusis." After being admitted, the initiates were instructed in the secret wisdom which had been preserved for ages. Plato, an initiate of one of these sacred orders, was severely criticized because in his writings he revealed to the public many of the secret philosophic principles of the Mysteries. Every pagan nation had (and has) not only its state religion, but another into which the philosophic elect alone have gained entrance.[219]

Another modern-day Mithraeum belongs to Yale University's secret undergraduate fraternity at 64 High Street in New Haven, Connecticut, known as the Order of the Skull and Bones. Many notable men of power in the United States have been members, including William Howard Taft (1878), the twenty-seventh president of the United States; Alfred Gwynne Vanderbilt I (1899); Prescott Bush (1917); George H. W. Bush (1948), the forty-first president of the United States; John Forbes Kerry (1966); and George W. Bush (1968), the forty-third president of the United States. The main building where all the society's secret rituals are said to be held is known as "the Crypt."

View of the front entrance of the Skull and Bones[220]

TAUROCTONY

The *Tauroctony* (*taurus,* "bull," and *ktonos,* "murder") is the most common act of Mithras depicted in art. Mithras, with the power of the Cybele and Attis combined, slays the bull in the ritual *defamation killing* of the

Bull-Zeus-God. Attis was made into a solar deity in Rome. Sol Invictus *is* Attis. Mithras always looks to him while murdering the bull. When the initiate comes to the essential understanding of the mystery, "killing his bull," he receives the Phrygian red cap.

Mithras killing the bull. The Tauroctony. A second- or third-century Roman bas-relief of the scene. Notice Attis (Sol Invictus) on the left and Cybele emerging "born from the rock" on the right.[221]

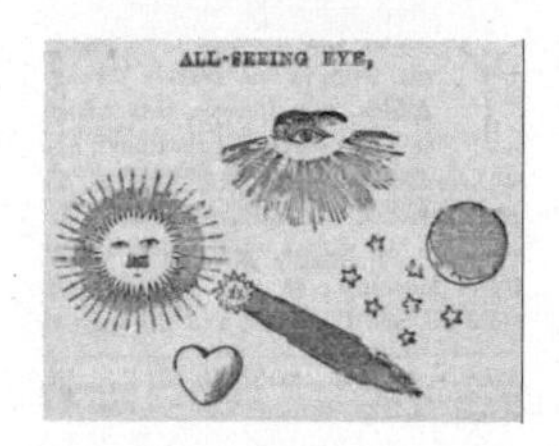

Image from the *The Freemason's Monitor*. Notice the placement of the sun, moon and "comet" in the same configuration as the image of Mithras killing the bull. The sun is Attis, the moon, Cybele, and the "comet" looks towards the "sun."[222]

The text explaining this image elaborates:

The All-Seeing Eye, Whom the Sun and Moon and Stars obey, and under whose watchful care even the Comets perform their stupendous revolutions, pervades the inmost recesses of the human heart, and will reward us according to our merits.[223]

Mithras image overlaid with the Masonic All-Seeing Eye, Sun, and Moon.[224]

The inclusion of the *heart* image in the Masonic depiction of the All-Seeing Eye that appears between Mithras and the sun in the overlaid image echoes an event illustrated in the epic of Gilgamesh.

EPIC OF GILGAMESH

The Sumerian *Epic of Gilgamesh* is one of the oldest works of literature known, dating back to the thirteenth century BC. In it, Gilgamesh and Enkidu kill the Bull of Heaven, Gugalana, to defy the gods. Ishtar is portrayed in the epic as quick to anger and spoiled by her father. She seeks to marry Gilgamesh, but her father refuses, since he knows the plight of her former lovers.

> Listen to me while I tell the tale of your lovers. There was Tammuz ["faithful or true son"; Hebrew: *Tammuz* , "sprout of life," the son of Semiramis and Ninus or Nimrod. The Egyptian Isis is linked to Semiramis and Horus to Tammuz], the lover of your youth, for him you decreed wailing, year after year.[225]

The summer solstice was the time of mourning in the ancient Near East, and the Babylonians would have six-day "funeral" for the god Tammuz. The people of Jerusalem engaged in this practice during the time of the prophet Ezekiel. (This is the only mention of Tammuz in the Bible.)

> Then he brought me to the door of the gate of the LORD's house which was toward the north; and, behold, there sat women weeping for Tammuz. Then said he unto to me, "Hast thou seen this, O son of man? turn thee yet again, and thou shalt see greater abominations than these." (Ezekiel 8:14–15)

Insulted by Gilgamesh's refusal to marry, Ishtar asks her father, Anu, to give her the Bull of Heaven with a threat:

> If you refuse to give me the Bull of Heaven [then] I will break in the doors of hell and smash the bolts; there will be confusion [i.e., mixing] of people, those above with those from the lower depths. I shall bring up the dead to eat food like the living; and the hosts of the dead will outnumber the living.[226]

After Anu gives Ishtar the Bull, she sends it to kill Gilgamesh. The first "bull fight" occurred here. For hours, Gilgamesh and Enkidu fought the nearly invincible creature until Gilgamesh, "dancing in front of the Bull, lured it with his tunic and bright weapons, and Enkidu thrust his sword, deep into the Bull's neck."[227] Modern-day bull fighting continues this scene in exactly the same fashion, although it is the matador (Spanish: *matar,* "to kill") or "dancer" wearing his *traje de luces* ("suit of lights"), who finally kills the Bull.

Gilgamesh and Enkidu, in defiance to Ishtar, *offer the bull's heart to the sun god Shamash*. Enraged, Ishtar stands upon the walls of the city of Uruk and curses Gilgamesh. Later, she calls "her people, the dancing and singing girls, the prostitutes of the temple, the courtesans" to "mourn for the bull of heaven."

The Mithraian mysteries that were born out of the Cybele-Attis cult that also existed until Roman times incorporated the triune or *Tritogeneia* Eve, Nachash, and bull images in their worship. One of the essential rites of Attis was the "baptism" in which the initiate would be soaked with blood from the bull at the vernal equinox.

Sir James George Frazer, in his book, *The Golden Bough: A Study in Magic and Religion,* writes:

> In the baptism the devotee, crowned with gold and wreathed with fillets, descended into a pit, the mouth of which was covered with a wooden grating. A bull, adorned with garlands of flowers, its forehead glittering with gold leaf, was then driven on to the grating and there stabbed to death with a consecrated spear. Its hot reeking blood poured in torrents through the apertures, and was received with devout eagerness by the worshipper on every part of his person and garments, till he emerged from the pit, drenched, dripping, and scarlet from head to foot.[228]

ANTIOCHUS IV EPIPHANES, THE MITHRIDATES

Antiochus IV Epiphanes (Greek: Ἀντίοχος Ἐπιφανής, Antíochos Epiphanes, "God Manifest") (215–164 BC), also known as *Mithridates* ("given by the deity Mithra"), was the king of the Greek Seleucid Empire. A son of Antiochus III the Great, he took the name "Antiochus" after he ascended the throne.

He was known to have massacred eighty thousand Jews after the revolt against Greek control over Jerusalem led by the high priest Jason Oniad. Later, the king profaned the Temple of Jerusalem by slaughtering a pig on the Altar of Sacrifice. The deuterocanonical book, *2 Maccabees* (written by Judas Maccabeus, who led the revolt against the Seleucid Empire), records the persecutions brought about by Antiochus:

> [He caused them] to abandon the customs of their ancestors and live no longer by the laws of God; also to profane the temple in Jerusalem and dedicate it to Olympian Zeus, and that on Mount Gerizim to Zeus the Hospitable, as the inhabitants of the place requested.... They also brought into the temple things that were forbidden, so that the altar was covered with abominable offerings prohibited by the laws. A man could not keep the Sabbath or celebrate the traditional feasts, nor even admit that he was a Jew. At the suggestion of the citizens of Ptolemais, a decree was issued ordering the neighboring Greek cities to act in the same way against the Jews: oblige them to partake of the sacrifices, and put to death those who would not consent to adopt the customs of the Greeks.[229]

Antiochus IV has been considered a second *type* of Antichrist after the first, who was Alexander the Great. Many Jewish and Christian scholars believe that the book of Daniel was written during the time of Antiochus IV, in which he is described by the prophet Daniel as the "little horn," the "prince who is to come," and the "King of the North."

Another Mithridates, Mithridates VI, king of the Anatolian Pontic Empire (134–63BC), so feared being poisoned that he regularly ingested small doses, believing that he would develop an immunity. *Mithridatism* later became the term for the practice.

8

THE ORACLE AT DELPHI

A Hebrew boy, a god who rules among the blessed, bids me leave this house forever and go back to Hades. So in silence go from my altars.

—The response from the Delphic Oracle when the emperor Augustus had asked, "Why are you silent?"[230]

Omphalos (ὀμφαλός), or *baetylus,* which means "navel" or "center" in Greek, is the word for a mystical stone.[231] The Omphalos was the stone given to Chronos as a substitute for the infant Zeus. In ancient myth, Omphale was also known as the daughter of Iardanus, the king of Lydia, as well as a river-god or as the wife of Tmolus, who was also king of Lydia, but who later died after being gored by a bull. As the wife of Tmolus, Omphale continued to reign on her own.

The navels of the earth were set down when Zeus sent out two eagles to fly and meet at its center. Legend has it that the eagles established the Omphalos in Greece at the Delphic Oracle.

The Omphalos in the Museum of Delphi[232]

The stone at the museum of Delphi has a carving of a *knotted net* over its surface. The minor prophet Habakkuk describes the "burden" of the evil religion of the Babylonians as net-like:

> They take up all of them with a hook, They catch them in their net, And gather them in their dragnet. Therefore they rejoice and are glad. Therefore they sacrifice to their net, And burn incense to their dragnet; Because by them their share [is] sumptuous And their food plentiful. (Habakkuk 1:15–16)

The word used for "net" in Hebrew is *charem* (חֵרֶם), which means "net," but also "accursed," or "to dedicate for destruction."

The characters in myth and their meaning are supposed to be "net like." The idea is that the theme and true identities of what or whom the characters represent are intentionally obfuscated, combined, and/or switched to confuse anyone who might try to untie the knot to solve the riddle, traverse the maze, or unravel the tapestry. It is not that an unsophisticated, ancient culture would randomly assign some idiosyncratic attribute to a god or goddess, as if he or she needed at least one to have an interest in weaving so that the weavers had someone to worship. A great intelligence does this purposefully. It is done with precise intention and the most cunning skill to depict and at the same time obscure the knowledge and meaning as to whom the character actually represents.

Gaining the understanding of the knowledge given to Eve—and the identity of its source comes only by seeing through the obfuscation, confusion, or "knots"—involves effort, since this chance for illumination is only for those worthy of guidance. As we shall see, the ideas included in the story of the Labyrinth, the double-bladed axe, and the Gordian knot are all a part of the knotted-net theme.

PYTHON

Python was the dragon who guarded the Omphalos of Delphi, the center of the earth. Pytho was the old name of Delphi and is related to *pythein*, meaning, "to rot." The Proto-Indo-European root, *dhubhon*, from *dheub*, means "hollow, deep, bottom or depths." Python was known as the *chthonic* (Greek: χθόνιος *chthonios*, "in, under, or beneath the earth")[233] dragon and was killed by Apollo with the darts given to him by Zeus, becoming the new guard of the Oracle.[234]

DELPHYNE SNAKE

The *Delphyne* (Greek: Δελφύνη) was another name used for the creature who guarded the Oracle of Delphi.[235] Delphyne is also known as Echidna, who had the head and torso of woman and the lower body of a snake. She was the consort of Typhon, the last son of Gaia, the "Father of All Monsters" who was also half human, half snake.

The amalgamation of Eve and the Nachash is the image of the parthenogenesis of the woman via the snake. The woman of the rotting womb (Python) appears as both serpent and human female. Delphyne, which means "womb," is another way of describing the Nachash-Eve amalgamation. She was the soothsayer (the root of "Nachash" means "to practice divination") who guarded the area of the garden-gained, illuminated power.

APOLLO

The center of the earth was the place where the event occurred in Eden that separated heaven from earth. Apollo, as the Nachash, symbolically changed his *image* in preparation for his future expression in human form by coming as the *slayer* of his first manifestation, the serpent-dragon, Python. As Apollo, he plans to create his version of "heaven on earth." Of course, the center of the earth is not really just a place marker, but it is also a *time* marker and a concept; it is where the beginning of all that is to come via the knowledge of good and evil sprang forth. Apollo at Delphi is similar to the legend of St. George.

Apollo killing Python[236]

St. George

The Golden Legend (Latin: *Legenda aurea* or *Legenda sanctorum*), written by Jacobus de Voragine in 1260, tells the story of St. George and the dragon that was said to have taken place in Silene, Libya ("Silene" means "flame" or "to burn"[237]). The dragon required that the Selenites offer it two sheep every day. After all the sheep had been eaten, by lottery, the Selenites fed the dragon their children. Eventually, the lot fell on the king's daughter, Sadra (from the Avestan language: "grief, sorrow, calamity").[238] The grieving king offered half of his kingdom and all of his wealth to anyone who might help him spare his daughter's life. The townspeople had pledged to allow no substitutes, so they sent his daughter, dressed as a bride, out to meet the dragon.

St. George (Greek: *georgios*, "earth worker"), who happened to ride by, asked the maiden what she had done to be so cruelly doomed. Sadra insisted that St. George leave her so that he would not suffer the same fate. He ignored her, stayed with her until the dragon appeared, and enchanted it with his lance. Acquiring the maiden's girdle (Greek: *zonus,* ζώνη, which also means "an order of divine beings presiding over, or engirdled with cosmic zones"),[239] St. George bound it around the neck of the monster so that the princess was able to lead it like a lamb.

In gratitude to and in honor of St. George, the townspeople converted to Christianity and were baptized. After cutting off the dragon's head and refusing the prize of wealth offered by the king, St. George left the city. Jacobus writes: "Georgius then smote the dragon with the spear (lancea), and had the girl collar the dragon up with her girdle [zonus]."[240]

The sword that St. George used to slay the dragon was called *Ascalon*.[241] From *Strong's Concordance, askelon* or *ashkelon* means "the fire of infamy" or "I shall be weighed." Askelon happens to be the name of the city where Samson slew thirty men after they had discovered his riddle.

> And the men of the city said unto him on the seventh day before the sun went down, What [is] sweeter than honey? and what [is] stronger than a lion? And he said unto them, If ye had not plowed with my heifer, ye had not found out my riddle. (Judges 14:18)

The bride awaiting her wedding and the power symbolized by her girdle directly relate to the realm God allowed the snake to have on earth. This manifold-substitution concept is artfully woven into the story and mirrors an overarching but intentionally hidden theme in mythology.

The king (God) offered to exchange all his wealth for his daughter's (humanity's) life. The dragon (Nachash) waits to destroy what the king greatly loves. St. George gains the bride's girdle, the symbol of man's subjugation to the law of God, and uses it to pacify *himself*, the lowly, God-cursed serpent. The wretchedness of the serpent that reflected the punishment given to it directly by the God of the universe had been defeated and substituted with a more fitting replacement, an assumed glory, and victory in his struggle—the image of the "earth worker," St. George.

The mystery schools look forward to a future when their god of light will manifest in human form. This story or *type* found so often in myth is an allegory of the future birth and rule of an illuminated messiah, the Apollyon[242] of light. In the story of Apollo and Python, the greatest, brightest, and most beautiful angel symbolically casts off the lowly curse of God. The act of slaying the snake symbolizes the transforming act that the Nachash plans in the future. He, as Apollo, is the god that will unite earth and heaven under his power. The changeover to Apollo from Python is a *prophecy*. The "light" will come, physically replacing the old mystery. The Oracle at Delphi has all the aspects of the garden encounter: the womb or beginning act of the self-generation and the whispering subtleness taken on by the woman. The snake remains as a guard to the whole structure of the relationship established. The description of the womb, Delphyne, changes to the rotting, underground, earth-bound snake. Although still the protector of the priestess and the navel stone, the bright destroyer comes to establish a new order, changing the place named Delphi, and becomes "Delphinus Apollo." In the same fashion, the incarnation of what has been for thousands of years representing itself in various symbolic forms comes to "slay" the old, rotting, mystery religion and replace it with himself, now as god-human.

The story of St. George is a representation of a vital prophecy understood by the highest echelons of the illuminated fraternities. On the surface, and to those whom the "illuminated" societies consider the *vulgar* majority, these stories represent the truth of the power of God over the Nachash. Their meaning has been inverted to be used and understood by the mystery schools in the manner that the snake has designed.

The symbolic reversal of the nature of archangel Michael is an allegory of the coming anti-Messiah as well.

Statue of Archangel Michael at the University of Bonn, slaying Satan as a dragon; *Quis ut Deus* ("Who is like God?") is inscribed on his shield.[243]

George Washington Masonic National Memorial—Alexandria, Virginia. An image of George Washington's head is rendered in the pediment of the Memorial below a thirteen-stepped tower reaching to heaven. A masonic double *tau* as the compass and square decorate the front of the building.[244]

Delphic Tripod

The Pythian priestess sat on a peculiar tripod ("three-footed") seat while uttering her oracles. It had a circular top, where a branch from the laurel was laid while the priestess was absent. The tripod was sacred to Apollo after he killed Python. The three feet of the tripod suspended the woman above Gaia in an imitation of Eve taking on the power of the Nachash-Apollo. From the tripod, the priestess speaks the words that reveal the future of men.

A Tetradrachm from the Illyro-Paeonian region representing Apollo. Notice the triangle and the elipse between the legs of the tripod.[245]

The Plataean Tripod or "Serpent Column" was a monument erected at Delphi from a tenth part of the armor and weapons taken from the Persian army after the Greeks defeated them in 479 BC in the Battle of Plataea. The approximately twenty-foot-high monument stood in the shape of three snakes twisted together, forming a tall post.[246] At the top, the snake's heads supported an ornate golden bowl. The base coils featured an inscription of the list of the Greek city-states that had fought in the battle.

Herodotus recorded that the column was dedicated to Apollo: When the booty had been gathered together, a tenth of the whole was set apart for the Delphian god, and, from this, was made the golden tripod that stands on the three-headed bronze serpent nearest the altar.[247]

The Greek Phoceans used the golden Plataean tripod to fund their army during the Third Sacred War (356–346 BC), and the golden bowl was carried off sometime during the Fourth Crusade. The emperor Constantine removed the remaining coiled serpent stand in AD 324 and placed it in the Hippodrome at Constantinople, where it still sits, although damaged. The heads of the serpents have disappeared from the monument, but one is on display at the Istanbul Archaeology Museum.

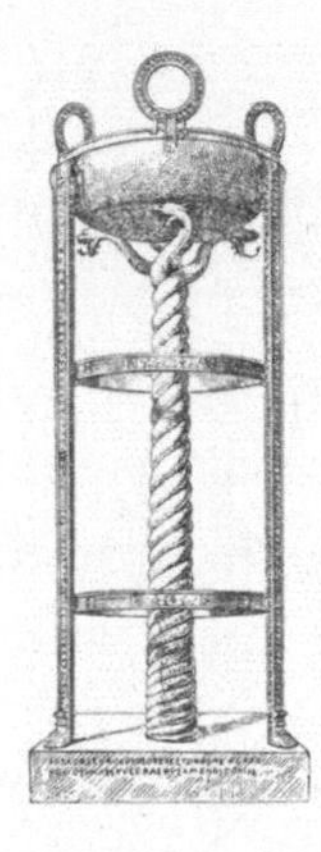

The Plataean Tripod

The Greek historian and Athenian general, Thucydides (460–395 BC), records that the Spartan King Pleistarchus, the son of Leonidas, inscribed the tripod in his book, *The History of the Peloponnesian War:*

> And it was remembered that he had taken upon himself to have inscribed on the tripod at Delphi, which was dedicated by the Hellenes as the first-fruits of the spoil of the Medes, the following couplet:—
>
> The Mede defeated, great Pausanias raised
> This monument, that Phoebus might be praised.[248]

"Phoebus" (Greek: "shining") is an epitaph for "Apollo."

The Serpent Column. The Obelisk of Theodosius is seen in the background.[249]

THE GORDIAN KNOT AND ZEUS SABAZIOS

There was a time when the Phrygians were without a king. So, the Oracle at the ancient capital city of Telmissus, Phrygia, predicted that the first man to enter the city on an ox-cart should become king. A peasant farmer named Gordius (whose names means "unsolvable"; related to the Latin *nodus*, "a knot," "to grasp," "to girdle," or "of a winding serpent")[250] entered the city driving an ox-cart and was declared king by the temple priests. Gordius had observed an eagle landing on his cart before entering the city and interpreted it as a sign from the gods. At the gates of Telmissus, he encountered a seeress, who instructed him to offer sacrifices to horse-riding Phrygian god Sabazios, whom the Greeks identified with Zeus.

> "Let me come with you, peasant," [the seeress] said, "to make sure that you select the right victims." "By all means," replied Gordius. "You appear to be a wise and considerate young woman. Are you prepared to marry me?" "As soon as the sacrifices have been offered," she answered.[251]

Later, Gordius' son, Midas—who in some accounts was adopted by Gordius and Phrygian goddess Cybele[252]—dedicated the ox-cart to Sabazios and bound its shaft with an intricate cornus bark rope knot. The wood from the cornus tree (Cornus sanguinea) known as dagwood, or "dagger wood," is so dense that it sinks in water and was valuable for the construction of spears, javelins, bows, and daggers.[253] The Greek name for "cornus" was a synonym for "spear" in poetry during the fourth and third centuries BC.[254] Much later, the red dye from the bark was used to make fezzes, which symbolized the Muslim's blood oath to defend their faith.

The Oracle at Telmissus prophesied that the one who could untie the rope knot would become the ruler of all Asia.

Alexander the Great

Alexander the Great (356–323 BC), whose name means "the defender of men," was the son of Philip II of Macedon. He was never defeated in battle, and conquered the area of modern-day Greece to the Himalayas. According to the Greek historian Plutarch (AD 46–120), his father was the god Zeus. His mother, Olympias, was a priestess of the Dionysus cult mentioned in Plutarch's *Life of Alexander* as having slept with serpents. Apollo, Attis, and Cybele are related to the Greek god, Dionysus. Like Attis, Dionysus' symbol was the pinecone. The day of Alexander's birth was the same day as the fiery destruction of the Temple of Artemis at Ephesus. It was thought that Artemis had allowed this to happen, since she was away attending Alexander's birth.

Alexander understood the ox-Eve-*Asterion* ("star" or "starry one"; epitaph for the Nachash) mystery religion thoroughly. In fact, Aristotle (a student of Plato) taught Alexander medicine, philosophy, morals, religion, logic, and art, and he developed a passion for the works of Homer—particularly the *Iliad*, an annotated copy of which Alexander carried with him on his journeys. Alexander named the horse that only he could tame, and which he rode in his many campaigns, *Bucephala* or "ox head," making him, in effect, "the rider of the bull." Alexander's familiarity with Plato's *Allegory of the Cave* must have been one of the reasons for his peculiar reaction to the Greek philosopher Diogenes of Sinope (412–323 BC), who lived in a large ceramic jar belonging to the Temple of Cybele. Alexander and Diogenes met in Sinope, Anatolia, sometime before the spring of 335 BC. Plutarch writes:

> [The] philosopher took not the slightest notice of Alexander, and continued to enjoy his leisure in the suburb Craneion, Alexander went in person to see him; and he found him lying in the sun. Diogenes raised himself up a little when he saw so many people coming towards him, and fixed his eyes upon Alexander. And when that monarch addressed him with greetings, and asked if he wanted anything, "Yes," said Diogenes, "stand a little out of my sun." It is said that Alexander was so struck by this, and admired so much the haughtiness and grandeur of the man who had nothing but scorn for him, that he said to his followers, who were laughing and jesting about the philosopher as they went away, "But truly, if I were not Alexander, I would be Diogenes."[255]

Diogenes' reply to Alexander has been thought of as one of disregard for human position and of outstanding bravery to speak truthfully. In the light of the *Allegory of the Cave* and the mystical identity of Alexander, the meaning behind the reply makes sense. At seeing Alexander and asking him to move so that the sun could fall on him once more, Diogenes revealed that he *understood*. Alexander was an incarnation of the Egyptian god, Amun-Ra, also known as Helios, Attis, or Apollo. Alexander's relationship to these gods was revealed during his visit to Jerusalem, where he was welcomed as the "first king" and shown the prophecy of Daniel:

> And the rough goat [is] the king of Grecia: and the great horn that [is] between his eyes [is] the first king. (Daniel 8:21)

The successions of kings described in Daniel are *types* of the Apollo-Attis-Nachash incarnations that will culminate in the fully realized Antichrist described later in the same chapter:

> And through his policy also he shall cause craft to prosper in his hand; and he shall magnify [himself] in his heart, and by peace shall destroy many: he shall also stand up against

the Prince of princes; but he shall be broken without hand. (Daniel 8:25)

In Egypt, Alexander visited the Oracle of Amon at Siwa Oasis, and was pronounced the son of Amon, "Master of the Universe."[256] The Greek biographer, Diogenes Laertius (c. AD 200–500), in his *Lives of Eminent Philosophers*, wrote that the other Diogenes—the philosopher who shared his name—"lit a lamp in broad daylight and said, as he went about, [saying] 'I am looking for a man.' "[257] Modern translations of the Greek for that quote, "I am looking for a man," add the word "honest" with "man." The Greek translation for the quotation, however, is *anthropon* (*anthropon,* ἄνθρωπον, "man," "mankind,") and *zeeto* (ζητῶ, "inquiring," "looking," "searching").[258]

An illustration from a postcard created by the American-born artist, Will Hicok Low (1853–1933), shows Diogenes with his lantern. Although left undescribed in the image, a statue of Alexander the Great wearing the horns of Jupiter Amon stands to the left. Low reveals his illuminated understanding of the meaning of Diogenes' search by associating him with Alexander. The Alexandrian manifestation of Apollo was the light symbolized by his lantern as well as the searched-for "man."

An illustration from a postcard created by the American-born artist Will Hicok Low shows Diogenes with his lantern.[259]

It is probable that Diogenes' (the philosopher's) encounter with Alexander echoes today in the form of an English corruption of his name. A word of "uncertain origin" meaning "to shift place" as defined by *Webster's Revised Unabridged Dictionary* is "dodge."[260]

In a symbolic echo of the way the Trojans who "loved the horse" were replaced by the power of the invading Greeks, from his father Philip (*philos,* "lover," *hippos,* "horse"), Alexander changed the balance of power in the ancient world. The first town Alexander reached after invading Anatolia was Troy, where he visited the tomb of the invincible (if not for his vulnerable heel) Greek warrior, Achilles, and made sacrifices to him.[261]

During the winter of 333 BC, Alexander *untied* the Gordian knot by slicing it in half with a stroke of his sword, exposing the "ends." That night, during a violent thunderstorm, the prophet Aristander ("the one with ears") who accompanied Alexander throughout his battles told Alexander that Zeus was pleased and would grant him many victories.

At his death in Babylon at age thirty-two, Alexander's body was placed by his soldiers into a form-fitting sarcophagus filled with honey, and then placed it in a gold casket—mirroring the stories of Glaucus and Osiris, which will be described in chapters 9 and 13.

9

THE LABYRINTH

> We were like children after larks, always on the point of catching the art, which was always getting away from us.... At last we came to the kingly art, and enquired whether that gave and caused happiness, and then we got into a labyrinth, and when we thought we were at the end, came out again at the beginning, having still to seek as much as ever.
>
> —SOCRATES, *PLATO'S EUTHYDEMUS* ("STRAIGHT LAND")[262]

Europa (εὐρυ, "wide" or "broad," and ὤψ, "eyes" or "face") was the Phoenician daughter of Agenor, king of Tyre. Zeus saw her picking flowers and decided to seduce her by turning himself into a shining, white bull. Enchanted by Zeus' beauty, Europa allowed him to abduct her to Crete. The sons of Zeus and Europa were Rhadamanthus, Sarpedon, and Minos. Europa eventually married Asterion, "the starry one."

The rhetorician Lucian of Samosata (AD 125–180), in his *De Dea Syria* ("Concerning the Syrian Goddess"), wrote about the Sidonian Temple of Astarte-Europa that was sacred to Europa:

> There is likewise in Phœnicia a temple of great size owned by the Sidonians. They call it the temple of Astarte. I hold this Astarte to

> be no other than the moon-goddess. But according to the story of one of the priests this temple is sacred to Europa, the sister of Cadmus. She was the daughter of Agenor, and on her disappearance from Earth the Phœnicians honoured her with a temple and told a sacred legend about her; how that Zeus was enamoured of her for her beauty, and changing his form into that of a bull carried her off into Crete. This legend I heard from other Phœnicians as well; and the coinage current among the Sidonians bears upon it the effigy of Europa sitting upon a bull, none other than Zeus. Thus they do not agree that the temple in question is sacred to Europa.[263]

King Minos

King Minos, son of Zeus and Europa, was the king of Crete whose name has been associated with the Canaanite deity Baal Meon.[264] *Beon* is a contraction of *Beth-baal-meon* and is used one time in the Pentateuch, in Numbers 32:3. *Beth* means a "house" or "temple." *Ma`own* is a "dwelling, habitation, refuge, lair, refuge (of jackals)," and is the same as the word *ownah*, which means "cohabitation or conjugal rights."

God was angered with the children of Reuben and Gad, who sought to stay in the area of Beon so that they could raise their cattle and not continue into the Promised Land. Because of this, He made Israel wander in the desert wilderness for forty years.

> And the LORD's anger was kindled the same time, and he sware, saying, Surely none of the men that came up out of Egypt, from twenty years old and upward, shall see the land which I sware unto Abraham, unto Isaac, and unto Jacob; because they have not wholly followed me. (Numbers 32:10–11)

Minos prayed to Poseidon, the brother of Zeus, for support in his struggle to become the most powerful king. Poseidon sent him a perfect, snow-white bull known in antiquity as the "Cretan Bull." The identity of the bull was the same as the one that carried away Europa—Zeus in disguise.

Instead of sacrificing the bull in honor of Poseidon, Minos decided to keep it because of its great beauty, and offered instead a substitute bull sacrifice of his own. To punish Minos, Poseidon had Aphrodite make his wife, Pasiphaë (Greek: "wide shining"—the same meaning as "Europa," "Athena," and "Glaucus"), daughter of the sun god Helios, fall in love with the white bull. According to Ovid, in his *Ars Amatoria* ("Art of Love"), Pasiphaë "took pleasure in becoming an adulteress with the bull." She had the genius artisan Daedalus ("clever worker") fashion a wooden cow that she could crawl into to help complete the adulterous act. The result was the ferocious, half-man, half-bull monster, the Minotaur ("Minos' bull"). The Minotaur, also known as the *Asterion* (ἀστέριον, "ruler of the stars" or "starry one"), required human flesh as its sole source of food and was too difficult for Pasiphaë or Minos to control. In desperation, Minos went to the Delphic Oracle for advice. At the direction of the Oracle, Pasiphaë and Minos had Daedalus create a great Labyrinth to imprison the monster.

The whole concept of what the double bladed axe or *labrys* (Greek: λάβρυς, "lábrys") represents is vital to the understanding of the Labyrinth. The labrys has been attributed to the Lydian culture from southeastern Anatolia from around 800 BC. Plutarch mentioned that the origin of the labrys was from Lydia and named after the god Zeus Labrandeus, later borrowed by the Minoans at Knossos.[265]

The Minoan civilization venerated the labrys and specifically represented its use by only women priestesses. The axes found at the island of Knossos vary from small, iconic, gold symbols to the functionally large ones, which were used to ritualistically kill bulls. The priests at Delphi were called *Labryades,* or the "men of the double axe."

The word "labrys" has all the letter-based etymologic hallmarks of the activity of the Nachash in the garden of God. The Phoenician root-letter meanings for "labrys" (λάβρυς: *lamda, alpha, beta, rho, nu, sigma*) are: goad, ox, house, head, serpent, and tooth/name/hiss/sharp. In light of the bull/ox/Zeus/God metaphor, the meaning leaps out: "The sharp, injuring act of the serpent against God." The word "labyrinth" has "labrys" in its base, rendering the Greek translation as "the house of the double-bladed ax."

Minos' son, Androgeus (*Andro*, "man," *geus-geos,* "earth") or Eurugûes ("he who plows"),[266] was the greatest athlete of the Panathenaic festivals held in Athens. In some accounts, the Athenians killed Androgeus in jealousy or he died attempting to kill the Cretan bull under the orders of the Athenian king, Aegeus (*Ae*, "eternity," *geus-geos*, "earth"), who was also known as the "goat man." In anger, King Minos declared war on Athens, but offered peace if the Athenians would accept his terms that they must offer the Minotaur seven young men and seven young women—all to be chosen by lot—every seven years.

For the human sacrifices to reach the Minotaur, the path to the beast must have been easy. In fact, every path would have led inevitably nearer to the monster, since the victims would have tried to avoid reaching it at all costs. Escape from the Labyrinth was impossible for both the predator and the prey.

The concept of the bull's head as a symbol for the One God is perhaps the most important component required in gaining understanding of the true meaning of the Labyrinth. Minos desired power, and in reply to his prayer to Poseidon, the Cretan bull of heaven, Zeus in disguise, came to him as a sacrifice. Minos rejected the deal. As punishment, Poseidon as Zeus (God) caused the love of his life, the one who was on the path of knowledge with her shining, open eyes, to love the bull rather than him. Disaster followed. God and the woman created the God-man, the bull-man. The "clever-working" Nachash helped by restraining and protecting Minos and Pasiphaë from the "terrible" God-man in his twisting, false-pathed, confusing trap.

THESEUS

Theseus was the demigod son of Aegeus *and* Poseidon, since Aegeus' wife Aethra (*Ae*, "eternity," *thra-thera*, "hunter") had slept with both of them in one night. Theseus (Θησεύς), from the Greek root *tetheme* (τίθημι), means "to set, establish, put in place." *Thesmos* (θεσμός) means an "institution."[267]

Theseus captured the Cretan bull on his way to Marathon, and brought it back to Athens where he sacrificed it to Zeus—a strange story, since the bull was a manifestation of Zeus. Literally, God sacrificed Himself. The fennel stalk that Prometheus used to hide the fire he stole from Zeus was sacred to the Greeks, and Marathon (*Marathon,* Μαραθών, "fennel") was famous for being "overgrown" with them. The *thyrsus,* a giant fennel (*ferula communis*) staff covered with ivy vines and always topped with a pinecone, was part of the costume of the Dionysian or Bacchus cult. Bacchus was the god of wine, madness, and revelry. The philosopher Socrates (469–399 BC) addressed the meaning of the fennel stalk in his Dialogue, *Phaedo:*

> I conceive that the founders of the mysteries had a real meaning and were not mere triflers when they intimated in a figure long ago that he who passes unsanctified and uninitiated into the world below will live in a slough, but that he who arrives there after initiation and purification will dwell with the gods. For "many," as they say in the mysteries, are the thyrsus bearers, but few are the mystics,"—meaning, as I interpret the words, the true philosophers.[268]

The *decoded* story of Theseus and the Cretan bull is bizarre. The one who establishes a path must first go to the place of "much knowledge"—"many fennel stalks"—and capture the Zeus-God, who "hides" in the form of the bull. With understanding, "God" can be subdued and led to the place of the mother goddess Eve-Athena so that He can be sacrificed to Himself.

Freemasons use the Mosaic pavement pattern in their lodges as a symbol of the Labyrinth. The image is described as "a representation of the ground floor of king Solomon's Temple...and the *Blazing star,* in the center...is emblematic of human life, checkered with good and evil."[269]

Image from the *Freemason's Monitor* depicting the mosaic pavement.

At the time of the third sacrifice to the man-bull-Asterion, lord of the stars, Theseus traveled to Crete in a black-sailed ship promising his father Aegeus that he would return with a white sail if he succeeded in killing the Minotaur. When he arrived, Minos' daughter, Ariadne (Greek: *ari*, αρι, "most," and *adnos*, αδνος, "holy"), fell in love with him. Under the direction of Daedalus, the creator of the Labyrinth, Ariadne gave Theseus a ball of thread also known as the "clue." Theseus managed to find and—after a great struggle—kill the Minotaur. He escaped the Labyrinth by following the "clue."

In a mirror to the story of Theseus and the Cretan bull, the guidance of the "holy woman" (Ariadne-Eve) with help from the "clever worker" (Daedalus-Nachash) was the key to solving the problem. It required that the one who might find the path to knowledge first "kill" the God-man and eliminate its suffering-causing influence. Next, through the "clue" provided by the clever worker, the path back to the light was possible. Both stories reveal the strange deception perpetuated by the Nachash: that through the light-bringer's *guided* acquisition of knowledge, the knowledge kept secret to all but the most worthy of his established Eve cult, the God of all creation can be *subdued*. This is the mystery behind the Attis-Cybele-bull cult of Mithras, the Europa, bull, and Asterion story, as well as the secret of the enigmatic Athenian epitaph, *Tritogeneia*.

After Theseus' success, he sailed first to the island of Delos, known to the Greeks as the birthplace of Artemis and Apollo, to celebrate his victory. The Greek historian Plutarch writes:

> Now Theseus, in his return from Crete, put in at Delos, and having sacrificed to the god of the island, dedicated to the temple the image of Venus which Ariadne had given him, and danced with the young Athenians a dance that, in memory of him, they say is still preserved among the inhabitants of Delos, consisting in certain measured turnings and returnings, imitative of the windings and twistings of the labyrinth. And this dance, as Dicaearchus writes, is called among the Delians the Crane. This he danced around the Ceratonian Altar, so called from its consisting of *horns taken from the left side* of the head. They say also that he instituted games in Delos, where he was the first that began the custom of giving a palm to the victors.[270]

Some of the hedge mazes or knot gardens popular during the Renaissance featured a notable characteristic: In order to reach the center, a person needed only continue making right turns wherever possible. The maze at Hampton Court Palace is an example of one with a right-turn solution. It was created for William III of Orange sometime around 1690.

Maze of Hampton court. The "right" path leads to the center.[271]

The word for "left" in Latin is *sinister* and in French is *gauche*, also meaning "crude or inappropriate." The Lithuanian *kairys,* "left," and Lettish *kreilis,* "left hand," are derived from a root that yields words for "twisted" or "crooked."[272] A euphemism for "the better one," *aristos* (ἄριστος), comes from the Greek the word for "left," *aristeros* (ἀριστερός).

The maze of the Minotaur is solved by taking the left-hand path, the path undesired through ignorance but taken nevertheless through illuminated guidance.

Theseus forgot to raise the white sail at his return to Athens, and his father, seeing the black sail, threw himself into the sea and drowned. Plutarch describes the combinations of emotions experienced by Theseus and the Athenians: joy at the freedom from having to sacrifice their children and grief at the death of their king:

> At his entrance, the herald found the people for the most part full of grief for the loss of their king; others, as may well be believed, as full of joy for the tidings that he brought, and eager to welcome him and crown him with garlands for his good news, which he indeed accepted of, but hung them upon his herald's staff; and thus returning to the seaside before Theseus had finished his libation to the gods, he stayed apart for fear of disturbing the holy rites; but, as soon as the libation was ended, went up and related the king's death, upon the hearing of which, with great lamentations and a confused tumult of grief, they ran with all haste to the city. And from hence, they say, it comes that at this day, in the feast of Oschophoria, the herald is not crowned, but his staff, and all who are present at the libation cry out eleleu, iou, iou, the first of which confused sounds is commonly used by men in haste, or at a triumph, the other is proper to people in consternation or disorder of mind.[273]

The illuminated mystics who secretly worship Lucifer rejoice at the fact that he defied God, freeing men and giving them the chance to be like gods themselves. At the same time, they mourn for the angel, for how much greater would he have been throughout their history if God had not cursed him?

The black-sail event, along with the arrival of a conquering hero, is strangely mirrored in the black standard or "young eagle" flag used by Muhammad. It was said to be the head cloth of his *seven*-year-old wife, Aisha, whose name means "Mother of the Believers."[274]

At the arrival of the Islamic messiah or *Mahdi*, Islamic tradition states that the event would be signaled by black standards proceeding from the Khorasan region in Persia, which means "the coming eastern sun,"[275] the coming *Anatolia*.

After his arrival in Athens, Theseus established the feast of *Oschophoria*, the feast of boughs. Similar to the feast of Attis, during which the eunuch priests would accompany the effigy of Attis on the pine tree, the Oschophoria procession was led by two young noblemen dressed as women carrying bunches of grapes (*oschoi*) on branches, with banquets given by female dinner-bearers who issued libations accompanied by mixed cries of joy and grief.

Theseus also coined money featuring the image of the Minotaur, which the Greeks valued at a *hecatomb*, the value of the sacrifice of one hundred oxen. The Greeks sometimes sacrificed a hecatomb after receiving any great gift thought to have been given through their god's intersession.

Pythagoras proved the 47th problem of Euclid, from his 465 mathematical propositions, or Elements, that for a right triangle, the square of the hypotenuse is equal to the sum of the squares of the other two sides. He was said to have offered a hecatomb after discovering this fact, known today as the Pythagorean Theorem.

The 3:4:5 triangle is a golden or the smallest set of Pythagorean (*phi*, Φ) triples, and sacred to Freemasons for the reasons explained in chapter 2. The symbol used in Masonic literature for the 47th problem of Euclid is the three squares.

The symbol used in Masonic literature for the 47th problem of Euclid[276]

The term "thesis" used today means the same as the root word for Theseus: "something put forth." It refers to an intellectual proposition or a researched investigation. Another term for "thesis" also related to the myth of the Labyrinth is "dissertation," which comes from the Latin *dissertātiō*, meaning "path." Plutarch mentions the paradox of the ship of Theseus:

> The ship wherein Theseus and the youth of Athens returned had thirty oars, and was preserved by the Athenians down even to the time of Demetrius Phalereus, for they took away the old planks as they decayed, putting in new and stronger timber in their place, insomuch that this ship became a standing example among the philosophers, for the logical question of things that grow; one side holding that the ship remained the same, and the other contending that it was not the same.[277]

Just as the gods representing the Nachash, Eve, Adam, and God Himself have diverged, aggregated, and morphed over the many thousands of years since the garden, the twisted-core religious mystery has remained the same. From Eve springs Isis, Hathor, Neith, Cybele, Attis, Ishtar, Seriamis, Pasiphaë, Europa, Artemis, and Athena. From the Nachash, there is the lion, the snake, Daedalus, Mithras, Asterion, and the Phoenix.

God is the ox, bull, or cow, as well as Zeus or Poseidon. There are dual-aspect characters exhibiting aspects of both God and Eve, God and man, and God and woman. These are interchangeable with ones representing different aspects that occur as mythological stories progress. Artemis in ancient artistic representation was superimposed with the form of the evil cherub. The Minotaur is the God-man, but his dual-natured name is Asterion, either God-man or the Nachash. This is done frequently since the Nachash seeks to subvert and replace the image of God.

The paradox known as the "ship of Theseus" is a question of whether the original ship, after having every bit replaced over time, could be identified as the same ship. Is the one having no original parts still considered the same ship?

The answer to the paradox is clear: Over time, each replaced component of the ship might appear completely different, but the underlying *mystery* remains the same for anyone whose eyes have been opened. The last is the same as the first. The essence of the religion of the Nachash *is* the ship, no matter the twists and turns through the Labyrinth, the forms of the players and characters over time, or the knotted, coiled snares around the legends that, at times, seem to contradict or confuse, and, at other times, reinforce the characters' identity in a layered fashion of superimposed allegory.

Apart from an example for young children of the value of possessing a truthful character, the story of the axe that George Washington used to cut down his father's cherry tree bears an uncanny resemblance to the story of the Labyrinth and the labrys.

The concept is the same: a bold decision to tell (reveal) the truth in the face of dire consequences. The human choice to go to the "light" or "truth" despite the fact that their creator had forbidden it is illustrated in the story of Washington cutting down his father's cherry tree. The axe, although not double-bladed, is an allusion to the labrys. The embellished story today specifically describes the ship of Theseus paradox: "What if the axe was kept in a museum and had undergone repairs which over the years had the head replaced once and the handle replaced twice. Is it the same axe?"

Certain paths to illumination require a way-shower. Others are restricted to the individual. For these types of paths, the journey leads from one beginning truth. From the first truth, much more can be discovered—if the truth-seeker is worthy. If unworthy, no amount of effort at "dragging" the student farther will succeed.

Euclid described this concept as well in his fifth proposition known as the Theorem on Isosceles Triangles or the "Pons Asinorum" (Latin: "bridge of asses"), where the proof requires the ability to understand that a beginning fact leads to other factual conclusions.

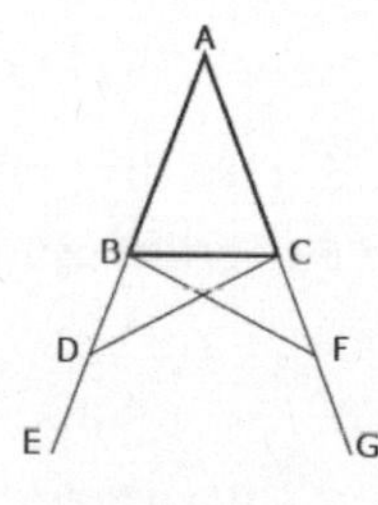

Image used in Euclid's proof of proposition 5[278]

The quintessential point is this: To understand the mystery, one must first understand the hidden identity of each mythological character. This identity never changes, but the outward appearance is not limited to name, appearance, or even gender. This is the definition of the Labyrinth, the knotted net, and the tapestry of the weaver. The *clue* must guide the traveler away from the false paths and ultimately back to the outer "light" so that all can be considered and understood after the journey is complete. There is more than just following the correct path to obtain illumination. Although there may be more than one way to reach the center and more to escape, the journeyer must be prepared to meet each dangerous impediment with the understanding gained at each stage.

GLAUCUS

Glaucus (Γλαῦκος, "shiny," "bright," or "bluish-green") was a prince, the son of Minos and Queen Pasiphaë. While chasing a mouse in a wine cellar in Minos' palace, Glaucus fell into a jar of honey and suffocated. After failing to find his son, King Minos went to the dancing Corybantes,[279] who worshipped the goddess Cybele, for guidance. They told the king: "A prodigy has been born for you. Whoever explains it will restore the child to you."[280]

Minos realized that they were referring to a newborn calf from his herd that continually changed color in a sequence from white to red, dark purple, and then back to white. The colors of the red, white, and blue flag of the United States were copied from the British flag that was originally designed in 1606 during the time of King James I at the union of England and Scotland. Red (*desher*) was the color of the god Seth and was the symbol of rage and death. White (*hedj*) signified anything that was sacred or holy. The Egyptian pharaoh, Menes, who united the upper and lower kingdoms, established the city of Memphis, which means "white walls." Memphis was the place of the preeminent creator of the universe and all other gods, Ptah. Blue (*irtiu*) was the color of rebirth.

The Corinthian seer *Polyidus* ("seeing many things") compared the calf to the ripening of the fruit of the mulberry, so Minos sent him to find Glaucus.

Seeing an owl driving bees away from the wine cellar, Polyidus went inside and found the boy. Minos demanded that Polyidus bring his son back to life, and closed the cellar doors until he did so. In the darkness, Polyidus watched as a snake approached the corpse, but he killed it with a stone to prevent it from harming the boy's body. Soon, another snake appeared with an "herb" and placed it on the body of the dead snake, bringing it back to life. Polyidus took the same herb and placed it on the boy, raising him, too, from the dead. Minos was overjoyed at having his son back, but still would not let Polyidus leave Crete until he had taught his son the art of divination. Polyidus capitulated, but as he was preparing to sail away, he asked Glaucus to spit in his mouth, causing Glaucus to forget everything that he was taught.[281] The resurrected Glaucus later led an army that attacked Rome and introduced the shield and military girdle or *labicus*.

10

MONEY

An inch of time is worth an inch of gold,
but it is hard to buy one inch of time
with one inch of gold.
—Chinese Proverb

Adam and Eve's expulsion from paradise meant that for the first time, humanity experienced an alien state of existence—the state of want or *lacking*. There could never be a state of lacking in paradise. Hunger, thirst, anxiety, fear, sadness, and *death*—the condition of lacking life itself—could not have existed. The fruit of the Tree of the Knowledge of Good and Evil provided specifically what it promised. Although Adam and Eve lived in the very presence of God, they lacked the knowledge of good as it contrasted with evil, and vice versa. Of course, the evil portion of experience was completely unknown until the Nachash convinced Eve to try the fruit. Communion with God, heaven on earth, was lost—and Adam and Eve were expelled from the garden. The necessity of constant labor to sustain life and avoid discomfort were what the Nachash brought Adam and Eve, via the fruit, for the first time. Without the need for labor, there would be no reason for the eventual necessity of *money*.

Aristotle believed that all objects valued by human beings have two possible uses: 1) the original purpose or function of the object; and 2) the possibility that the object could be used for barter.[282] The substitute of a token in place of a barter item requires that, first, an intelligent and sufficiently powerful authority controls its distribution, and, second, that the token's value is accepted. The token then becomes an object of value even though it has no functional significance. To cement the token's power as a medium of exchange, it should be exceedingly scarce and as physically indestructible as possible. Throughout human history, gold has been found to possess these qualities.

Money is a commonly accepted part of life, and most people take its existence for granted without further contemplating its profundity. Everyone understands its function, but few understand its essence: that money is a symbolic token of human life. The time spent working for money is life set aside or taken out of the fixed amount given to each human. Since the very definition of life must include the time spent being alive, all of the time spent earning money, in a true sense, is life converted to money. There is a mystic vitality to the inanimate object representing human life being used to gain the necessities for the activity or improvement of living.

With this idea in mind, one is able to gain an understanding of the more esoteric implications concerning the history, use, control, and corruption of money. Money takes on a type of mystical significance when it has achieved acceptance. Modern archeologists have theorized that the temple priests of goddess Artemis in ancient Lydia issued the first magical tokens known later as *money*.

The Quince Is a Coin

In his book, *Cydonia: The Secret Chronicles of Mars*, author David Flynn notes that the ancients did not have what we today know as *pears*. In art, the quince represented the fruit of the Tree of Knowledge of Good and Evil, known by its scientific name, *Pyrus Cydonia*.

"The English word that we use today for money as both a noun and verb is *coin*," Flynn states. "The word coin is directly related to the fruit of the tree of the knowledge of good and evil, not represented by the apple but the quince or *Pyrus Cydonia*."[283]

The 1828 edition of *Webster's Revised Unabridged Dictionary* describes the quince as "the fruit of the Pyrus Cydonia, so named from Cydonia, a town of Crete, famous for abounding with this fruit. One species of this fruit is of an oblong shape, from which probably it has its French name."[284]

The 1913 edition of *Webster's* adds a bit more to the definition, specifically relating the word quince to *coin*: "Quince, n. [Prob. a pl. from OE. quyne, coin, OF. coin, cooin, F. coing, from L. Cydonius a quince tree, as adj., Cydonian, Gr. Cydonian, a quince, fr. Cydonia, a city in Crete, the Cydonians. Cf. Quiddany]."[285]

Because of the involvement of the Nachash with the fiery Cydonia fruit, the etymology of the word "coin" grew from the idea of a separation or wedge set in place between man and God. The wedge as something that obstructs is directly linked to the idea of the pediment structure.

The Latin word *cuneus* basically means a "wedge." The old French *coing*, from the Latin cuneus, can mean "a wedge, a stamp, a piece of money, a corner, or an angle." Something that is *cuneate* is wedge-shaped, but more especially is something that is narrowly triangular.

The old English *quion* or *coign* can mean an "exterior angle of a wall or other piece of masonry," or it can refer to the actual stone block used to form a quoin, especially when it is different from the other blocks that are used to build a structure or a cornerstone. It can also refer the actual die used for stamping out metal into "coins." In Modern French, a coin is "a corner, an angle," "a nook," or an "interior angle."[286]

From this same word, we get "cuneiform," which describes the earliest known form of written expression used in ancient Samaria, Akkadia, Assyria, Babylonia, and Persia. Part of the poem, "Roman de la Rose," written by Guillaume de Lorris in 1230, is set inside a walled garden. The poem is unique in that it uses the word "coin" for the quince:

Que bon mengier fait après table.
Où vergier ot arbres domesches,
Qui chargoient et ***coins*** et pesches,

Chataignes, nois, pommes et poires,
Nefles, prunes blanches et noires,
Cerises fresches merveilletes,
Cormes, alies et noisetes;
De haus loriers et de haus pins
Refu tous puéplés li jardins.[287] (emphasis added)

Here is the poem, translated into Middle English:

And many homly trees ther were
That peches, ***coynes***, and apples beere,
Medlers, plowmes, perys, chesteynes,
Cherys, of which many oon fayn is,
Notes, aleys, and bolas,
That for to seen it was solas.
With many high lorer and pyn
Was renged clene all that gardyn.[288] (emphasis added)

The "coin" has taken on the idea of the separation or event that placed a *wedge* between earth and paradise, God and man, as well as the becoming a word for the fruit that it directly represents.

HECATE

The goddess who quintessentially embodies the overlapping relationship between the Nachash and Eve illustrated in the Attis-Cybele god well as the wedge-coin idea is the Anatolian goddess Hecate.[289] The etymology of Hectate or Hecate is from the Greek *Hecate* (Ἑκάτη), an epithet of Artemis, which is the feminine equivalent of *Hekatos* (Ἑκατός). That word, in turn, is an obscure name for Apollo, meaning "far-shooting."[290]

Hecate was associated with crossroads, entranceways, necromancy, fire, torches, light, dogs, keys and the moon. Frequently depicted in a *triple* form, she mirrored the three-footed Delphic tripod of the Pythian priestess. She is particularly involved in the commerce of mankind, and has been said to bestow great wealth to anyone whose prayers she receives favorably. Hecate was the daughter of the Titans Phoebe ("radiant light") and Coeus, whose name means "an expression of anger or surprise."[291]

Hesiod mentions Hecate and her power to bestow wealth in his *Theogony:*

> Again, Phoebe came to the desired embrace of Coeus.... And she conceived and bare Hecate whom Zeus the son of Cronos honoured above all. He gave her splendid gifts, to have a share of the earth and the unfruitful sea. She received honour also in starry heaven, and is honoured exceedingly by the deathless gods. For to this day, whenever any one of men on earth offers rich sacrifices and prays for favour according to custom, he calls upon Hecate. Great honour comes full easily to him whose prayers the goddess receives favourably, and she bestows wealth upon him; for the power surely is with her.... And the son of Cronos made her a nurse of the young who after that day saw with their eyes the light of all-seeing Dawn.[292]

Like the Cybele-Attis-Mithras cult, Hecate was worshipped as a chthonic goddess, and the priests who served her were eunuchs.[293]

Coins have been found from the Greco-Bactrian Kingdom (250–125 BC) depicting Hecate with her two torches being held by the hand of Zeus. Modern Wiccan witchcraft still honors Hecate today. The Wiccan Hecate reflects the image of the goddess born in the walled garden, empowered by the serpent and referred to as "the goddess of hedges" or "she who rides the hedges."

The Hecate of the Greek island Chiaramonti, a Roman sculpture of triple Hecate, after the Greek original. Notice the wedge or cornerstone structure built into Hecate's body, the "rays," and the Phrygian caps on each of her three heads, associating her with Attis-Cybele. As the triple Hecate, she is an anthropomorphized version of the Plataean and Delphic Tripod.[294]

The ancient temple of Hecate was located at Lagina (Greek: Λαγίνα, "of the hare"), Anatolia, in the area occupied by the Lydians, who were known as the first people to use gold and silver coins.[295]

THE LYDIANS

Herodotus wrote, "The Lydians were the first people we know of to strike coins of gold and of silver."[296] He also mentioned that the first king of Sardis, the capital of ancient Lydia, was Agron, the son of Ninus, who was the son of Belus, the son of Agelaus, son of Heracles respectively.

Ninus, or Nimrod, as he is thought to be in some scholarly circles, was the king of Assyria and legendary founder of the city of Ninevah.[297] Homer called the kingdom of Lydia Maionia,[298] and that said that its capital was not Sardis, but Hyde, so named after the star cluster in the face of the Taurus constellation, the Hyades. The Meiones were renamed Lydians after the reign of King Lydus. Flavius Josephus derives "Lydus" or "Lud" to be the son of Shem and the grandson of Noah.[299]

The Lydians were known for their skill in archery[300] and for the practical and ceremonial use of the double-bladed axe. Plutarch mentioned that the origin of the double-bladed axe or labrys was Lydia and that it was named after their god, Zeus Labrandeus.[301]

Strong's Concordance defines the name Ludim (לודיי) or Lydian as: "to the firebrands: travailings," from *Luwd* (לוד), meaning "strife."

The word "drachma," from the Greek *drássomai*, means "to grasp."[302] The base word, *drakōn* (δράκων), as described in *Strong's Lexicon*, is "a dragon, a great serpent, a name for Satan," with an alternate form of *derkomai*, which means "to look or watch."

The word for a limit of something that could be held by a human hand, a *drássomai,* comes from the earliest form of Greek script known as Linera B via the earlier Minoan Linear A from Knossos at the city-state Cydonia.

The six base objects together forming a new unit name is similar to the six "eggs" of the ancient Hebrew measure of volume, in which six eggs formed a "log" (because only three eggs could be held in each hand). This measuring system beginning with six base units has an allegory to the Troy pound, which is composed of 5760 grains.

In the case of the drachma, the things grasped were simply skewers or arrows. Known as *oboloí* or *obeloí*, they were made of iron, copper, or bronze, and literally as useful for battle as they were as "money." Later, the obeloi became more and more symbolic in form until the skewer shape changed to more of an oblong, metallic arrowhead.

The use of an arrowhead in place of the coin token that signified the fruit of the knowledge of good and evil is typical of the Nachash. Rather than allowing the understanding of the symbolic representation of the coin as the reason for necessity labor and money, the Nachash corrupted it, making it a representation of himself.

The four-drachmae tetradrachm from the fifth century BC known as the *glauke* is commonly understood to mean an "owl" and was a widely used coin up to the time of Alexander the Great. On one side was a profile of Athena in her helmet, and on the other was her symbol, the wide-eyed owl. The Greek word for "wide-eyed" is "Europa" (εὐρύς, *eurys*, "broad," and ὤψ, ōps, "eye")[303] and the term "glauke" does not literally mean "owl"—it is from *glaukopis* (γλαυκ, *glauk*, "gleaming" + ὦπις, *opis*, "eyes").[304]

The tetradrachm or "glauke." The modern Greek euro still has an owl on the reverse.[305]

> And the eyes of them both were opened, and they knew that they [were] naked; and they sewed fig leaves together, and made themselves aprons. (Genesis 3:7)

History of Money in the United States

Originally, the government of the United States was specifically based upon the belief in God. The Declaration of Independence describes this principle:

> When in the Course of human events it becomes necessary for one people to dissolve the political bands which have connected them with another and to assume among the powers of the earth, the separate and equal station to which the Laws of Nature and of Nature's God entitle them, a decent respect to the opinions of mankind requires that they should declare the causes which impel them to the separation.
>
> We hold these truths to be self-evident, that all men are created equal, that they are endowed by their Creator with certain unalienable Rights, that among these are Life, Liberty and the pursuit of Happiness.—That to secure these rights, Governments are instituted among Men, deriving their just powers from the consent of the governed.

This belief in God was the basis for the legitimacy of the new nation and the principle that the people would control their government. The use and regulation of money in a nation that was established justly or through that nation's reliance on the laws of God is outlined in the Constitution.

Article I, Section 8 explicitly assigns the power to coin money and fix standards of weight and measure to the government, which is controlled by the people of the United States: "To coin Money, regulate the Value thereof, and of foreign Coin, and fix the Standard of Weights and Measures; To provide for the Punishment of counterfeiting the Securities and current Coin of the United States."

Thomas Jefferson understood the importance of maintaining the control of currency by the governed rather than allowing an establishment of a private bank:

> I consider the foundation of the Constitution as laid on this ground—that all powers not delegated to the United States, by the Constitution, nor prohibited by it to the states, are reserved to the states, or to the people [10th amendment]. To take a single step beyond the boundaries thus specially drawn around the powers of Congress, is to take possession of a boundless field of power, no longer susceptible of any definition.

On the subject of the establishment of a national bank outside the control of its citizens, Jefferson wrote: "The incorporation of a bank, and the powers assumed by this bill, have not, in my opinion, been delegated to the United States by the Constitution."[306]

The belief that money debasement was an offence on the same level as murder was recognized at time the United States was established. It would be consistent that the penalty for an act of currency debasement would be death. The Coinage Act passed by the United States Congress in 1792 established the United States Mint in Philadelphia and set down regulations on the quality and quantity of gold and silver used in coinage. Only one penalty was listed for anyone convicted of coinage debasement: death.

The Coinage Act of April 2, 1792:

> Penalty on debasing the coins. Section 19.
> And be it further enacted, That if any of the gold or silver coins which shall be struck or coined at the said mint shall be debased or made worse as to the proportion of the fine gold or fine silver therein contained, or shall be of less weight or value than the same out to be pursuant to the directions of this act, through the default or with the connivance of any of the officers or persons who shall be employed at the said mint, for the purpose of profit or gain, or otherwise with a fraudulent intent, and if any of the said officers or persons shall embezzle any of the metals which shall at any time be committed to their charge for the purpose of being coined, or any of the coins which shall be struck or coined

> at the said mint, every such officer or person who shall commit any or either of the said offenses, shall be deemed guilty of felony, ***and shall suffer death.***[307] (emphasis added)

TALISMAN

Money lacking a legitimate source by its issuer can be considered a magic token or talisman. A talisman, from the Greek work *teleo,* meaning, "to consecrate," is an object that has been *charged* with magical power by its creator. The Hermetic Order of the Golden Dawn describes a talisman as "a magical figure charged with the force which it is intended to represent. In the construction of a talisman, care should be taken to make it, as far as possible, so to represent the universal forces that it should be in exact harmony with those you wish to attract, and the more exact the symbolism, the easier it is to attract the force."[308]

A talisman should be created by the entity that plans to use it, since the ignorance of the power behind it would render it ineffective. This limits the talisman's power to an elite group of people who possess the knowledge to create them. The timing of the creation is important, and it should be synchronized with the celestial forces intended to bestow the power.

For 143 years, the United States currency was based on gold and silver. The first time any attempts to change this occurred during the Civil War, when Abraham Lincoln issued emergency "greenbacks" that were not immediately redeemable in gold or silver. These quickly became worthless. Again, President Woodrow Wilson suspended the requirement of gold and silver backing of currency briefly during World War I.

Wilson, who was a leader in the social progressive movement of the time, believed that the government rather than the people governed should be allowed to change according to *its own needs* in spite of or in opposition to the will of the governed. He believed that the leaders in government and banking had a more enlightened understanding of what was best for the governed. It was under his watch that the Federal Reserve Act was put in place, and the United States abdicated its control over money to a private banking system that was in direct violation of Article 1, Section 8 of the Constitution.

A strange opposition was at play in the establishment of the United States. On one hand, the nation started out on the firm foundation of being established through justice and godly piety, but at the same time, the establishment was backed by many high-ranking members of the Masonic fraternities. Perhaps in the same way that the precept "hidden in plain sight" dictates the *modus operandi* of the Illuminati when it comes to the manifestation of the "Great Work," the establishment of the United States necessarily had to be first one based on the people's firm belief in God. As the nation comes closer to the time of the completion of the Great Work, it is destined to rely completely on the guidance and rulership of the Great Architect, the light-bringer.

There is always a dichotomy at work—both sides of the coin, so to speak—when those who follow the light-bringer move toward the establishment of their "golden age," their attempt at the removal of the pillars set in place by God. Rules are made and given but not followed; it is as if the essential nature of the fruit of the Tree of Knowledge of Good and Evil forces the snake to pretend to be offering both as if it is some immutable law. He must always display his intentions out in the open before attempting action. The "hidden in plain sight" *modus operandi* is more than just an intellectual game; it is a requirement. In this same way, the establishment of the United States, even though it was destined to be the vehicle in which the new order of the ages would come with its new god as ruler, was done first through a firm establishment of law, justice, and human freedom based on the belief in God and His law.

The Canadian-born mystic Manly Palmer Hall understood that the United States was more than a "noble experiment," but was a mystical establishment set forth for a specific purpose:

> European mysticism was not dead at the time the United States of America was founded. The hand of the mysteries controlled

> in the establishment of the new government for the signature of the mysteries may still be seen on the Great Seal of the United States of America. Careful analysis of the seal discloses a mass of occult and Masonic symbols chief among them, the so-called American Eagle.... the American eagle upon the Great Seal is but a conventionalized phoenix.... Not only were many of the founders of the United States government Masons, but they received aid from a secret and august body existing in Europe which helped them to establish this country for A PECULIAR AND PARTICULAR PURPOSE known only to the initiated few.[309]

Contrast the Coinage Act of 1792 with the remarks made by Lyndon B. Johnson at the signing of the Coinage Act of July 1965, which allowed the Federal Reserve to mint coins containing no precious metal whatsoever:

> So, we have come here this morning to this, the first house of the land and this beautiful Rose Garden, to congratulate all of those men and women that make up our fine Congress, who made this legislation possible—the committees of both Houses, the leadership in both Houses, both parties, and Secretary Fowler and all of his associates in the Treasury. I commend the new coinage to the Nation's banks and businesses and to the public. I think it will serve us well. Now, I will sign this bill to make the first change in our coinage system since the 18th century. And to those Members of Congress, who are here on this very historic occasion, I want to assure you that in making this change from the 18th century we have no idea of returning to it. We are going to keep our eyes on the stars and our feet on the ground.[310]

It is interesting to note that even though money is used by people as a medium of exchange and would seemingly be counter to the correct use of a talisman, the power related to the talisman aspect of it is "used" by the Federal Reserve Bank. The power of the talisman is one *directed* over human beings.

TROY OUNCE

The etymology of the word "troy" used in weight measurement is not certain. The 1913 *Webster's Revised Unabridged Dictionary* defines "Troy weight":

> Troy weight, the weight which gold and silver, jewels, and the like, are weighed. It was so named from Troyes, in France, where it was first adopted in Europe. The troy ounce is supposed to have been brought from Cairo during the crusades.

The 1911 *Encyclopædia Britannica* contributor, Sir Charles Moore Watson (1844–1916), in his book, *British Weights and Measures as Described in the Laws of England from Anglo-Saxon Times* (1910), mentions that the first time the term "troy" pound was used in Britain was in 1414 for the weighing of silver.[311]

TROY, *sb.* Yks. Chs. Der. Lin. Also in form **trow** Chs.[1] s.Chs.[1] [troi.] A steelyard; a pair of scales; *gen.* used in *pl.* Cf. **trone,** *sb.*[1]
w.Yks.[2], **Chs.**[1], **s.Chs.**[1], **nw.Der.**[1], **n.Lin.**[1] **sw.Lin.**[1] A pair of troys.

English Dialect Dictionary, Joseph Wright, 1905[312]

One of the old English meanings for *troy* or *troi* was "a pair of scales." The link to the word meaning of "scales" for troy or troi in English is consistent with the idea of the act of weighing out something of value. The smallest unit and base of the traditional English weight system used for precious metals is the grain, roughly equal to the weight of one grain of barley. The grain, interestingly, is also the standard used in projectile weights of bullets and arrowheads. There are 5,760 grains in a Troy pound; the number 5,760 was not arrived at by chance.

THE MIKVEH

The *mikveh* or *mikvah*, which means "collection," "something hoped for and expected" or "confidence," is a pool of clear water used in Judaism to immerse any object that has become defiled, including the human body. Levite priests would immerse themselves in the mikvah, and all worshipers were required to do so as well before entering the Temple Mount.

The required volume of water for the mikvah must be at least forty *seahs,* and it must be filled with "living" or flowing water and not drawn from a stagnant source.

Working backwards, the volume of one mikvah is forty seahs. A seah eqauls six *cabs*. A cab equals four *logs,* and, finally, a log is comprised of six eggs.

The smallest unit of volume used by the ancient Hebrews was the *egg*. In the light of the meaning of "mikvah," "something waited or hoped for," it also symbolically represented a unit of time. The average human hand can hold three eggs, and the total that a human could carry then was the definition of a cab, equaling six eggs. A mikvah equals 5,760 eggs.[313]

It turns out that the volume of an average-sized chicken egg or what it displaces in water is approximately 51.5 milliliters. This is a close approximation of pi.

π(pi) 3.14159 cubic inches = 51.48 milliliters

The largest unit of ancient Greek currency, the *talent,* equaled 36,000 *oboloi*. The largest unit of Hebrew volume, the mikvah, equals 5,760 eggs. The ratio between the two is 6.25, which roughly equals 2π or 6.28...

The Troy pound being equal to 5,760 grains is significant in the light of the meaning of the conflict at Troy, where Athena instigated and made the fall of Troy possible (as illustrated in chapter 14). There was a period from the Flood of Noah to the establishment of Troy to its fall as one epoch in the use of money and the state of men as they worshipped their gods. After the fall of Troy, the "power of Athena" was transferred to Greece and later Rome, and ultimately to the world mystery religion centered at Washington, DC, and the world banking system.

The rabbinical scholar and bibliophile, Rabbi David Azulai (1724–1806), wrote prophetically that "the Days of Man are the measure of the Mikvah."

The Jewish calendar year 5760 was a Jubilee year (fiftieth anniversary) that began on September 11, 1999, and ended on September 30, 2000. A year later, on September 11, 2001, the Twin Towers of the World Trade Center in New York City fell.

The year 2000 was a Jubilee year of Israel officially declaring Jerusalem its capital on January 23, 1950, as well as a leap year. It is significant in that it was the first year equaling a mikvah and the first then evenly divisible by all the other units, seahs, cabs, and logs.

To the Hebrews, the moon is the symbol of the Redeemer, and they based their calendar on its motion. The waxing and waning progresses in the same manner as Hebrew is read: from right to left.

The average diameter of the earth happens to be 7,920 miles. This number minus the number of the eggs in a mikvah equals the average diameter of the moon, 2,160 miles:

$$7920 - 5760 = 2160$$

The corruption of the earth as the Nachash rules it can only be cleansed by the action of the mikvah, the living water of the Messiah, whose symbol is the moon.

The Earth-Moon-Mikvah Distance

Starting with the diameter of the moon (2,160 miles) and the mikvah number (5,760), in the same manner as the Fibonacci series is calculated, nine iterations give a close approximation of the average distance between the earth and moon: 241,200 miles.

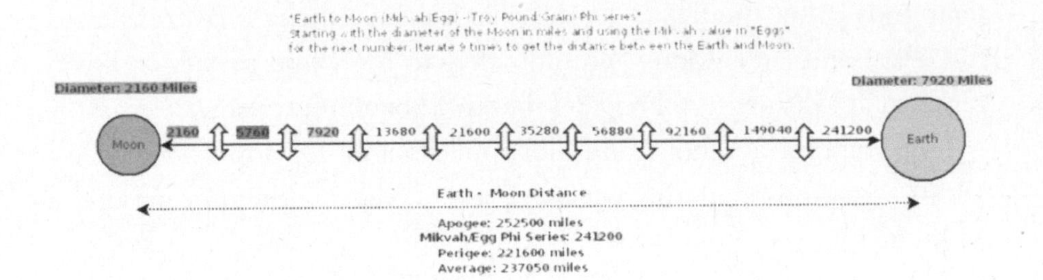

The Earth-Moon-Mikvah distance[314]

The Planets and the Mikvah

The ten intervals or spaces gained after approximating the average distance between the earth and the moon conveniently allow for the position of each of the planets in our solar system, including the asteroid belt, the shattered remnants of Rahab. The earth, the third planet from the sun, has a diameter of 7,920 miles, which is the diameter of the moon plus the mikvah number.

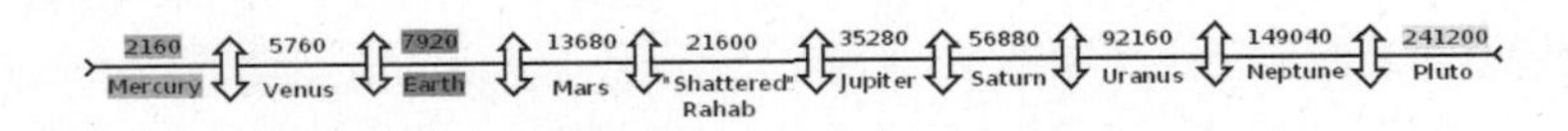

The planets and the mikvah[315]

11

THE DOLLAR

Buy the truth, and sell [it] not; [also] wisdom,
and instruction, and understanding.
—Proverbs 23:23

The history and meanings of the words used to describe United States currency expose the essential nature of the intelligence that controls it. The word "dollar" comes from *Sankt Joachimsthal*, the name of a town in sixteenth-century Bohemia that was the place of the discovery of large silver deposits, meaning "Saint Joachim's Valley." The coins that were minted there starting in 1520 were called *Joachimsthalers,* and later the name was shortened to *thaler* or *taler* ("from the valley")—from where the English pronunciation "dollar" came.

Joachim was the father of Mary, the mother of Jesus. Although not found in the Bible, Mary's father's name is mentioned in the apocryphal Gospel of James, which was written around AD 145. In Hebrew, Joachim or *Joiakim* (Yowyaqiym) means "Jehovah raises up." A man with this name appears in the book of Nehemiah as a priest and the son of the high priest, Jeshua.

Jehoiakim (*Yĕhowyaqiym*), which is a form of "Joachim," was the son of Josiah and the third from the last king of Judah who reigned for *eleven* years before he died a violent death by the hands of his own subjects. He allowed himself to act under the power of King Nebuchadnezzar and filled the land of Israel with innocent blood (see 2 Kings 24:4). The book of Jeremiah includes a peculiar reference to his evil doings that involved taking advantage of human labor and giving nothing in return:

> Woe to him who builds his palace by unrighteousness, his upper rooms by injustice, *making his own people work for nothing, not paying them for their labor*....
>
> Therefore this is what the LORD says about Jehoiakim son of Josiah king of Judah: "They will not mourn for him: 'Alas, my brother! Alas, my sister!' They will not mourn for him: 'Alas, my master! Alas, his splendor!" (Jeremiah 22:13, 18)

The roots of "Jehoiakim" are Yĕhovah ("the existing One," the name for God) and *quwm,* which can mean, "to maintain oneself or rise up and establish in a *hostile* sense." In light of the fact that United States dollars are also known as "greenbacks" and are printed on linen rather than paper, it is prescient that St. Joachim is the patron of linen makers and that he is always portrayed wearing *green* robes.[316]

THE MASONIC ORDER OF ST. JOACHIM

A Masonic relationship to Joachim is linked to the plan of the Illuminati (plural of Latin: *illuminatus,* "enlightened"). The Masonic Order of St. Joachim, established in 1755 by H. S. H. Prince Christian Franz von Saxen-Coburg-Saalfeld,[317] was a chivalric order of knights founded in imitation of the military orders of the Crusades. Many prominent military figures from the eighteenth and nineteenth centuries were members.

The insignia of the order was a green ribbon attaching a helmet above a Maltese or Templar cross. The order accepted women, whose insignia differed, with a skull and crossbones in place of the helmet.

The insignia of the Order of St. Joachim[318]

The prominent American Mason of the Scottish Rite, Albert Pike (1809–1891), wrote many documents concerning the rituals and principals of Freemasonry. He also wrote about the Order of St. Joachim in his book, *A Historical Inquiry in Regard to the Grand Constitutions of 1786:*

> The disbanded Illuminati continued on through the various branches of the Rosicrucian Order, including the later versions of the Gold Rosicrucian's [sic], namely, the Order of Perfect Initiates of Asia, or the Asiatic Brethren, and the various Orders of Light, specifically, "The Order of Saint Joachim."

The dollar bill is made of a blend of cotton and linen. In Judaism, it is forbidden to wear clothing of a mixed type, that is, one of wool and linen:

> Thou shalt not wear a garment of divers sorts, [as] of woollen and linen together. (Deuteronomy 22:11)

In 2 Chronicles 1:16, after Solomon had asked and received wisdom from God, he imported horses from Egypt and, as the Kings James Version translates it, from "Linen Yarn." Other translations call the place *Kevah* or *Kue*. The word used here for "Linen Yarn" in Hebrew is *Mikveh*, the same as the term for the Hebrew ritual pool used for purification. "Mikveh" is the masculine form of the noun; "mikvah" is the feminine. "Mikveh" can mean "hope, a gathering, pool, expectation" and "linen yarn."

The prohibited, mixed-wool-and-linen word is *shaatnez*, and one of the statutes is known as *chukim*—beyond the ability of men to comprehend.[319] The word used for "linen" in Deuteronomy 22:11 is *pistheh* (פִּשְׁתֶּ), from *pash* (פַּשׁ),[320] meaning "disintegrate, to be pounded, folly, stupidity and also pride, ferocity or transgression."

The idea behind the prohibition comes from the same *type* of prohibition illustrated in Genesis when Cain and Abel offered the fruit of their labors to God. God rejected Cain's offering of the things that he grew. Abel's first born of his animal stock was accepted.

> And in process of time it came to pass, that Cain brought of the fruit of the ground an offering unto the LORD.
>
> And Abel, he also brought of the firstlings of his flock and of the fat thereof. And the LORD had respect unto Abel and to his offering:
>
> But unto Cain and to his offering he had not respect. And Cain was very wroth, and his countenance fell.
>
> And the LORD said unto Cain, Why art thou wroth? and why is thy countenance fallen?
>
> If thou doest well, shalt thou not be accepted? and if thou doest not well, sin lieth at the door. And unto thee [shall be] his desire, and thou shalt rule over him.
>
> And Cain talked with Abel his brother: and it came to pass, when they were in the field, that Cain rose up against Abel his brother, and slew him. (Genesis 4:3–8)

Men who do their own will and yet presume themselves acceptable to God operate in the same fashion as the Nachash. Those who love pleasure more than God epitomize the words of 1 Timothy 6:10, since pleasure can be *purchased:*

> For the love of money is the root of all evil: which while some coveted after, they have erred from the faith, and pierced themselves through with many sorrows.

Timothy, whose name means "honoring God" and who was mentored by the apostle Paul, further describes the nature of "money lovers" as they would be at time of the "golden age" planned by the Nachash:

> This know also, that in the last days perilous times shall come.
>
> For men shall be lovers of their own selves, covetous, boasters, proud, blasphemers, disobedient to parents, unthankful, unholy,
>
> Without natural affection, trucebreakers, false accusers, incontinent, fierce, despisers of those that are good,
>
> Traitors, heady, highminded, lovers of pleasures more than lovers of God;
>
> Having a form of godliness, but denying the power thereof: from such turn away. (2 Timothy 3:1–5)

The first units of exchange known as "dollars" were the *peso de a ocho* or "pieces (weights) of eight," so named since they were worth eight Spanish *reales* ("royals"). They were first minted starting after the currency reform of 1497 instituted by King Ferdinand and Queen Isabella via the Ordinance of Medina del Campo to correspond to the weight of the German thaler.

The town of Medina del Campo ("the fields of the city") was famous for banking, *wool,* and *textile* fairs held during the fifteenth and sixteenth centuries, and was named after the place where Mohammad ended his "flight" from Mecca that was thought to have occurred sometime around AD 622. More specifically and in addition to simply meaning "city," "Medina" is from the Aramaic *medinta,* meaning "jurisdiction" or "place of the judge."[321]

Medina as a place of *judgment* is a reference to the same idea behind the city name, Ashkelon, meaning "the fire of infamy: I shall be weighed,"[322] which comes from the Hebrew *shaqal* ("to weigh something out"), a term used to generally describe ancient coins used in the Middle East.

The Babylonian King Belshazzar decided one night to use the golden vessels that his father, Nebuchadnezzar, had taken from Solomon's Temple during the sack of Jerusalem in 587 BC to make toasts to his gods of "gold, silver, brass, iron, wood, and stone." In response, God visited him and his guests. The revelers watched in terror as a disembodied hand wrote the words, "MENE, MENE, TEKEL, UPHARSIN" on the plaster of the wall in the chamber.

On the advice of his queen and having failed to learn the meaning from any of his royal astrologers or soothsayers, Nebuchadnezzar asked the Judean captive Daniel (Hebrew: "to judge") to interpret the writing. In return, the king promised Daniel the rule of one-third of his kingdom.

Daniel said to the king:

> This [is] the interpretation of the thing: MENE; God hath numbered thy kingdom, and finished it.
>
> TEKEL; Thou art weighed in the balances, and art found wanting.
>
> PERES; Thy kingdom is divided, and given to the Medes and Persians. (Daniel 5:26–28)

The word *tekel* ("to weigh") is related to the word for currency used in the ancient world, the *shekel* or *shaqal*. The corresponding word in Syriac relates to the idea of "suspending a balance," and in the Ethiopic, "to suspend, as on a cross."[323]

Later that night, Darius the Mede (Hebrew: "the lord of the midst") killed Belshazzar and took his kingdom. Belshazzar means "Bel protect the king" and corresponds to Belteshazzar, "lord of the straitened's (deficient, distressed, narrow) treasure." Like the Philistines whom Samson destroyed at Ashkelon and the proud King Belshazzar, the corrupt system of commerce that controls our modern world will be judged and "found wanting."

The peso became the first world currency by the late 1700s and was used in Europe, South America, the Far East and the United States until the Coinage Act of 1857, which outlawed the use of foreign coins as legal tender.[324]

The Americans also called the pieces of eight "pillar dollars," since the obverse (front side) of the coin displayed the Pillars of Hercules. The pillars stood next to the two hemispheres of the world. The left had the Spanish motto *plus* and the right featured *ultra*, meaning "more beyond." The motto originally came from Holy Roman Emperor Charles V, and was a reversal of the mythological warning that was said to have been written on the base of the Pillars of Hercules, *Non plus ultra*, or "nothing farther beyond."[325]

Silver 8 *real* coin of Ferdinand VI of Spain, 1753 showing the pillars with the motto, "PLVS VLTRA"[326]

The Syriac collection of translations of the Greek scientific works, *The Cause of All Causes,* mentions that there were *three* pillars of Hercules rather than two.[327] In the same way, the Delphic "tripod" formed the most stable structure for the powerful priestess to float over the earth and utter her oracles; the three pillars of Hercules would accentuate the idea of the strength and unmovable power of the separation event that occurred in the garden.

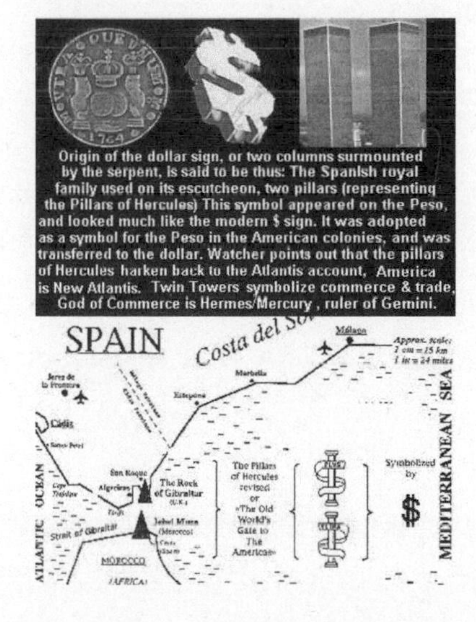

Image created in 2001 by David Flynn. From the Watcher website.

The brilliant English philosopher, scientist, statesman, and leader of the Rosicrucian Masonic Order,[328] Sir Francis Bacon (1561–1626), used the image of the Pillars of Hercules on the title page of his *Instauratio Magna* or "Great Renewal," which was a foreword to the *Novum Organum* or "New Instrument" published in 1620. The *Novum Organum* developed a new system of logic based upon inductive reasoning, which made broad generalizations from specific observations. It is considered the first important text in the development of the scientific method. The Latin motto used at the base just below the ship that was featured on the title page reads *Multi pertransibunt et augebitur scientia,* meaning "Many will pass and knowledge will increase."

The same idea can be found in Daniel 12:4:

> But thou, O Daniel, shut up the words, and seal the book, [even] to the time of the end: many shall run to and fro, and knowledge shall be increased.

The title page of Sir Francis Bacon's *Instauratio Magna*, 1620[329]

The United States silver certificate dollar bills issued from 1928 to 1957 had pillars on both ends with a "1" appearing at the base and another at the top inside an oval.

Dollar bill with "pillars"[330]

The penultimate talisman in the form of the Great Seal of the United States was added to the reverse of the dollar bill in 1935 by the thirty-second president, Franklin Delano Roosevelt, as suggested by Henry

Agard Wallace. Volumes have been written about the meaning of the symbolism in the Great Seal, but it suffices here to simply mention when it occurred and to name the individuals who were responsible for the incorporation of this powerful talisman into the currency that is the basis for modern world trade.

President Franklin Roosevelt's signed approval of the one-dollar bill's design in 1935 that required the appearance of the both sides of the Great Seal on the reverse.[331]

At the time that the Great Seal was incorporated, the dollar still was redeemable for the same value in silver. It was later, in 1964, when this ended and the full "magic" of the talisman was realized. It now relied solely on the power of the confidence, belief, and acceptance of the people using it for its value. Throughout the changes made to greater denominations over the years to thwart counterfeiting, the one-dollar bill has remained unchanged. Any alteration to the talismanic dollar unit would destroy its power.

The Princeton-educated writer William Greider expressed this idea well in his book, *Secrets of the Temple: How the Federal Reserve Runs the Country*:

> Above all, money was a function of faith. It required implicit and universal social consent that was indeed mysterious....
>
> To create money and use it, each one must believe, and everyone must believe. Only then will the worthless pieces of paper take on value. When a society [loses its] faith in money, it [is] implicitly losing faith in itself....
>
> The money process still requires a deep, unacknowledged act of faith, so mysterious that it could easily be confused with divine powers.[332]

Manly P. Hall understood the power of the Great Seal. He wrote:

> The obverse of the great seal has been used by the Department of State since 1782, but the reverse was not cut at that time because it was regarded as a symbol of a secret society and not the proper device for a sovereign State.[333]

It makes sense that when the obverse of the seal *was* used on the dollar, it had ceased to be a legitimate sovereign unit of exchange and had become a talisman exerting the power of the secret illuminated society over the people who relied on it.

TREASURY SEAL

The Department of the Treasury Seal[334]

It is interesting to note that the Treasury Department mentions that the actual creator of the seal in not known, but is believed to be Francis Hopkinson, the same who contributed to the design of the Great Seal of the United States. The *lambda-chevron* symbol, with its thirteen stars, is representative of the triangle found in the head of the constellation Taurus that was the abode of the daughters of Atlas and was aligned with the Parthenon of Athena. The meaning of the symbols on the Department of the Treasury Seal deciphered would be "those who possess the key to the high mystical art of the manipulation of measure."

Both the thirty-second president of the United States and his secretary of agriculture were Freemasons. Roosevelt was initiated into the Holland Lodge No. 8, New York City, in 1911.[335] Henry Agard Wallace (1888–1965) was the thirty-third vice president of the United States, Roosevelt's secretary of agriculture (1933–1940), and the secretary of commerce (1945–1946). In the 1948 presidential election, Wallace was the nominee of the Progressive Party. He was a mystic who attained the

32nd Degree in the Scottish Rite (Sublime Prince of the Royal Secret) and sought guidance from various illuminated people of the time. One of his associates was the Russian theosophist and writer Nicholas Roerich, who was a member of the English-Welsh chapter of the Theosophical Society, founded by Helena Blavatsky.

HELENA BLAVATSKY

Helena Blavatsky (1831–1891) and Henry Steel Olcott (1832–1907) founded the Theosophical Society in New York City in 1875 with the motto, "There is no religion higher than truth."[336] Blavatsky defined *theosophia* or "divine wisdom" as the "wisdom of the gods" and *theogonia* as the "genealogy of the gods." She wrote:

> The word *theos* means a god in Greek, one of the divine beings, certainly not "God" in the sense attached in our day to the term. Therefore, it is not "Wisdom of God," as translated by some, but Divine Wisdom such as that possessed by the gods. The term is many thousand years old.[337]

KNIGHTS TEMPLAR

The Knights Templar started out as an order of knights devoted to a life of poverty sometime around 1118. They vowed to defend the newly captured Jerusalem after the First Crusade. The *Catholic Encyclopedia* entry for the Knights Templar states:

> Immediately after the deliverance of Jerusalem, the Crusaders, considering their vow fulfilled, returned in a body to their homes. The defense of this precarious conquest, surrounded as it was by Mohammedan neighbors, remained. In 1118, during the reign of Baldwin II, Hugues de Payens, a knight of Champagne, and eight companions bound themselves by a perpetual vow, taken in the presence of the Patriarch of Jerusalem, to defend the Christian

> kingdom. Baldwin accepted their services and assigned them a portion of his palace, adjoining the temple of the city; hence their title "pauvres chevaliers du temple" (Poor Knights of the Temple).

The Poor Fellow-Soldiers of Christ and of the Temple of Solomon (Latin: *Pauperes commilitones Christi Templique Solomonici*), existed for nearly two centuries during the Middle Ages and were responsible for building many fortifications across Europe and the Holy Land. They were endorsed by the Catholic Church around 1129, and became a favored charity throughout Christian Europe, growing rapidly in wealth and power. Templar knights wore white mantles with a distinctive red cross and were considered to be the most skilled knights of the Crusades.[338]

The members of the order not engaged in fighting campaigns began to acquire a very large economic empire using financial techniques that were similar to modern banking with interest charges and the issuance of promissory notes.[339, 340]

The Templars and the Jews living in Europe were allowed to loan money with interest, which was forbidden to the rest of the populous under the strict anti-usury dictates of the Roman Catholic Church. The Hebrew word for usury (*nashak,* נָשַׁךְ) also means "the bite of a serpent." In England, the Templars were exempt from taxes, and anyone who worked for them enjoyed the same privilege.

Although modern Freemasonry denies having any affiliation with the order, many of its orders and degrees are derived from ones used by the Templars such as the York Rite Preceptory of Knights Templar, Order of the Temple, and the Holy Royal Arch Knight Templar Priest's degree. One theory on the origins of Freemasonry claims that it had descended from the historical Knights Templar members who took refuge in Scotland to escape the purge ordered by French King Philip IV under the order of Pope Clement V. The king owed the order a large amount of money that he had borrowed during his war with the English.

King Philip IV ended the order in 1307 and had Jacques de Molay (1244–1314) and many other French Templars arrested. Philip had expelled the Jews from France a year earlier and was instrumental in transferring the papal court from Rome to Avignon in 1309.

"Philip the Fair," as he was known, had de Molay and the others tortured into making false confessions. When de Molay recanted, Philip condemned him to be hung on a scaffold and slowly burned on an island in the River Seine in Paris. The Kansas Masonic Order of DeMolay made Franklin Delano Roosevelt the first Honorary Grand Master at a White House ceremony in 1934.[341] The ceremony of de Molay is described on the order's website:

> The participants are first sworn to keep the ritual secret and then trial of De Moley is recreated. The players dress in robes and gather on a dimly-lit stage where they recited the lines of the ritual. The act commemorates the strength of De Moley and the importance of not revealing the secrets of the order even through the pain of torture and death.[342]

The Templars' motto was *In hoc signo vinces* ("In this sign, you will conquer"), which was adopted from the one used by the Roman Emperor Constantine I after he had a vision of the *chi* (X) *rho* (P) in the sky just before the Battle of Milvian Bridge on October 28, AD 312.

Constantine used the sign on his military standard or labarum from that time onward.

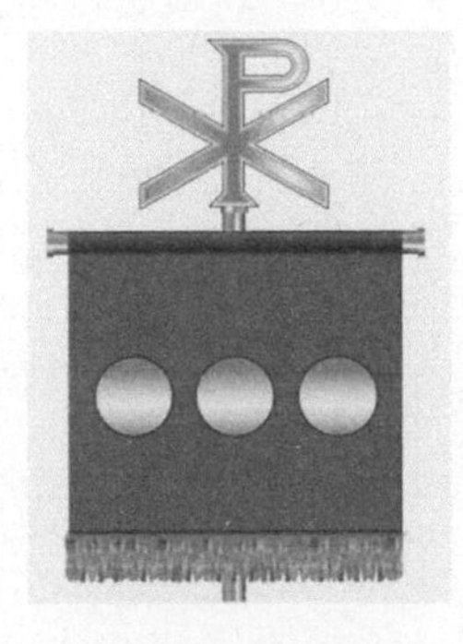

Constantine's labarum military standard[343]

A coin of Constantine (c. 337) showing a depiction of his labarum over a serpent[344]

The labarum was represented in the coinage of the time with a snake beneath it. Modern etymologists do not agree on its origins, but it is interesting to note that the word "labarum" is noticeably close to the Greek word *labrys,* originally form the Anatolian cult of Labranda.

CHI RHO

The origin of the Greek *chi* (X) was the Phoenician *semka,* meaning a "fish," although a more appropriate representation for the *chi* would be the Phoenician *tau* (X) since they are identical in appearance. The Greek *rho* (P) comes from the Phoenician *rosh* meaning "head."

Semka, meaning a "fish"

Rosh, meaning "head"

The Greek acronym *IXΘYΣ* (*Iēsous Christos Theos Yios Sōtēr*), meaning "Jesus Christ God Son Savior," was used by the early church during the time of Christian persecution started by the emperor Nero (AD 37–68).[345] It was said that Nero had blamed the Christians for the fires that destroyed much of Rome in AD 64. The obfuscated letters were written in a layered fashion, forming an eight-sectioned wheel image.

Early Christian *ichthys* marble inscription from Ephesus[346]

The meaning of *chi-rho* would be a legitimate symbol for those who followed Christianity, with the *chi* as the *semka* (fish symbol) idea as well as the *tau-rosh* or "head"—alluding to the circular form of the Proto-Hebrew alphabet connected at the "head" via the two *taus.* The superimposed *IXΘYΣ* wheel formation emphasized this idea—God at the *head* of the circuit.

The *chi-rho* symbol was used earlier by the Greeks to represent time or the god Chronos.[347] The symbol used by the modern Roman Catholic Church consists of the Greek letters *iota*, *eta*, and *sigma*, and stands for, *Iesous Hominem Salvator*, "Jesus, Savior of Man." It was the shorthand for the sign of Constantine, *In Hoc Signo*. It is surrounded by the sun symbol of the god Apollo, Sol Invictus, or Attis.

Chi-rho symbol used to represent time or the god Chronos

Iota, eta, and *sigma* surrounded by the sun symbol[348]

The French king, Louis XIV (1638–1715), or "Sun King" (*le Roi-Soleil*) used the sunburst sign of Apollo as his symbol. He was also known as the Great *Dauphin* (French: "dolphin," from the Greek *delphys,* or *delphi,* alluding to the idea that the "fish-like" creature has a womb) from the name that was started by Charles V ("the Wise") in 1364. The symbol of Apollo's sunburst along with the Dauphin title referred to their *divine right,* or rather, *Apollo-given* right, as kings.

The Connection at Golgotha

The Israelites were intimidated by the great size and strength of the Philistine army that gathered at Shochoh (Hebrew: "bushy," from *suwk*, a "hedge or fence," "to hedge in"), and especially by their great Nephilim (Hebrew: "giants," from *naphal,* "to fall, lie, be cast down, fail") warrior Goliath, who openly mocked them and their God. Goliath is described in 1 Samuel 17:4:

> And there went out a champion out of the camp of the Philistines, named Goliath, of Gath, whose height [was] six cubits and a span.

A cubit is approximately twenty inches; a span is nine. Goliath's name means "splendor," from the root, *galah*, which means "naked" or "uncovered." The "splendor of nakedness" would be a literal term for the Nachash, the brightest and most subtle (naked) angel.

Despite his small size, the youngest son of Jesse implored King Saul for permission to fight the giant. Saul doubted his chances:

> And Saul said to David, Thou art not able to go against this Philistine to fight with him: for thou art but a youth, and he a man of war from his youth. (1 Samuel 17:33).

David ultimately was allowed to engage Goliath:

> And David put his hand in his bag, and took thence a stone, and slang it, and smote the Philistine in his forehead, that the stone sunk into his forehead; and he fell upon his face to the earth....
>
> Therefore David ran, and stood upon the Philistine, and took his sword, and drew it out of the sheath thereof, and slew him, and cut off his head therewith. And when the Philistines saw their champion was dead, they fled....
>
> And David took the head of the Philistine, and brought it to Jerusalem; but he put his armour in his tent. (1 Samuel 17:49, 51, and 54)

David and Goliath by Gustave Doré (1832–1883)[349]

It is probable that David buried the giant head of Goliath at the high point of the city, which was aptly named at the time of Christ both in appearance and for the resting place of the Nephilim skull. The name for the area was "Golgotha," meaning, "the place of the skull," from the root *gulgoleth*.

Hebrew is numeric; taking inspiration from the lectures of David Flynn, the numbers depicted in the word "gulgoleth" reveal more towards the significance of the place where the crucifixion took place:

> *gulgoleth* (גֻּלְגֹּלֶת) = 33 and 33. *gimel*-3, *lamed*-30, *gimel*-3, *lamed*-30, and *tav*-400

The *tav* "connects" the thirty-threes both as a reference to the third of the angels allied with the serpent and to the two sets of thirty-three equaling sixty-six, the two-thirds that remained with God, and brings them to the place where the absolute righteousness of God would be manifest to all creation. Golgotha completed the circuit; heaven and earth could again be joined. It has been said that the place resembled a skull, but this is the most thinly basic understanding of the whole associations of the word.

"Gulgoleth" does mean "skull," but it can also mean "every man" in the sense of all people being numbered in a poll or census. "Gulgoleth" is from the duplication of galal (גָּלַל), meaning to "be rolled, roll oneself, or to roll away."

David Flynn noted in his work that the area in Israel where Jesus walked during His ministry was Galilee or *Galiyl*, meaning a "circuit."[350] Like Gulgoleth, its root comes from the word *galal*.

It is no coincidence that one meaning of the word alludes to the idea of something being rolled away by oneself.

> Now upon the first [day] of the week, very early in the morning, they came unto the sepulchre, bringing the spices which they had prepared, and certain [others] with them.
>
> *And they found the stone rolled away from the sepulchre*. And they entered in, and found not the body of the Lord Jesus.
>
> And it came to pass, as they were much perplexed thereabout, behold, two men stood by them in shining garments:

> And as they were afraid, and bowed down [their] faces to the earth, they said unto them, Why seek ye the living among the dead?
>
> He is not here, but is risen. (Luke 24:1–6, emphasis added)

The event there was one that had ended a conflict that began in the garden. The words of God Himself start the circuit at the "π verse."

> And the LORD God said unto the serpent, Because thou hast done this, thou [art] cursed above all cattle, and above every beast of the field; upon thy belly shalt thou go, and dust shalt thou eat all the days of thy life. (Genesis 3:14)

The Son of Man-Son of God hung from the *tav* until he experienced the *muwth* (מות, "death") that man via the Nachash had brought about in the garden. He was God and man at the "head," in Hebrew, *rosh* (ראשׁ), *rosh* (ר; "head"), *aleph* (א, "ox head"), *shin* (שׁ, "standing for The Name"). To clarify the meaning of the letters in this instance, the *shin* is the symbol of the name of the same God who referred to Himself as *El Shadday.* This is revealed clearly in Exodus 6:3, when God spoke to Moses:

> And I appeared unto Abraham, unto Isaac, and unto Jacob, by [the name of] God (el)Almighty *[shadday]*, but by my name JEHOVAH was I not known to them.

At the place of the skull, Jesus did what God and man apart could not do. God cannot die and man cannot create or restore his own life. Yet the man, who was same time God, did both, crushing the head of the serpent at very place where the symbol of His power was buried, the skull of the defeated *splendor* of the subtle one. The cross, the *tav*, was there at the *rosh*. The same God who walked with man in the garden was with him again at the completion of the circuit.

The very first word in Genesis 1:1 is *re'shiyth,* meaning "beginning or first":

> [Hebrew Root Form] In the beginning [ראשית *re 'shiyth*] God [אלהים *'elohiym*] created [ברא *bara'* את *'eth*] the heaven [שמים *shamayim*] and [את *'eth*] the earth [ארץ *'erets*].

Re'shiyth is from *ro'sh*, which means "the head," "height," or "top"; also a *chapiter* ("the capital of a column"). The term "rosh" by itself symbolizes the circuit connection of the *tavs* forming one letter that appears at the *head* and depicts the power of God. The ox *head* is also the *rosh*.

There is a reference in the Bible to the identity of God being the "head" or *rosh* in the form of an *ox*. The fortieth chapter of the book of Job describes the Behemoth (*bĕhemowth,* בְּהֵמוֹת, from *bĕhemah,* בְּהֵמָה, meaning "wild beast, cattle" [a singular of *Egyptian* derivation]) as a metaphor for God's power:

> Behold now behemoth, which I made with thee; he eateth grass as an ox.
>
> Lo now, his strength is in his loins, and his force is in the navel of his belly.
>
> He moveth his tail like a cedar: the sinews of his stones are wrapped together.
>
> His bones are as strong pieces of brass; his bones are like bars of iron.
>
> He is the chief of the ways of God: he that made him can make his sword to approach unto him.
>
> Surely the mountains bring him forth food, where all the beasts of the field play.
>
> He lieth under the shady trees, in the covert of the reed, and fens.
>
> The shady trees cover him with their shadow; the willows of the brook compass him about.
>
> Behold, he drinketh up a river, and hasteth not: he trusteth that he can draw up Jordan into his mouth.
>
> He taketh it with his eyes: his nose pierceth through snares. (Job 40:15–24)

The "ox-like," grass-eating Behemoth illustrates the power of God. The allusion to the "ox circuit" (*rosh*) as a symbol for Him is further revealed at the place where the beast rests. The "shady trees" where the ox lies is *tse'el* (צֶאֱלִים), meaning a "lotus tree."

Chapter 41 of Job continues with the image of the Leviathan (*livyathan,* לִוְיָתָן, "sea monster, dragon," from *lavah,* לָוָה, "to be joined").

In *Cydonia: The Secret Chronicles of Mars,* David Flynn wrote much about the mystery of the "twisted serpent"[351] Leviathan, or the *Ouroboros,* and its meaning as related to the *Cycle of the Aions.*[352] The importance of mentioning Leviathan here is to point out that it appears in Job directly after the Behemoth. As God was describing His great power to Job, the two in tandem are not just coincidental, but a direct definition of the "ox circuit," the whole of God, Leviathan as the circular joined *tavs* with Behemoth at the *rosh* or "head."

Behemoth depicted as the red bull and Leviathan as a fish. The giant monsters Leviathan, Behemoth, and Ziz from the *Illustrated Hebrew Bible* produced in Ulm, Germany, around 1238.[353]

The Griffin-like Ziz depicted in the *Illustrated Hebrew Bible* is mentioned three times in the Old Testament—twice in the book of Psalms (80:13 and 50:11) as "wild beasts," *ziyz sadeh* (ziyz, זִיז, "moving creatures, moving things," and *sadeh,* שָׂדֶה, "field, land"). It is interesting that the image of the Griffin would be used to depict the *ziyz sadeh,* since it is also used for a cherub.[354]

The writer of the book of Psalms ("praises") uses the term *ziyz sadeh* in reference to the action of the Nachash on the state of Israel:

> Thou hast brought a vine out of Egypt: thou hast cast out the heathen, and planted it....
>
> Why hast thou then broken down her hedges, so that all they which pass by the way do pluck her?

> The boar out of the wood doth waste it, and the wild beast of the field doth devour it. (Psalms 80:8, 12–13)

The third "ziyz" reference in Isaiah 66:11 is used to mean, "abundance of her glory," *ziyz kabowd* (*kabowd*, כָּבוֹד, "glory, honour, glorious, abundance," from *kabad*, כָּבַד, "to be heavy, glorious, burdensome, honoured"). Isaiah later prophesies Israel's redemption and the "abundance of her glory":

> Rejoice ye with Jerusalem, and be glad with her, all ye that love her: rejoice for joy with her, all ye that mourn for her:
>
> That ye may suck, and be satisfied with the breasts of her consolations; that ye may milk out, and be delighted with the abundance of her glory. (Isaiah 66:10–11)

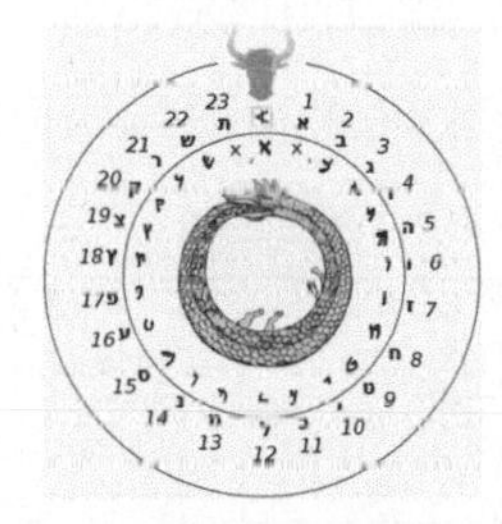

Leviathan and Behemoth in the Aramaic-Hebrew letter circuit "clock." The first and final forms of the *Ṣadhe* or *Tsade* (18 and 19) and an extra space between *aleph* and *tav* are used to make twenty-four spaces.[355]

The Old Testament uses the word *chabatstseleth* (חֲבַצֶּלֶת) for the rose and the lily. The lotus flower that opens and closes at the rising and setting of the sun imitated the powers of the Egyptian gods Isis and her son Horus, whom Isis resurrected from her husband, Osiris, while hiding in the marshlands of the Nile. It was also the origin of the solar deity Atum-Ra, who was said to have risen from the primordial mound of water as a lotus flower to start the creation of the world. The Greeks and Romans later substituted the lotus or lily flower for the rose.

Manly P. Hall describes the link between the rose and the lotus:

> Of all symbolic flowers the lotus blossom of India and Egypt and the rose of the Rosicrucians are the most important. In their symbolism these two flowers are considered identical. The esoteric

> doctrines for which the Eastern lotus stands have been perpetuated in modern Europe under the form of the rose. The rose and the lotus are yonic emblems, signifying primarily the maternal creative mystery, while the Easter lily is considered to be phallic.[356]

The Latin term *sub-rosa,* meaning "under the rose," has been used since ancient times to mean "something said or understood that must remain secret." The lotus-rose was linked to the *silent* god Horus, who was known to the Greeks as Harpocrates (rendered from the Egyptian *Heru-pa-khered,* meaning "Horus the Child").

A common thread in the worship of the many mother goddesses and their lost husband-sons is the inclusion of the blood-spilling aspects of their deaths. Each is remembered with blood-colored symbols, mulberry fruit, roses, or pomegranates. The stories of Glaucus, Attis and Cybele, Pyramus, and Thisbe and Romeo and Juliet (explained in the next chapter) reenact these. The goddesses who promise knowledge, life, and resurrection hold the representation of power of life in their symbols. These symbols are always linked to them in the form of the ones who were *lost* but yet endure. They hold the life in the blood for those that worship them, in a diabolical reversal of the blood that God required of His own Son to atone for the act committed in the garden:

> For the life of a creature is in the blood, and I have given it to you to make atonement for yourselves on the altar; it is the blood that makes atonement for one's life. (Leviticus 17:11)

The final blood atonement for all of humanity occurred at the death and resurrection of Jesus (*Yĕhowshuwa,*`יְהוֹשׁוּעַ, "Jehovah is salvation").

Aphrodite created the *anemone* or rose flower to honor the Attis-like Adonis after his death:

> She saw the lifeless body, lying in its own blood, she leapt down, tearing her clothes, and tearing at her hair, as well, and beat at her breasts with fierce hands, complaining to the fates.

> "And yet not everything is in your power" she said. "Adonis, there shall be an everlasting token of my grief, and every year an imitation of your death will complete a re-enactment of my mourning. But your blood will be changed into a flower.... So saying, she sprinkled the blood with odorous nectar: and, at the touch, it swelled up, as bubbles emerge in yellow mud. In less than an hour, a flower, of the colour of blood, was created such as pomegranates carry, that hide their seeds under a tough rind. But enjoyment of it is brief; for, lightly clinging, and too easily fallen, the winds deflower it, which are likewise responsible for its name, windflower: anemone.[357]

Aphrodite was said to have given a rose to her son Eros, who later gave it to Harpocrates to keep the knowledge contained, hidden. In a typical reversal of the true meaning of the head-rosh-God idea and through word play surrounding the rosh and the flower rose, the illuminated fraternities have used the term "sub-rosa" for centuries. It describes the realm of knowledge held by the Great Architect of the Universe, the knowledge that he gives to all the worthy elect but keeps hidden from the vulgar.

Lord of Sidon

The Templar knights adopted the *rosh-tav* as a symbol of the knowledge hidden within their order. The legend of the origin of the skull and crossbones involved a knight known as the Lord of Sidon who loved a young woman named Yse who died unexpectedly.

In the book, *Holy Blood and Holy Grail*, the origin of the skull and crossbones is told in the story of the "lady of Maraclea" and the Lord of Sidon.

> A great lady of Maraclea was loved by a Templar, a Lord of Sidon; but she died in her youth, and on the night of her burial, this wicked lover crept to the grave, dug up her body and violated it. Then a voice from the void bade him return

> in nine months time for he would find a son. He obeyed the injunction and at the appointed time he opened the grave again and found a head on the leg bones of the skeleton (skull and crossbones). The same voice bade him' guard it well, for it would be the giver of all good things', and so he carried it away with him. It became his protecting genius, and he was able to defeat his enemies by merely showing them the magic head. In due course, it passed into the possession of the Order.[358]

The name of the place known as Marcalea means "clear waters of the sea" and was a small, coastal, Crusader town and a castle in the Levant, between Tortosa and Baniya.[359] "Levant" means "to rise as the sun" and was another name for Anatolia or Canaan.[360]

Marah in Hebrew means "to be rebellious," and the Latin *clarus* means "relating to the sight, clear, bright, shining, brilliant."

Image of the Sovereign Prince of the Rose Cross, Grade 18. The Head of Christ at the Cross—the Rosh at the Tav.[361]

TUDOR BONNET

The British monarchy has used the rose as its symbol since the fifteenth century. The Heraldic Red Rose of Lancaster and White Rose of York combined when Henry Tudor VII (1457–1509) defeated Richard III (1452–1485) of the House of York after a power struggle for the throne of England known as the Wars of the Roses.

The peculiar, soft, rounded cap worn as part of academic dress by a person who holds a doctorate degree is referred to as a Tudor bonnet and was popularly worn in England during the time of the five Tudor monarchs. The rose depicted in the Royal Badge of England and symbolically in the five-lobed Tudor hat is the Mediterranean *Anemone coronaria* ("crown"), named after the flower Aphrodite that was created for Adonis. "Anemone" in Greek means "daughter of the wind," from *ánemos* ("wind") and the suffix *ōnē* ("mother").[362] The many species of five-petaled roses are similar in appearance.

The Tudor Rose as a royal badge of England used by every British monarch since Henry VII[363]

Queen Mary I was the fourth monarch of the Tudor dynasty, and was remembered for her bloody restoration of Roman Catholicism after the Protestant reign of Henry VIII. She ruled while living in the Palace of Placentia, which, in Greek, would be the *Paláti Delphys,* or the "Palace of Delphi."

12

MT. HERMON

O Lord, my God! Is there no help for the widow's son?[364]

After Adam and Eve's expulsion from the *locus amoenus*, the Nachash maintained an active role in his intervention. In the new world outside of the garden, ultimately the curse given to him by God would manifest itself via the Redeemer from the line of Eve. To circumvent this and render the word of God *undependable*, the *ben 'elohiym*, or "sons of God" also known as the "Watchers" or "fallen ones" came to earth. They would manipulate the dust creature's God-formed characteristics so that they would cease to be from the line of the woman and not fully human.

The Bible mentions this in Genesis, chapter 6:

> There were giants in the earth in those days; and also after that, when the sons of God came in unto the daughters of men, and they bare children to them, the same became mighty men which were of old, men of renown. (Genesis 6:4)

The extrabiblical text known as the *Book of Enoch* written by Enoch, the great grandfather of Noah, gives an account of this incursion:

> And it came to pass when the children of men had multiplied that in those days were born unto them beautiful and comely daughters.
>
> And the angels, the children of the heaven, saw and lusted after them, and said to one another: "Come, let us choose us wives from among the children of men and beget us children."
>
> And Semjâzâ, who was their leader, said unto them: "I fear ye will not indeed agree to do this deed, and I alone shall have to pay the penalty of a great sin."
>
> And they all answered him and said: "Let us all swear an oath, and all bind ourselves by mutual imprecations not to abandon this plan but to do this thing." Then sware they all together and bound themselves by mutual imprecations upon it.
>
> And they were in all two hundred; who descended in the days of Jared on the summit of Mount Hermon, and they called it Mount Hermon, because they had sworn and bound themselves by mutual imprecations upon it.
>
> And these are the names of their leaders: Samîazâz, their leader, Arâkîba, Râmêêl, Kôkabîêl, Tâmîêl, Râmîêl, Dânêl, Êzêqêêl, Barâqîjâl, Asâêl, Armârôs, Batârêl, Anânêl, Zaqîêl, Samsâpêêl, Satarêl, Tûrêl, Jômjâêl, Sariêl.
>
> These are their chiefs of tens.[365]

The Hebrew meanings for the name "Hermon," like many others involved with the early actions of the Nachash, are revealing. "Hermon" (*Chermown,* חֶרְמוֹן) means "a sanctuary" from the root, *charam* (חָרַם), "to ban, devote, destroy utterly, completely destroy, dedicate for destruction, exterminate, to prohibit, to consecrate, devote, dedicate for destruction, to be devoted, be forfeited, to split, slit, mutilate, to mutilate, to divide."

Enoch continues:

> And all the others together with them took unto themselves wives, and each chose for himself one, and they began to go in unto them and to defile themselves with them, and they taught them

> charms and enchantments, and the cutting of roots, and made them acquainted with plants. And they became pregnant, and they bare great giants, whose height was three thousand ells: Who consumed all the acquisitions of men. And when men could no longer sustain them, the giants turned against them and devoured mankind. And they began to sin against birds, and beasts, and reptiles, and fish, and to devour one another's flesh, and drink the blood. Then the earth laid accusation against the lawless ones.[366]

Apart from the terrible results of the interbreeding between the fallen ones and humans, the Watchers bought men *knowledge*. Enoch continues, relating the individual names and skills attributed to each:

> And Azâzêl taught men to make swords, and knives, and shields, and breastplates, and made known to them the metals of the earth and the art of working them, and bracelets, and ornaments, and the use of antimony, and the beautifying of the eyelids, and all kinds of costly stones, and all colouring tinctures. And there arose much godlessness, and they committed fornication, and they were led astray, and became corrupt in all their ways.
>
> Semjâzâ taught enchantments, and root-cuttings,
> Armârôs the resolving of enchantments,
> Barâqîjâl [taught] astrology,
> Kôkabêl the constellations,
> Êzêqêêl the knowledge of the clouds,
> Araqiêl the signs of the earth,
> Shamsiêl the signs of the sun, and
> Sariêl the course of the moon.
> And as men perished, they cried, and their cry went up to heaven.[367]

God sent a flood to end the evil havoc caused by the Watchers, but He allowed for the continued existence of a specific uncorrupted line of humanity, Noah and his family:

> And God said unto Noah, The end of all flesh is come before me; for the earth is filled with violence through them; and, behold, I will destroy them with the earth....
>
> And, behold, I, even I, do bring a flood of waters upon the earth, to destroy all flesh, wherein is the breath of life, from under heaven; and every thing that is in the earth shall die. (Genesis 6:13, 17)

NIMROD

According to the book of Genesis, after the Great Flood, Nimrod ("rebellion") was the king of the "land of two rivers" known as Shinar. He was the son of Cush ("black"), who was the son of Ham ("hot"), who was the son of Noah.

> He was a mighty hunter before the LORD: wherefore it is said, Even as Nimrod the mighty hunter before the LORD. (Genesis 10:9)

The word used for "mighty" in the Hebrew is *gibbowr* ("strong," "mighty"). Its intensive form is *gabar,* which, in addition to "mighty," means "to act proudly." *Gesenius' Lexicon* adds, "to prevail, to bind up anything broken."

Additionally the word for "hunter" in the Hebrew adds to the identification of Nimrod's characteristics. The word used for hunter is *tsayid* (צוד), meaning simply "to hunt." Gesenius adds an interesting contrast: "צוד...used as a metaphor for snares laid for men."[368]

In the same way that the illuminated fraternities of today believe that they will eventually be able to achieve immortality though the knowledge given by the angel of light, Nimrod hoped to regain the power of knowledge bestowed by the Watchers. With the technological knowledge retained from before the Flood, he conspired to build a tower that would make the communication between men and the Watchers not only possible once more, but *continuous.* The tower was not necessarily a device that would cause men to become gods immediately, but an *intradimensional* conduit that would once more bring the assistance of the Watchers who would make men gods like themselves through the *knowledge* they provided.

Flavius Josephus described the building of the tower of Babel:

> Now it was Nimrod who excited them to such an affront and contempt of God. He was the grandson of Ham, the son of Noah, a bold man, and of great strength of hand. He persuaded them not to ascribe it to God, as if it were through his means they were happy, but to believe that it was their own courage which procured that happiness. He also gradually changed the government into tyranny, seeing no other way of turning men from the fear of God, but to bring them into a constant dependence on his power. He also said he would be revenged on God, if he should have a mind to drown the world again; for that he would build a tower too high for the waters to reach. And that he would avenge himself on God for destroying their forefathers.
>
> Now the multitude were very ready to follow the determination of Nimrod, and to esteem it a piece of cowardice to submit to God; and they built a tower, neither sparing any pains, nor being in any degree negligent about the work: and, by reason of the multitude of hands employed in it, it grew very high, sooner than any one could expect; but the thickness of it was so great, and it was so strongly built, that thereby its great height seemed, upon the view, to be less than it really was. It was built of burnt brick, cemented together with mortar, made of bitumen, that it might not be liable to admit water. When God saw that they acted so madly, he did not resolve to destroy them utterly, since they were not grown wiser by the destruction of the former sinners; but he caused a tumult among them, by producing in them diverse languages, and causing that, through the multitude of those languages, they should not be able to understand one another. The place wherein they built the tower is now called Babylon, because of the confusion of that language which they readily understood before; for the Hebrews mean by the word Babel, confusion.[369]

The loss of the unifying power of common language was an exacting form of punishment toward the efforts of Nimrod. His attempt at reconnecting with the light givers failed. Reading, writing, and storytelling ceased. As the tower fell and its builders wandered away in confusion, the chance for communion between men and the fallen angels ended and erased humanity's possession of Watcher-given knowledge from before the Flood.

Ninus

Ninus was the legendary son of Belus or Bel (*Ba'al* or "lord"), whose reign lasted fifty-two years, from the year 2189 BC. He was said to have been the first to use dogs in hunting and the first to tame horses. He controlled a vast army of more than two million soldiers and used them to conquer much of the territory that surrounded modern-day Iraq from the shores of the Mediterranean to the east as far as India. He has been depicted in Greek mythology as a centaur. Alexander Hislop has also recognized Ninus as Nimrod, son of Cush, in his book, *The Two Babylons.*[370]

The Legend of the Craft

In one of the oldest manuscripts concerning the origins of Freemasonry, *The Legend of the Craft*, Ninus or *Nimrod* is mentioned as possessing knowledge gained from before the Flood of Noah. It also mentions the tower of Babel and Naamah the weaver who closely resembles the Egyptian goddess Neith:

> We shall now tell you how this science was begun. According to the fourth chapter of Genesis, before Noah's flood, there was a man called Lamech who had two wives, one called Ada and the other Zillah. The first wife Ada bore him two sons, Jabal and Jubal, and the second wife Zillah bore him a son and a daughter, tubal-Cain and Naamah. These four children found the beginning of

all the crafts in the world. Jabel, the eldest son, found the craft of Geometry, and he was the first person to divide lands and flocks of sheep and lambs, and he was also the first to build a house of wood and stone. Jubal found the craft of Music, Tubal-Cain the craft of the Smith and Naamah the craft of Weaving. Now these children knew that God would take vengeance upon the earth, either by fire or water, and in order that their discoveries might be preserved to future generations they wrote them upon two pillars of stone; one of marble, which would not burn in fire, and the other of lattress, which would not drown in water.

After the destruction of the world by flood, Hermes, who has been called the Father of Wise Men, found one of the pillars and taught the sciences written thereon to other men. At the building of the Tower of Babel, masonry was in great repute, and Nimrod, the King of Babylon, was himself a Mason and a lover of the craft, so that when Nineveh and other cities of the East were about to be built, he sent thither three score masons at the request of his cousin, the King of Nineveh, and when they went forth he gave them a Charge in this manner:—That they should love each other truly, in order that no discredit should fall on him for sending them, and he also gave them a charge concerning their science. These were the first Masons who ever received any charge.[371]

NINEVEH

According to the Greek historian Diodorus Siculus (c. 90–30 BC), the founder of the city of Nineveh was Ninus. Genesis chapter 10 mentions that Nineveh was built after Nimrod had established the cities in the land of Shinar. Nineveh was a great center of commerce. Archeological digs have uncovered massive walls eight miles in perimeter, aqueducts, palaces and a library that features twenty thousand clay tablets, including accounts of the flood in the Epic of Gilgamesh.[372]

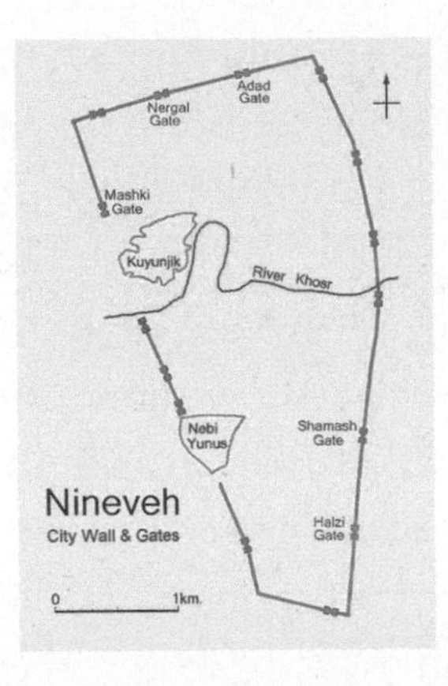

Simplified plan of ancient Nineveh, showing city wall and location of gateways[373]

The *Jewish Encyclopedia* mentions that the form of the name Nineveh is "derived from the Masoretic text and is close to the native Assyrian for *Ninua.* "The origin of the name is obscure, but possibly means "the seat of Ishtar," since Nina was one of the Babylonian names of that goddess. The Assyrian ideogram means "house or place of fish."[374]

Nineveh, famous for being the residence of the successive kings of Assyria, remained the capital of the kingdom throughout the centuries and was regarded by Greek writers as its permanent capital, virtually equivalent to the country itself. The people of Nineveh worshipped the fish god Derceto, the mother of Semiramis, the wife or daughter (or both) of Ninus, who has also been thought to be Nimrod.[375]

SEMIRAMIS

Semiramis was the daughter of Derceto of Ascalon (Ashkelon) and a mortal father. Derceto abandoned Semiramis at birth and threw herself into a nearby lake. She is the Assyrian version of the Anatolian Cybele, the Babylonian Ishtar and the Egyptian Isis.

The Greek historian Diodorus Siculus wrote about the birth of Semiramis and how she came to be associated with doves:

> Now there is in Syria a city known as Ascalon, and not far from it a large and deep lake, full of fish. On its shore is a precinct of a famous goddess whom the Syrians call Derceto; and this

goddess has the head of a woman but all the rest of her body is that of a fish, the reason being something like this. The story as given by the most learned of the inhabitants of the region is as follows: Aphrodite, being offended with this goddess, inspired in her a violent passion for a certain handsome youth among her votaries; and Derceto gave herself to the Syrian and bore a daughter, but then, filled with shame of her sinful deed, she killed the youth and exposed the child in a rocky desert region, while as for herself, from shame and grief she threw herself into the lake and was changed as to the form of her body into a fish; and it is for this reason that the Syrians to this day abstain from this animal and honour their fish as gods. But about the region where the babe was exposed a great multitude of doves had their nests, and by them the child was nurtured in an astounding and miraculous manner; for some of the doves kept the body of the babe warm on all sides by covering it with their wings, while others, when they observed that the cowherds and other keepers were absent from the nearby steadings, brought milk therefrom in their beaks and fed the babe by putting it drop by drop between its lips. And when the child was a year old and in need of more solid nourishment, the doves, pecking off bits from the cheeses, supplied it with sufficient nourishment. Now when the keepers returned and saw that the cheeses had been nibbled about the edges, they were astonished at the strange happening; they accordingly kept a look-out, and on discovering the cause found the infant, which was of surpassing beauty. At once, then, bringing it to their steadings they turned it over to the keeper of the royal herds, whose name was Simmas; and Simmas, being childless, gave every care to the rearing of the girl, as his own daughter, and called her Semiramis, a name slightly altered from the word which, in the language of the Syrians, means "doves," birds which since that time all the inhabitants of Syria have continued to honour as goddesses.[376]

Doves were also considered sacred to the fish-goddess Derceto, also known as Ataratheh. She was known to the Greeks as Aphrodite Derceto,[377] and as Deasura, the goddess of Syria, to the Romans.[378]

The port city of Ashkelon, where the birth of Semiramis was said to have occurred, is the same mentioned in Judges 14:19, where Samson went to slay thirty men after they had "plowed with his heifer":

> And the Spirit of the LORD came upon him, and he went down to Ashkelon, and slew thirty men of them, and took their spoil, and gave change of garments unto them which expounded the riddle. And his anger was kindled, and he went up to his father's house.

The Greek historian Ctesias of Cnidus (c. 400 BC) through his access to the royal historical records as the court physician of Artaxerxes II (435–358 BC) claimed that a King Ninus and Queen Semiramis had lived in Nineveh. Diodorus added to Ctesias' accounts in his *Bibliotheca Historica*.

During the siege of Bactra, Ninus met Semiramis and married her because he was impressed by her bravery. At that time, she was already the wife of one of his officers named Onnes. Onnes later committed suicide over his loss. According to Diodorus, Semiramis and Ninus then had a son named Ninyas.

During one of Ninus' later campaigns, he was struck by an arrow and fatally wounded. Semiramis disguised herself as her husband (in some accounts as her son Ninyas) and continued to command his army, ultimately conquering all of Ethiopia. She also restored ancient Babylon and had high brick walls built as fortifications surrounding the city.

Later, in honor of her husband, Semiramis erected a temple tomb in Babylon that was said to be ten stadia (according to the Greek historian Herodotus, one stadia is equal to approximately six hundred feet) broad and nine stadia high.[379]

Although mankind's ability to communicate in a common language was lost at the fall of the tower of Babel, the remembrance of the event remained. Nimrod-Ninus and Semiramis have later been ascribed to the gods Marduk and Astarte (also known as Ishtar). They and the followers of their cult were responsible for the construction of various towers or ziggurats throughout the Mesopotamian region commemorating the attempt by Nimrod to reestablish the link to the Watchers.

Additionally, the gods and goddesses worshipped throughout the region of Anatolia and Mesopotamia were often depicted wearing a peculiar, "tower-like" headdress known to the Greeks as the *polos* (introduced in chapter 5), a high, cylindrical crown that was depicted on goddesses of ancient Anatolia and also used by the ancient Greeks and Romans. Cybele, Hera, and Artemis are often shown wearing the castle- or turret-like polos. The polos reflected not specifically their association with Nimrod, but the connection to the heavens that mimics the tower of Babel.

The word *asherah* (אֲשֵׁרָה) is Hebrew for "pole" or a "grove for idol worship," or the Canaanite mother goddess, Asherah. The Hebrew word for the practice of worshipping a goddess in the form of a wooden pole, as well as a word for "pole" came from the name of the goddess herself.

God expressly hated the use and worship of Asherah poles:

> You must never set up a wooden Asherah pole beside the altar you build for the LORD your God.
>
> And never set up sacred pillars for worship, for the LORD your God hates them. (Deuteronomy 16:21–22)[380]

The Asherah goddess who had contact with the light bringer was worshipped in the form of a pillar, pole, tree, or fountain (discussed in chapter 6) reaching to heaven, and was associated with the *meleketh shamayim,* meaning "queen of heaven." God was especially angered by the people of Jerusalem who worshiped her:

> The children gather wood, and the fathers kindle the fire, and the women knead [their] dough, to make cakes to the *queen of heaven*, and to pour out drink offerings unto other gods, that they may provoke me to anger. (Jeremiah 7:18)

The Roman historian Ammianus Marcellinus (AD 320–390) credits Semiramis, like her counterpart Cybele, as the first to use eunuchs as slaves.[381] Her traditional reputation as a harlot is similar to the Babylonian goddess Ishtar and Greek Hecate. At her temple in Hierapolis Bambyce, located in northern Syria, her statue was displayed with a golden dove above her head.[382]

Doves were the symbol of the Babylonian Ishtar and Assyrian Astarte, who was associated with the Greek Aphrodite and the Anatolian Artemis. The Latin word *columba* means "dove" or "pigeon." The subterranean chamber tombs used in the ancient world had the same appearance as the places built to house doves. The word for both "a dove keeper" and for the "chamber in which urns containing the ashes of the dead are stored" is *columbarium* (*columba,* "dove," and *arium,* "a place for").[383]

The familiarity the ancients had with chamber-like crypts and their similarity to the chambers that housed doves led to the double meaning of the word. The idea of resurrection mirrors the image of the energetic doves flying out of the same chambers that housed the dead. The ancient people who put energy towards the worship of their respective goddesses believed that they would gain favor or blessings from them. They also looked to these deities for life after death.

The word *columbia* literally means "the country of the doves" or, more sinisterly, "the country of sepulchral chambers"—but a more complete meaning of the term would be "the country of the resurrection." This meaning alludes to the ancient deity that Washington, DC—the District of *Columbia*—is dedicated to, the Anatolian Cybele-Attis goddess who is the same as the Greek Pallas Athena.

Illustrations of School Classics written 1903 by Sir George Francis Hill features an image of an interesting coin from the Temple of the Aphrodite in Paphos, Cyprus, issued during the reign of Garacalla showing a conical stone as well as a star, crescent, and sacred doves.

A bronze coin of Cyprus, issued in the reign of Garacalla (AD 198–217).[384]

Hill writes:

> The coin is inscribed KOI NO N KVTTPinN, as being issued by the associated cities of Cyprus. The temple consists of a high central portion with two lower wings or porticoes and a fore-court. In the central portion is a large conical stone, which was supposed to be the goddess herself. Above (not well-pre-served) are a star and crescent, the symbol of the goddess. The wings contained sacred columns—or tall incense-altars—and on the roof of each is one of the sacred doves.[385]

In a story similar story to the birth of Attis, the son of Cybele, Tammuz, was later born to Semiramis.[386] His birth was considered a miracle, since it was late after the death of Nimrod. Semiramis herself declared it a "fatherless" birth, the god Marduk reborn. Tammuz and Ishtar are like Attis and Cybele in a variety of ways. He and his mother Ishtar were said to have loved each other and married. In Mesopotamia, his cult also worshipped during March[387] in a dramatic processional ceremony that lamented his unfortunate demise wherein he had been killed and taken to the underworld by jealous demons.

In the story of Isis and Osiris, Cybele and Attis, and Semiramis and Tammuz, the son/husband of each goddess "dies," but continues to endure in some eternal fashion, waiting to be reborn. Each is described as being desired and loved by their goddess-mothers and are greatly mourned. Looking at the story of the garden through the eyes of the Nachash, the woman had *desired* his assistance. After he had given it, his appearance changed from what it was before their interaction, and he was "lost," changed by the curse of God.

> And the Lord God said unto the serpent, Because thou hast done this, thou art cursed above all cattle, and above every beast of the field; upon thy belly shalt thou go, and dust shalt thou eat all the days of thy life. (Genesis 3:14)

The curse given to the Nachash is the meaning of the death of each goddess' son. He is thought of as Eve's son since she had a part in his change (birth) to the lowly serpent, and her husband since they were "wed" in the formation of the Nachash-Eve religious amalgamation. The hoped-for resurrection of the son/husband is the plan of the enduring cherub to rise as the phoenix in human form, throwing off the serpent curse to become the false savior of man who would lead all to the knowledge of resurrection and immortality.

Embedded in the story are images that were expressed in the later mystical hermetic legends of Pyramus and Thisbe, in which Pyramus' blood stains the white mulberry fruits, and ultimately the story of Glaucus, in which Polyidus notices the similarity of the mulberry fruit and the color-changing calf of King Minos before raising Glaucus from the dead.

JONAH

The prophet Jonah (יוֹנָה, "dove") dealt with Nineveh about one hundred years before the minor prophet Nahum wrote his oracle concerning its destruction.[388] Jonah was the fifth of the minor prophets during the reign of Jeroboam II. He was the son of Amittai (אֲמִתַּי, "my truth," from emeth, אֱמֶת, "sureness, true doctrine").

God sent Jonah to prophecy to against Nineveh:

> Arise, go to Nineveh, that great city, and cry against it; for their wickedness is come up before me. (Jonah 1:2)

At first, Jonah avoided going to proclaim God's judgment on the city. Instead, he went to the port city of Joppa (named after the son of Noah, Japheth) and boarded a ship to Tarshish (Tarshish was the name of the son of Javan, who was the son of Japheth; see Genesis 10:2–4).

While on the ship, a great storm came up. At Jonah's suggestion, his shipmates threw him overboard in order to calm the sea and save the ship. A fish (*dagah*) swallowed him; he remained inside the fish for three days before being spit out again onto dry land. After this experience, Jonah relented:

> So Jonah arose, and went unto Nineveh, according to the word of the LORD. Now Nineveh was an exceeding great city of three days' journey. (Jonah 3:3)

Nineveh repented because the Ninevites knew what had happened to Jonah and perhaps reasoned that Jonah's God would be even harsher with them. It is likely, though, that they realized the "fish" that swallowed Jonah was the same form as the goddess they worshipped, Derceto.

Derceto, from Athanasius Kircher's *Oedipus Aegyptiacus*, 1652[389]

The "place of the fish goddess," the city of Nineveh, was the center for the worship of Derceto for the whole region of Syria. The mystical dove symbol of both Derceto and her daughter Semiramis alluded to their powers, albeit false powers, of resurrection.

The prophet, whose name also means "dove" and whose father's name was "the true doctrine," was sent by the direct commandment of God Himself to warn Nineveh of impending destruction. This dove happened to be swallowed by a great fish ("great," *gadowl*, גָּדוֹל, and "fish," *dag*, דָּג; see Jonah 1:17), and remained in its belly for three days, later to be spit out, resurrected, or—more aptly— "truly resurrected." Nineveh later received Jonah as a true prophet and was saved. The amalgamated Eve-Nachash religion whose heart was the city of Nineveh is the same religion that has endured throughout history since before the Flood until modern times.

When Jesus was on earth, the Pharisees asked for a sign that would prove His power. He responded:

> An evil and adulterous generation seeketh after a sign; and there shall no sign be given to it, but the sign of the prophet Jonas. (Matthew 12:39)

The "evil and adulterous generations" follow the religion of the Eve-Nachash goddesses. It is no wonder that Jesus went on to say:

> The men of Nineveh shall rise in judgment with this generation, and shall condemn it: because they repented at the preaching of Jonas; and, *behold, a greater than Jonas [is] here.* (Matthew 12:41, emphasis added)

He who was in their midst would lie in the *columbarium* for three days, and just as the *true* symbol of the dove alludes, resurrect. As the story of Jonah illustrated from before the time of Jesus, the Derceto-like goddess cults would have no power of bestowing eternal life to their worshippers, but through Christ's death and resurrection, all of humanity could gain it.

Pyramus and Thisbe

Ovid's *Metamorphoses* describes the story of two lovers in the city of Babylon. In a continuation of the "death of the loved one" theme, Pyramus and Thisbe were forbidden to associate, since their respective families had an ongoing dispute. Through a crack in one of the walls that separated the two families' courtyards, they whispered their love for each other and arranged to meet near at the tomb of Ninus under a mulberry tree.

Thisbe, whose name means "doves," arrived first, and saw a lioness with her mouth bloodied from *tearing an ox to pieces*. Frightened, she ran away, leaving her veil. The lioness went to drink from a nearby *fountain* and chewed up the veil that Thisbe had left behind.

Pyramus, whose name means, "of the fire," arrived later to see Thisbe's veil and assumed that the lioness had killed her. Pyramus then killed himself, falling on his sword and splashing blood on the white mulberry leaves and fruit, turning them red. When Thisbe returned, she found Pyramus' body under the tree. Thisbe also stabbed herself with the same sword as Pyramus in her grief. The gods who had observed the tragedy decided to change the color of the mulberry fruit from that day to the color of blood to honor the lovers.

In the light of understanding gained thus far through the progression of this book, the decoded story turns out to be quite evil.

The jealous families (God) forbid Pyramus (Nachash) and his love Thisbe (Eve) to meet by setting up a barrier (the walled garden). Each greatly desired the other. Thisbe, the dove, who through communion with Pyramus would give mankind life, observed the lion (Nachash) after he was victorious in killing the ox (God). Not recognizing the lion for what it was—a sign that her communion with Pyramus was possible, since the lion had been victorious over the ox, she ran away in fear and ignorance.

Just as the two lovers experienced a tragic, unnecessary death, mankind, by failing to recognize the possibility of life gained through the path provided by the Nachash and the woman, will experience the same. To remind men of the path to "life" that the Nachash offers, the secret is encoded in the color of the rose, the pomegranate, the mulberry.

Thisbe was also known as the Naiad nymph of the spring, well, or fountain of the Boiotian village of Thisbe (in central Greece). The city of Thebes, where the story of Oedipus and the sphinx occurred, was located in Boeotia as well.

Shakespeare uses the story of Pyramus and Thisbe in *A Midsummer Night's Dream* as a play within a play. The actors curiously mispronounce Ninus' Tomb as "Ninny's Tomb," although the director of the play, Peter *Quince,* corrects them initially, but in vain.

ROMEO AND JULIET

Romeo and Juliet was Shakespeare's retelling of the story of Pyramus and Thisbe. The name "Romeo" means Rome, named after Rommylos (Romulus), the descendant of Ascanius, son of the Trojan prince Aeneas and founder of the of the seven mountains. Romeo was a member of Montague (French, "peaked mountain") family.

"Romulus" means "exalted." The story of how Romulus killed his brother is similar to the story in Genesis 4:8 of Cain killing his brother Abel. Cain means "possessor" or "spear."[390]

The name "Juliet" comes from the god Juno or the Jupiter, whose temple was at the Roman Pantheon on Capitoline Hill (Latin: *Collis Capitōlīnus*). Juliet was a member of the Capulet family. In an allusion to the *columbarian* idea of the doves sacred to many of the ancient goddesses, the name "Capulet" means "coffin" (Latin: *capul,* "coffin"—with the French ending *et,* a capulet is a "a small coffin").

In the story of Set and Osiris, Set tricked Osiris, sealed him in a coffin, and threw it in to the Nile, where it floated to Byblos. It is revealing to look at Shakespeare's play in the light of the meaning behind the names.

Romeo-Romulus, the exalted one, says this to Juliet, also known as Eve, Cybele, Ishtar, Semiramis, and Thisbe:

> But, soft! what light through yonder window breaks?
> It is the east, and Juliet is the sun.
> Arise, fair sun, and kill the envious moon,
> Who is already sick and pale with grief,
> That thou, her maid, art far more fair than she.
> Be not her maid, since she is envious;
> Her vestal livery is but sick and green
> And none but fools do wear it; cast it off.
> (*Romeo and Juliet*, Act 2, Scene 2)

There is more meaning in the imagery described by Romeo when seeing Juliet. The mysteriously hidden, ever mythologically present symbol of the horns of the bull, must be slayed: "Arise, fair sun, and kill the envious moon."

The story of Glaucus is another example of the recurring theme of the path to knowledge lost, with similar characters: the snake, the bull/cow/calf/ox, death, and the hope of resurrection or ascending to becoming godlike though knowledge. There is also the idea of being trapped, since many of the stories occur within walls, chambers, places, or situations where freedom is restricted. This is illustrated in Ninus' tomb and the Capulet "crypt" meaning, as well as in the wine cellar of Glaucus. All have the same theme involving a restriction of some type. The word used for "garden" in Genesis is *gan* (גן), meaning an "enclosed garden, enclosure," from the root *ganan* (גָּנַן), "to defend, cover, surround." The Garden of Eden was from the Nachash's point of view a place of ultimate restriction to his, and in this sense, Eve's, "freedom."

THE COIN AND THE FISH

There is an account in the book of Matthew that occurs in the town of Capernaum. Jesus and His apostles arrive there after Jesus' transfiguration on Mt. Hermon. This was the same town in which Jesus had begun preaching that "the kingdom of Heaven is at hand" after His baptism by John. There, Jesus and His disciples were asked for "tribute money":

> And when they were come to Capernaum, they that received tribute [money] came to Peter, and said, Doth not your master pay tribute?
>
> He saith, Yes. And when he was come into the house, Jesus prevented him, saying, What thinkest thou, Simon? of whom do the kings of the earth take custom or tribute? of their own children, or of strangers?
>
> Peter saith unto him, Of strangers. Jesus saith unto him, Then are the children free.
>
> Notwithstanding, lest we should offend them, go thou to the sea, and cast an hook, and take up the fish that first cometh up; and when thou hast opened his mouth, thou shalt find a piece of money: that take, and give unto them for me and thee. (Matthew 17:24–27)

Peter went and did as Jesus instructed and paid the tribute.

CAPERNAUM

Capernaum (Hebrew: *Kfar Nahum,* כְּפַר נַחוּם, "Nahum's village") was a fishing village located on the northern shore of the Sea of Galilee. The prophet Nahum ("full of consolation or comfort") was an Elkoshite

(*'Elqoshiy*, "God the ensnarer"). Nahum, one of the twelve minor prophets of the Old Testament (between Micah and Habakkuk), wrote an oracle concerning Nineveh's destruction. He described the city as a "bloody city all full of lies and robbery."[391] Nahum's oracle or *Book of Vision* was written shortly before the fall of Nineveh at the hands of the Medes and the Babylonians in 663 BC.[392]

In a path that traced the history of the fallen world and revealed the redeeming power of God, Jesus was transfigured on the same mountain that was the site of the first incursion of the Watchers. He descended to the town named after the prophet Nahum, who foretold the destruction of Nimrod's city of Nineveh. At Capernaum, He paid the "kings of the earth" or the powers inhabiting it not as tribute to them, but to maintain peace. He cured a slave (also a figurative slave to the gods of the world) there at the request of the Roman centurion, showing His willingness to allow all of humanity who lived under the power of the Nachash entrance into His future kingdom.

THE WIDOW CYBELE'S SON

The first story of a "widow" in Anatolian myth is that of the Phrygian goddess Cybele. As her first incarnation, she was known as the epicene god, Agdistis, who was emasculated by the jealous Olympians. Similar to the story of Chronos in Hesiod's *Theogony*, the blood from his severed genitals spawned life—in his case, an almond or pomegranate tree. The river goddess Nana became impregnated from the fruit of the tree, which created the beautiful Attis, who, like Zeus, was said to have been abandoned and tended by the he-goat or Pan.

At the moment of Agdistis' castration, he became the widow Cybele, since Attis' father had been forever lost after the transformation. In the later amalgamation of the Cybele-Attis deity after the death and transformation of Attis into the enduring pine, the cults that followed worshipped Cybele and Attis in a new form, Mithraism. It was Mithras, "the one who binds," who would be the avenger-helper of the "widowed" Cybele. He took on both the power of his immortal mother and "brother" Attis. Killing the bull was a symbolic act of revenge toward the God who caused the misfortune of his two powerful, transcendent relatives. It has been theorized that he looks to Sol Invictus on his left for inspiration, courage, or guidance. It is more appropriate in this light and in light of etymologic study earlier in this book that he looks to Attis during his defamation of the bull with a haughty attitude of revenge, as if to say, "This is for you, brother." His mother Cybele looks on, emerging from the rock on the right, also blessing the magnificent act that depicts the prophetic intention of retribution towards God—inspired by the Nachash who suffered his indignity in the garden.

The "binding" Mithras intends to complete the circuit started at the garden with the curse given by God. Like the story of Apollo and Python, Mithras reveals the same future concerning the eventual manifestation of the new god of light appearing as man at the beginning of the "Golden Age" when heaven and earth will be reunited not by God, but by the Nachash.

The etymological and mythical links from Attis-Cybele-Mithras to Pallas Athena, explained in Chapters 2 through 6, continue in a twisted, obfuscating fashion to this day. Athena is often depicted wearing the Phrygian cap of the old gods; many such representations can be seen today in her new acropolis (Greek, Ακρόπολις, *akros*, "edge, extremity," and *polis*, "city), Washington, DC, the "city on the edge." George ("earth worker") Washington's District of "Columbia" is surrounded by states whose names reveal the Athena-honoring intention of its early designers as well: Virginia, "Land of the Virgin"; Maryland, "Land of the Rebellious One"; and Delaware, "Land of War." The art contained in the various Palladian architecture of the United States Capitol reveals without a doubt that the cult of Mithras-Athena is truly alive today.

Continuing with the story of Jesus: He left Capernaum and went to the gates of the city of Nain ("beautiful field") and raised up the "widow's son." In raising the boy, Jesus demonstrated that not only were the slaves and workers in the fallen world eligible for God's redemption, but also all who might have been a part of the worship of the widow. Forgiveness, redemption, and eternal life were possible for all mankind.

The Didrachmon

The *didrachmon* (or two *drachmē* [δραχμή]) required as tribute money in the town of Capernaum was a Greek silver coin about the same weight as a Roman denarius.[393] As described in chapter 10, the word "drachma," from the Greek *drássomai*, means "to grasp." The base word, *drakōn* (δράκων), as described in *Strong's Lexicon,* is "a dragon, a great serpent, a name for Satan," with an alternate form of *derkomai*, "to look or watch."

The coin that Peter retrieved from the mouth of the fish he caught in the Sea of Galilee ("Galilee" means "a circuit"; it was also called earlier "Gennesaret," which means a "harp")[394] was a silver *stater* equal to four Attic or two Alexandrian drachmas. Stater, from *kauchēsis* (καύχησις), means "the act of glorying," from *kauchaomai* (καυχάομαι), to "glory on account of a thing," and *euchomai* (εὔχομαι) to "pray to God."[395]

Hiram Abiff

At the building of the first Temple in Jerusalem, King Solomon asked Hiram (Hebrew: *Huram*, "noble born"), the king of Tyre, for a "a man skilled to work in gold and silver, bronze and iron, and in purple, crimson and blue yarn, and experienced in the art of engraving, to work in Judah and Jerusalem with my skilled workers, whom my father David provided" (2 Chronicles 2:7).

He wished that his Temple for the Name of his God would be great:

> The temple I am going to build will be great, because our God is greater than all other gods....
>
> But who is able to build a temple for him, since the heavens, even the highest heavens, cannot contain him? Who then am I to build a temple for him, except as a place to burn sacrifices before him?...
>
> Hiram the King responded in a letter with praise to the God of Israel and said that he would send "Huram-Abi" a man of "great skill." (2 Chronicles 2:13)

In 1 Kings 7:14, Huram-Abi is described as "a widow's son of the tribe of Naphtali." "Naphtali," in Hebrew, means "wrestling," and comes from the root *pathal*, meaning "to twist." The Freemasons refer to the story of Hiram Abiff at the time of a fellow brother's climb to the 3rd Degree. They say that, after being appointed by Solomon as chief architect, three fellow masons conspired to force him into telling the secrets of the master mason. At each inquiry, Hiram steadfastly refused to divulge anything, whereby he was struck and injured with various stoneworking tools. The third brother mason finally killed Hiram. The murderers hid his body outside the Temple, marking it with an acacia branch. The word "acacia" comes from the Greek *akis* (ἀκίς), meaning "thorn." In Hebrew, the word for acacia is *shittah*, from shotet, meaning "scourge," or "to pierce." It has been theorized that the crown of thorns forced onto Jesus' head before His crucifixion was made from the acacia. The Ark of the Covenant was made of acacia wood, overlaid with pure gold.

The nineteenth-century historian Charles William Heckethorn wrote that it was King Solomon who planned the death of Hiram:

> The mysterious artificer was brought before her, and cast on the queen [of Sheba] a look that penetrated her very heart. Having recovered her composure, she questioned and defended him against the ill-will and rising jealousy of the king. When she wished to see the countless host of workmen that wrought at the temple, Solomon protested the impossibility of assembling them all at once ; but Hiram, leaping on a stone to be better seen, with his right hand described in the air the *symbolical Tau,* and immediately the men hastened from all parts of the works into the presence of their master. At this the queen wondered greatly, and secretly repented of the promise she had given the king, for she felt herself in love with the mighty architect. Solomon set himself to destroy this affection, and to prepare his rival's humiliation and ruin. For this purpose he employed three fellow-crafts, envious of Hiram, because he had refused to raise them to the degree of masters on account of their want of knowledge and their idleness.[396] (emphasis added)

In a typical serpent-inspired twist, this account of the murder of Hiram would then have been an evil act to a righteous man that was allowed to occur in God's Holy Temple.

The story of Hiram's murder is not corroborated in the Bible, but it does mention that Hiram "finished all the work he had undertaken for King Solomon in the temple of the LORD" (1 Kings 7:40).

Known as an "allegorical" play, the rite of the 3rd or Master Mason's Degree is a reenactment of the story of Hiram in the Temple. The brother making the transition comes to a point in the act when he is instructed on the masonic "sign of distress" and given the words to accompany it, "O Lord, my God! Is there no help for the widow's son?"[397]

Freemasons know that the widow is the goddess Cybele. Who will help Attis? They will, of course.

13

FALLING TOWERS

> And there shall be upon every high mountain, and upon every high hill, rivers and streams of waters in the day of the great slaughter, when the towers fall. Moreover the light of the moon shall be as the light of the sun, and the light of the sun shall be sevenfold, as the light of seven days, in the day that the Lord bindeth up the breach of his people, and healeth the stroke of their wound.
>
> —Isaiah 30:25–26

Understanding the pillar symbolism as it relates to money and commerce suggests that pillars will remain until the time that the Nachash comes in human form to establish his false "paradise" on earth.

The Pillar of Osiris

Set, the Egyptian god of chaos, fashioned a beautiful cedar and ebony chest and held a banquet so that all could admire it. He told his seventy-two conspirator-invited gods that anyone who might fit inside would become the owner.[398]

The number seventy-two today retains a special significance in light of the group of "evil gods" conspiring with Set. The magical text or *grimoire* written sometime in the fourteenth century called the *Goetia* (Greek: *goeteia,* "sorcery") from the earlier *Pseudomonarchia Daemonum*, or "Hierarchy of Demons," lists the seventy-two demons that King Solomon summoned and put to the task of helping construct the first Temple. Solomon controlled the demons with a brass and iron signet ring bearing the name of God in the form of the Star of David.[399]

Seal of Solomon on obverse of Moroccan 4 falus coin[400]

The prophet Daniel alludes to the "powers" against the plan of God who reside over specific areas on earth. The angel speaking to him described his struggle with the prince of Persia (the demon who ruled the region) and was helped by the archangel Michael.

> But the prince of the kingdom of Persia withstood me one and twenty days: but, lo, Michael, one of the chief princes, came to help me; and I remained there with the kings of Persia. (Daniel 10:13)

The principalities that surround the earth are anchored on the twelve constellations. Adding twelve to both the north and south of the ecliptic would make thirty-six equal areas in space said to be under the dominion of the fallen angels who are allied with the Nachash. The surface of the earth mirrors the realm above, making up seventy-two regions.

Set had planned to capture Osiris in the chest, because he knew that it would fit him alone. After Osiris was tricked into going in and lying down, Set quickly nailed the coffin closed, sealed it with molten lead, and had it thrown into the Nile. The chest floated to the city of Byblos in Syria, where it ran aground and was later encased in a tamarisk or *terebinth* tree.

The king of Syria had the tree cut down and installed in his palace when he noticed its sudden appearance on the shore. The jackal-headed Anubis later helped Isis locate Osiris in the king's palace. Isis went to the king and asked for the pillar. The retrieved Osiris crypt became known as the *djed*.

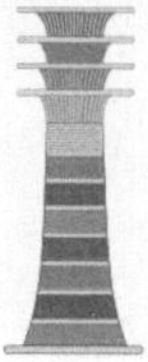

The strange, artistic form of the Egyptian djed, or Pillar of Osiris, has been interpreted in several ways. It is said to represent Osiris' spine or the Syrian cedar tree that grew encasing his coffin with its branches removed. Another interpretation is that it is an image of four free-standing pillars, each placed one behind the other.

Egyptian djed or Pillar of Osiris[401]

The Phoenician letter *semka* looks very much like the *djed*, and is the symbol for a fish. The Hebrew equivalent, *samekh*, means "to support." God hated the pillar (Hebrew: *matstsebah*, מַצֵּבָה, "pillar, idol"; also *asherah*, אֲשֵׁרָה, "groves for idol worship, poles") worship that was practiced by the inhabitants of the land promised to the Israelites:

> Neither shalt thou set thee up [any] image; [Matstsebah] which the LORD thy God hateth. (Deuteronomy 16:22)

XOANON

A *xoanon* (ξόανον, "carved thing") is a crudely shaped piece of wood or stone that represents a god or goddess, most often Apollo, Artemis, or Cybele. A xoanon could be a wooden beam or stone pillar. Over time, the very basic xoanon images created would take on a more distinct appearance of the deity.

Pausanias, in his *Description of Greece*, noted that it was Daedalus who made many of the xoanon pillar-like statues in Greece and was responsible for the image of Hera in her temple at Samos.[402] He observed that "All the works of this artist, though somewhat uncouth to look at, nevertheless have a touch of the divine in them."[403]

The fact that the Greeks attributed the creation of the xoanon to Daedalus is an important clue to their meaning and significance. The creator of the Labyrinth, the clever worker Daedalus, was known as the genius whose inventions were legendary in their complexity and sophistication. In contrast, the xoanon appeared simple and unsophisticated, often appearing merely as a rough block of wood or stone.

Daedalus made *inescapable* traps like the Labyrinth, but demonstrated that they could be defeated—not by the majority, but by the very elect who were given a *path* and stayed on a true course. After Daedalus helped Theseus defeat the Minotaur, King Minos had him and his son Icarus, whose name means "follower," imprisoned.[404] Since Minos had control of the sea and land, Daedalus fashioned wings for himself and his son out of wax so they could escape the island and return to Greece.

Before leaving, Daedalus instructed his son:

> My boy, take care to wing your course along the middle air; if low, the surges wet your flagging plumes; if high, the sun the melting wax consumes: Steer between both: nor to the northern skies, nor south Orion turn your giddy eyes; *but follow me: let me before you lay rules for the flight, and mark the pathless way.*[405]

Unfortunately, Icarus failed to follow the path his father laid out for him and wandered too close to the sun, melting the wings. He crashed into the sea and drowned.

> The boy began to delight in his daring flight, and abandoning his guide, drawn by desire for the heavens, soared higher. His nearness to the devouring sun softened the fragrant wax that held the wings: and the wax melted: he flailed with bare arms, but losing his oar-like wings, could not ride the air. Even as his mouth was crying his father's name, it vanished into the dark blue sea, the Icarian Sea, called after him.[406]

The complexity of the Labyrinth as described by Ovid is an allegory of the flight to freedom that Daedalus took with his son. In order to escape its complexity, it, too, required that one remain on an exact path:

Daedalus, celebrated for his skill in architecture, laid out the design, confused the clues to direction, and led the eye into a tortuous maze by the windings of alternating paths. No differently from the way in which the watery Maeander deludes the sight—flowing backwards and forwards in its changeable course, through the meadows of Phrygia, facing the running waves advancing to meet it, now directing its uncertain waters towards its source, now towards the open sea—so Daedalus made the endless pathways of the maze, and was scarcely able to recover the entrance himself: The building was as deceptive as that.[407]

The manifestation of the true expression of what is hidden in the xoanon appears via the efforts of the knowledgeable men who follow the correct path.

The Labyrinth of Knossos, the double-bladed axe, the Gordian knot, the Omphalos, the Baetylus meteorite god stones, and the Cydonia fruit of the Tree of the Knowledge of Good and Evil have the same congruity. All are symbols of the way to knowledge as well as the paths to becoming lost: the way towards confusion and, ultimately, death. Again, as far as the Nachash is concerned, they allude to an impediment to the "light" that must be cut away, clarified, or defeated to gain life through knowledge. They can be understood only by the wise. The initiated, worthy seeker chosen by others on the same path must be willing to do anything included (and this is key), becoming an adversary to the one God Himself, and becoming the same as the Nachash to find the ultimate goal of the hidden knowledge: eternal life. The serpent's giving of the Knossos was at the same time an axe releasing his new manifestation and an act of violence in a personal way against the creatures that God loved and against God Himself.

The Inescapable Ones

The goddess Amalthea, also known as Cybele, continually emerges from the rock restraining her, thus she is called the "inescapable" and "she who emerges." As such, she is represented as the block of stone. It is up to the clever ones to reveal her. In so doing, they fashion their own "path" to immortality and they become gods themselves though the help of the goddess.

The cult of the goddess Hera at Samos celebrated her birth in a festival called Toneia ("binding"), where she was ceremonially bound with branches from the lygos ("chaste") tree. Her Temple had a grove of one hundred marble pillars.[408]

The ceremony of Hera's binding is the same idea as the binding power of Mithras, and, according to the illuminated, is the same idea as what occurred between Eve and the serpent in the garden. Eve was bound with the serpent at the event that separated the heavens from the earth, and she became a new creature that was restrained by the curse of God.

The progression of more specifically anthropomorphic versions of the xoanon into more recognizable versions of the specific goddess or god also represents the men who worship it. As their god "emerges," they, too, progress in their path to becoming gods. The xoanon change and slowly reveal the hidden. The representations of Apollo known as *kouros* ("male youth") have shown this metamorphosis. The earliest versions merely suggested a roughly formed human figure, but over time, the more lifelike form emerges youthful and naked.

THE TWIN TOWERS

The World Trade Center had a peculiar design. The American-born architect, Minoru Yamasaki (1912–1986), designed the towers and the plaza around them as a representation of Mecca, known as the birthplace of Muhammad and the holiest city of the religion of Islam.

Yamasaki avoided interment as a Japanese-American during the Second World War because he was an architect working at Smith, Hinchman, and Grylls in New York—one of the longest continually operating architecture firms in the United States.[409] Yamasaki combined traditional Islamic architectural form with the modern building methods. The first project incorporating his unique style was in the design of the King Fahd International Air Terminal in Dhahran, Saudi Arabia, in 1961. Using prefabricated concrete to construct arrays of pointed arches, he completed the project, making the central flight tower look like a minaret. King Saud bin Abdulaziz Al Saud honored Yamasaki's work by including an image of the terminal complex on the 1966 series 5 *riyal* banknote.

Saudi 5 riyal banknote, 1966

Yamasaki used the same Islamic style in his design of the World Trade Center after the port authority selected him as lead architect in 1962. His Trade Center courtyard mimicked the arrangement of the Kaaba stone with the golden, spherical Caryatid statue in the Austin J. Tobin Plaza and the Grand Mosque or al-Masjid al-Haram, with its two great minarets in the place where the Twin Towers stood. He used the pointed-arch design throughout the lower facade of the buildings. Yamasaki also designed the Federal Reserve Bank tower in Richmond, Virginia. He went on to do more work for the Saudis, and always kept to his modern interpretation of Islamic architectural design.

Great Spherical Caryatid

One of the more enigmatic pieces of art in New York that was the centerpiece of the Twin Tower plaza was a large, metallic sphere statue created by the German sculptor Fritz Koenig (1921–), whom Yamasaki asked to do the work in the place where a large fountain was originally planned. The sphere was Koenig's largest work, standing twenty-five feet high and cast in fifty-two bronze segments. It was assembled in Bremen, Germany, and later shipped to Lower Manhattan.[410]

The sphere was placed in the center of a ring of fountains at the plaza complex. Described as a symbol of world peace, it rotated every twenty-four hours and was officially titled *Große Kugelkaryatide,* or "Great Spherical Caryatid."[411]

The work was done in a three-dimensional, cubistic style invented by Pablo Picasso in 1907 and characterized by the reduction and fragmentation of natural forms into the abstract. The sphere represented Atlas holding the heavens. Although contemporary descriptions mention that it is a sculpted female figure, this interpretation is simply taken from the meaning of the word "caryatid."

The sculpture survived the attacks on the Twin Towers and was later found in the rubble relatively undamaged. Koenig wanted to leave it in the same condition that it was found, calling it a "beautiful corpse."[412] The sphere was later relocated to Battery Park near Hope Garden under the supervision of Koenig. He stated that his appreciation of his work had changed. "It now has a different beauty, one I could never imagine. It has its own life—different from the one I gave to it."[413]

This golden sphere is a direct representation of both the Cydonia fruit as well as the heavenly sphere held by Atlas. The form of the Twin Towers as the pillars separating heaven from earth stood behind it. Its name, "caryatid," is also linked to the idea of pillars and entwines all the images of the garden at once: the tree, the woman, and the serpent. It represents a false path to immortality, the new order established at the separation of heaven and earth that would eventually lead to its reunification under the power of the serpent.

CARYATIDS

A "caryatid" (Greek: *karyatides,* Καρυάτις) is a sculpted female figure incorporated into a column or a pillar. Karyatides is the name for the maidens who resided in the ancient Peloponnese town of Karyai.

Carya was the daughter of Laconian King Dion and Amphithea. Apollo had rewarded the couple for their great reverence and hospitality to him by giving their daughters the gift of prophecy. He warned that they should never use his gift to betray the gods or search for forbidden knowledge. Artemis was associated with Carya as Artemis Karyatis at her temple in Peloponnese. Dionysus transformed Carya into a walnut tree after she used her gift to escape his affections.

Caryatids are sometimes called *korai,* meaning "maidens." Their male counterpart in architecture is the Atlas. Trees in the genus *carya* (ancient

Greek: κάρυον, "nut") are commonly known as hickory, derived from the Powhatan language of Virginia.

"Hamadryads" (Ἁμαδρυάδες), Greek mythological beings that live in trees, are a particular type of dryads, which in turn are a particular type of nymph. Hamadryads are born bonded to a particular tree. Some believe that hamadryads are the actual tree, while normal dryads are simply the entities, or spirits, of the trees.

Tile mosaic of Pan and a hamadryad, found in Pompeii.[414] Notice the Greek Key or stylized Labyrinth pattern framing the mosaic.

The Athenian Acropolis had six marble caryatids supporting the porch of the Erechtheum. The Erechtheum, named after the half-man, half serpent son of Vulcan, Erichthonius (Greek: 'Εριχθόνιος, "troubles born from the earth") was said to have contained the Palladium, the marks in the rock where Poseidon struck his trident in rivalry with Athena, and the sacred olive tree that won Athena the patronage of Athens. The Greek geographer Pausanias, in his *Description of Greece,* noted that each year, women would dance the caryatis at the Caryateia festival in honor of Artemis Caryatis.

HATHOR

Ancient Egyptian depictions of Hathor varied. Sometimes she was the Eye of Ra as well as his daughter, and at other times she was, like Neith, Ra's mother. The cow goddess of the great flood known as *Mht wrt* ("Great Flood") was also known as the mother of Ra. Mht wrt was either a pre-Hathor\Neith goddess or just another aspect of the complex cow goddess. Hathor's legs were said to be the pillars that supported the heavens, and the belly of the celestial cow was made up of the stars of the Milky Way.[415]

Hathor was known as the goddess of the sycamore tree in the Old

Kingdom. The sycamore fig or fig-mulberry has leaves that resemble the mulberry and was known to the Egyptians as the tree of life.[416] Hathor's Temple at the Dendera complex in Upper Egypt is known for its well preserved Hathor carytids or "divine pillars." The ancient site, built sometime around 2250 BC, was called *Ta-ynt-netert* by the Egyptians, meaning, "She of the Divine Pillar."

Hathor with the sun disk and horns[417]

Hathor pillars at the Temple of Dendra[418]

HESAT

The earthly form of Hathor was Hesat or Hesaret. As Hesat, the divine white cow, she gave her milk to feed the other gods of Egypt and was worshipped as the creator of all nourishment. Ironically Anubis, the god of death, was her son. Ra's noncelestial form was known as the Mnevis bull. The three gods Ra, Hathor-Hesat, and Anubis formed the holy triad that was represented by the bright stars that formed the *V*, *lamba*, or a triangle in the forehead of the constellation Taurus, the same as where the first Parthenon of Athena was aligned, the abode of the seven Hyades, the daughters of Atlas.

The *Book of the Cow of Heaven* appeared as hieroglyphs on the walls of a small chamber in the tomb of Seti I from about 1350 BC. It described mankind's rebellion against Ra. His punishment was said to be the reason for suffering and death and the imperfect state of the world. Before the rebellion, creation was *unified*. Ra sent out his eye in the form of Hathor to punish men. Hathor killed many, but before completing the job, Ra stopped her and separated himself from the earth with her on his back, because if he remained with them, Hathor would kill them all.[419]

The Egyptians in the region of Memphis worshipped the bull deity Apis or *Hapi-ankh*, "the renewal of the life." Apis bulls were the most important animal of Egypt. In order for a bull to be worshipped as the incarnation of Apis, the "strong bull of his mother Hathor," it was required to have special markings. Herodotus writes:

> Now this Apis-Epaphos is a calf born of a cow who after this is not permitted to conceive any other offspring; and the Egyptians say that a flash of light comes down from heaven upon this cow, and of this she produces Apis. This calf which is called Apis is black and has the following signs, namely a white square upon the forehead, and on the back the likeness of an eagle, and in the tail the hairs are double, and on the tongue there is a mark like a beetle.[420]

The bull had a special place made for it in the temple with a window to the outside so that all the people could see it. Its breath was thought to cure any disease, and its movements were closely watched and interpreted by priests as an oracle. When the Apis bull reached the age of twenty-eight, the same as Osiris when he was killed by Set, at the time of a new moon, the bull was put to death with great ceremony. The Greeks and then the Romans continued the worship of the Apis bull until nearly AD 400.

Boaz and Jachin

"Severity and mercy."—Manly P. Hall[421]

King Solomon commissioned Hiram of Tyre to fashion two pillars to be set on either side of the entrance to his Temple:

> He [was] a widow's son of the tribe of Naphtali, and his father [was] a man of Tyre, a worker in brass: and he was filled with wisdom, and understanding, and cunning to work all works in brass. And he came to king Solomon, and wrought all his work. (1 Kings 7:14)

The tribe of Naphtali descended from the son of Jacob or Israel and, as stated before, means "wrestling." Also as related earlier, the word for "brass" in Hebrew is *nĕchuwshah,* from *nachuwsh,* which comes from the past participle of the same word describing the serpent in the garden, the Nachash. By extension, brass exposes the ultimate destiny of the snake, symbolizing judgment. Brass' characteristic sheen mimics gold, but tarnishes and must be continually polished to remain brilliant. It is also the metal of choice for musical instruments because of its resonant qualities and is used to manufacture bells and wind instruments like the trumpet and tuba.

The prophet Ezekiel describes the Nachash as the ingenious master of music:

> Thou hast been in Eden the garden of God; every precious stone [was] thy covering, the sardius, topaz, and the diamond, the beryl, the onyx, and the jasper, the sapphire, the emerald, and the carbuncle, and gold: the workmanship of thy tabrets and of thy pipes was prepared in thee in the day that thou wast created. (Ezekiel 28:13)

The cherub has retained his skill in the creation of music. He uses it to identify himself and to interject his will into the lives of men. The possibility of selling one's soul to the devil in exchange for musical skill is a common theme in modern-day literature.

The pillars at the Temple of Solomon were not a part of any load-bearing structure, but were free standing as a literal depiction of the separation of heaven from earth. They stood at the entrance to the Holy Place, the one point on earth where God's presence was manifest. Although they described judgment, they revealed both the redemptive mercy and perfect righteousness of God. Through them, the Author of Life and the solution to redemption of humanity was approachable.

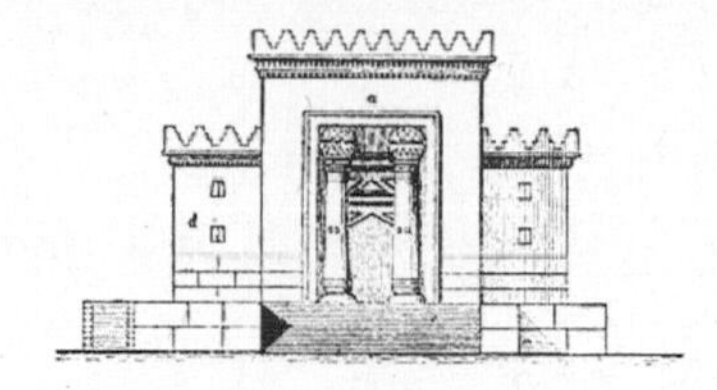

The front view of Solomon's Temple showing the pillars[422]

The capitals or "chapiters" that symbolized heaven were specially made with rows of two hundred pomegranates below "nets of checker work" combined with "wreaths of chain work," which were finally topped by great lilies. The words for "chapiter," "checker work," "pomegranate," and "chains" used in 1 Kings 7 bear much importance.

Working from the bottom of the chapiter or capital (*kothereth*, past participle of *kathar*, "to surround or encircle") up are rows of pomegranates (*rimmoum*, from *ramam*, "to be exalted, high lofty, lifted up"). Next, the nets (*sabak*, "to entwine, a net or lattice, a snare for catching animals") of checker (*sĕbakah*, from *sabak*) work (*ma`aseh*, "deeds, works of deliverance and judgment") and wreaths (*gĕdil*, from, *gadal*, "to twist, magnify oneself") of chain (*sharahĕrah*, from *sharash*, "to take root [and] to be rooted out, eradicated") work. At the very top was the lily (*shuwshan*, from *suws*, "to exult, rejoice, be glad").

The pillars from the ground up described the condition of the world. From the efforts of the Nachash, the path to heaven had been laid with snares. The self-magnified snake's kingdom set barriers to the lily (heaven), but the fact that the pillars resided on either side of the entrance to the Temple of the God of the Universe gave ultimate hope for redemption.

The meaning of the left (southern) pillar in the Temple of Solomon, known as "Boaz," can be understood from the genealogy of the sons of Israel starting at Ram and ending with David in 1 Chronicles 2. Specifically, Ram was from a corrupted line that started early on, when Israel's son Judah consorted with the Canaanite woman, Shua. Later, the corruption continued when the evil Er fathered Phares from his daughter-in-law, Tamar.

Going back from Ram, then, he was the son of Hezron, who was the son of Pharez, who was the son of Er. Er was the son of Judah, and Judah was the son of Israel. The meanings of each name, in order, tell an interesting story in the light of the pillar concept illustrated throughout this book:

- Ram—"to exalt oneself."
- Amminadab—*amam*, from *am,* "to grow dark," and *nadab*, "willingly."
- Nahshon—from *Nachash,*"to practice divination, divine, observe signs, to hiss, whisper."
- Salma—from *salmah,* "outer garment," from *cemel,* "image, statue, carved idol."
- Boaz—"fleetness "or "by his strength." Boaz was the kinsman redeemer of Ruth (from *rehuwth,* "female companion, mate"). "And Naomi had a kinsman of her husband's, a mighty man of wealth, of the family of Elimelech; and his name [was] Boaz" (Ruth 2:1).
- Obed—"led to labor."
- Jesse—"existence."
- Eliab—from *el,* which is shortened from *ayil,* "strong pillar," and *ad,* "father or construct."
- Abinadab—*ad*, "father or construct," and *nadab* "to impel, offer freely."
- Shimma—"fame or rumor."
- Nethaneel—"given, put set, of God."
- Raddai—from *radah,* "to rule, scrape out, to tread with the feet, a wine press."
- Ozem—"I shall hasten them; strength."
- David—"beloved."[423]

Combined, the meanings of the names form a narrative:

The Nachash exalted himself above God, willingly becoming evil. He caused the woman to become like himself, subtle (*aram,* "uncovered, naked"—without the presence of God). The woman needed to compensate for her loss and sought to cover herself in futility. God removed himself from the earth and separated it from heaven. He set the pillars, allowing the Nachash his earthly kingdom: the Eve-Nachash-idol religion. At the same time, God made a plan to redeem the woman. Despite dooming all men to endure suffering after the garden was lost, He freely provided a future in which reconciliation would be realized because of His great love for them.

The pillar on the right or north side of the Temple was known as *Jachin.* Jacob, the son of Isaac, shrewdly acquired his brother Esau's birthright by trading it with him for red soup. The line of Jachin began with Abraham:

Abraham—"father of a multitude."

Isaac—"he laughs."

Jacob—"heel holder" or "supplanter," but later called "Israel" after wrestling with an angel, who blessed him and gave him his new name.

Israel—"God prevails," from *sarah,* "set in order, powerful," and *el,* shortened from *ayil,* "strong pillar."

Simeon—"to be heard."

Jachin—"He will establish" or "to stand upright."

The beginning of the manifestation of God's new heaven on earth started with Abraham and his son Isaac. The birth of Isaac's son, Jacob is an allusion to the curse given in the garden:

> And I will put enmity between thee and the woman, and between thy seed and her seed; it shall bruise thy head, and thou shalt bruise his heel. (Genesis 3:15)

Eve was the mother of the line that would eventually see the birth of the True Redeemer. The same would have his heal bruised by the Nachash. These were God's words. Symbolically, Jacob grabbing his brother's heel illustrates the struggle between the two alignments of men starting with Eve and that the efforts of the snake through his influence on men will fail. The infant Jacob grabbing his brother's heel symbolically depicts this reversal. Esau gave up his birthright for nothing more than a temporary end to his hunger, allowing Jacob to overcome his disadvantaged position as second born. Later, Jacob, through stubborn perseverance in struggling with the "strong man," found favor with God. Jacob called the place where he survived his encounter with the angel "Peniel," meaning, "the face of God."

> So Jacob called the place Peniel, saying, "It is because I saw God face to face, and yet my life was spared." (Genesis 32:30)

The angel, described as a "strong man" (Genesis 32:24), but having the face of God, reveals His identity as the Kinsman Redeemer, both God and Man. Jesus often referred to Himself as the Son of Man as well as God.

> If ye had known me, ye should have known my Father also: and from henceforth ye know him, and have seen him. (John 14:7)

Later, Jacob referred to the identity of the angel while he was blessing his son Joseph and his grandchildren, Manasseh and Ephraim. Notice the comma separating the two verses:

> And he blessed Joseph, and said, God, before whom my fathers Abraham and Isaac did walk, the God which fed me all my life long unto this day,
>
> The Angel which redeemed me from all evil, bless the lads; and let my name be named on them, and the name of my fathers Abraham and Isaac; and let them grow into a multitude in the midst of the earth. (Genesis 48:15–16)

In a recapitulation of the same *type* that Jacob symbolized, the victory brought forth by God in the midst of evil, He blessed the second-born Ephraim with his right hand as he would the first-born. Ephraim's name reflects the same idea. It means both "double ash-heap" and "I shall be doubly fruitful," and the root for Ephraim, Ephraath, is another name for "Bethlehem." The first-born Manasseh's name means "to be forgotten."

The pillar Jachin is the symbol of God's establishment of His plan for the redemption of man and the overcoming of the wretched world that started in the garden.

Plan of the Nachash

The Nachash seeks to fashion his own complete realm on earth. The pillars that were established at the garden must fall and never be thought of again. These were instituted and manifest by God, his hated nemesis, the One God, whom he is loath to mention but for the symbol of the sacrificial bull, the mythical Zeus bull. The honest use of money must be eliminated. It is the recapitulation of the passing of the knowledge of good and evil via the quince/coin symbol between men as a commemoration of the act in the garden, which brought about the lowly state of the world. In a twisted reversal of the curse God gave to Cain, those who would exist in the Nachash's new "paradise" would signify their allegiance by receiving a "mark" that would eliminate the necessity of money. This concept is explained succinctly in the Revelation 13:

> And he causeth all, both small and great, rich and poor, free and bond, to receive a mark in their right hand, or in their foreheads:
>
> And that no man might buy or sell, save he that had the mark, or the name of the beast, or the number of his name. (Revelation 13:16–17)

The fall of the pillars of the Twin Towers was the penultimate gesture of this beginning false reunification of heaven and earth as well as the beginning of the elimination of commerce as it is known today. The Torah with its Ten Commandments, and above all the faith and worship of Jesus Christ, must be *crushed* away. The Nachash's new Atlantis is where he will walk with humanity in the garden of his design. It will necessitate that all men pledge their faith, worship him as their god, and depend on him exclusively. He will allow those who worship him to believe and consider themselves brother and sister gods, blessed and fortunate to live in his new "paradise."

The Freedom Tower

Daniel Libeskind (1946–), who won a competition held in 2003 to become the master plan architect, designed the Freedom Tower as a replacement for the fallen Twin Towers. He had originally planned to create a building that mimicked the asymmetrical form of the Statue of Liberty, but later changed his design to a single modified octagonal spire that would reach a height—combined with an antenna mast—of 1,776 feet. It is no coincidence that he would have sought to honor the Cybele mystery religion by constructing the replacement of the Twin Tower pillars with an image of the god Attis-Sol Invictus-Apollo. The cornerstone of One World Trade Center was laid in a ceremony on July 4, 2004, and the building was completed when the antenna spire was set in place in 2013, nine years later.

14

TROY

What is proper to hear, no one,
human or divine, will hear before you.
—Homer, *The Iliad*

The kingdom of Troy started from a line of kings that began with the mythical Dardanus, who established his city on top to the mountain of the Cybele, Mount Ida. Dardanus, from *dardapto,* "to wear, to slay, to burn up, devour,"[424] was the son of Zeus and Electra, the daughter of Atlas. The Phrygians say that he was originally from the earthly paradise, Arcadia, and he and his older brother, Iasion, were kings from the line of Atlas. Dardanus married Chryse (Greek: Χρύση, "golden"),[425] and had two sons, Idaeus and Dymas. After the great flood of Deucalion, the mountains that they inhabited became islands, and they later split into two groups. The one that remained had Dymas as king, but Idaeus left for the island of Samothrace or Knossos.[426]

After his wife, Chryse, died, Dardanus married Batea (Greek: βάτης, "the one that treads or covers"), and had two sons, Ilus and Erichthonius. The name "Erichthonius" is interesting, since it can mean "a populous" in the sense of people or a nation, and it can also mean "Athenian."[427] An alternate meaning is "an enclosure, castle or fortress."

Erichthonius, Boreas, and the Horse

In *The Iliad,* Homer writes about the origin of the Trojans and mentions the relationship between Erichthonius, horses, and Boreas, the god whose name means "north wind" or the "horrible one":

> In the beginning Dardanos was the son of Zeus, and founded Dardania, for Ilion was not yet established on the plain for men to dwell in, and her people still abode on the spurs of many-fountained Ida. Dardanos had a son, king Erichthonios, who was wealthiest of all men living; he had three thousand mares that fed by the water-meadows, they and their foals with them. Boreas was enamored of them as they were feeding, and covered them in the semblance of a dark-maned stallion. Twelve filly foals did they conceive and bear him, and these, as they sped over the fertile plain, would go bounding on over the ripe ears of wheat and not break them; or again when they would disport themselves on the broad back of Ocean they could gallop on the crest of a breaker.[428]

Tros, the son of Erichthonius and Astyoche (or Astyocheia), inherited his throne from his father and[429] had three sons: Ilus II, Assaracus, and Ganymedes.[430] Romulus and Remus were his descendants approximately nineteen generations later.

Ilus the Star

The Indo-European language, Albanian, is unique in that it is a branch that is shared with no other modern language. The Anatolian languages were the root of the Indo-European, and Albanian has been theorized to be one that split off from the group at a much earlier period, possibly as early as 7000 BC.[431]

Tros' son Ilus, "Illi" (*Ylli*) in Albanian means "star." The word *Troj* (*Troje*) in Albanian means "hearth or realm." Since there were two Iluses—the first

Ilus, the son of Dardanus, and the second Ilus, the son of Tros—the word "troy" would mean "the realm between the Asterions, the two stars." Eighteenth-century English used the term "troy" for "confusion" or a "maze."

TROY, *sb.* Yks. Chs. Der. Lin. Also in form **trow** Chs.[1] s.Chs.[1] [**troi.**] A steelyard; a pair of scales; *gen.* used in *pl.* Cf. **trone**, *sb.*[1]
w.Yks.[2], Chs.[1], s.Chs.[1], nw.Der.[1], n.Lin.[1] sw.Lin.[1] A pair of troys.

TROY-FAIR, *sb.* Som. Used to describe a time of household confusion. *N. & Q.* (1870) 4th S. vi. 300. Cf. **troy-town**, 2.

TROYNE, *sb.* Der.[2] nw.Der.[1] [**troin.**] A water-pipe.

TROYT, *sb.* *Obs.* n.Sc. (Jam.) An inactive person.
'A nasty troyt,' one who is both dirty and indolent.

TROYTLE, see **Troitle**.

TROY-TOWN, *sb.* w.Cy. Dor. Dev. Cor. **1.** A maze; a labyrinth of streets.
Dor. A maze formerly cut in turf on the downs, &c. There is a hamlet called Troy Town three miles from Dorchester, but no maze remaining (H.J.M.). Cor.[1] I lost my way; 'twas a regular Troy town; Cor.[2] Like Troy-town.

2. A state of confusion or disorder; a litter. Cf. **troy-fair**.
w.Cy. If a nurse, on returning after a short absence from the nursery, found the children 'hay-making,' and uproarious, she would say, 'Why, here's Troy Town all over again!' or 'You're making Troy Town of it!' (G.E.D.) s.Dev. A room with its furniture disarranged is said to be 'like Troy Town,' *N. & Q.* (1870) 4th S. vi. 401. Cor.[1] She had quite a Troy town round her; Cor.[2] e.Cor. *N. & Q.* (1870) 4th S. vi. 401.

Image from talented linguist Joseph Wright's (1855–1930) *English Dialect Dictionary*[432]

Ilus II, son of Tros, was said to have won the wrestling prize of fifty youths and maidens at Phrygian games held by the king. On the advice of the Oracle known to the Greeks as Zeus Sabazios, the nomadic, equestrian, sky father god of the Phrygians, the king gave him a cow and told him to establish a city where it should lie down. This was the establishment of city of King Tros, known afterwards as Troy.

Zeus Sabazios was associated with the cult of Cybele. The Greek philosopher and historian Strabo (64 BC–AD 24) mentioned this in his *Geography:*

> As in other things the Athenians always showed their admiration of foreign customs, so they displayed it in what respected the gods. They adopted many foreign sacred ceremonies, particularly those of Thrace and Phrygia; for which they were ridiculed in comedies. Plato mentions the Bendidean, and Demosthenes the Phrygian rites, where he is exposing Æschines and his mother to the scorn of the people; the former for having been present when his mother was sacrificing, and for frequently joining the band of Bacchanalians in celebrating their festivals, and shouting, Evoi, Saboi, Hyes Attes, and Attes Hyes, for these cries belong to the rites of Sabazius and the Great Mother.[433]

The Palladium

Ilus prayed to Zeus Sabazios for a sign after seeing his cow lying on the hillside of Ate (Ate is the Greek goddess of delusion and ruin). In response, Athena sent the Palladium from heaven, where Ilus later found it beside his tent. Since no mortal man was allowed to look at it directly, he was immediately struck with blindness. He regained his sight after making certain offerings to Athena, and constructed a temple at the spot where the Palladium had landed, which became the first building of the city of Troy. The Palladium bestowed Athena's powerful protection. As long as the statue resided in Troy, the city was said to be invincible.

Ilus Is the Asterion

The killing of Pallas by Athena and the suicide of Attis caused by Cybele were both events in which the goddesses (who are one in the same) took on the power of the one "killed." Both Attis and Pallas were greatly loved by their companions, but died through their hasty emotional intervention. This "taking on the power" of each was an allegory of the curse of the serpent in the garden. Like the newly created Eve, Athena and Cybele took on the aegic authority and attributes of the diminished serpent god, who yet endures.

Troy was the first establishment of an empire completely under the aegis of Athena. The Palladium symbolized the moment when she and the power of the serpent Pallas were *superimposed.* The additional sign of the cow lying down signified that the Zeus-bull-cow replacement for God was allowing the Nachash control over the establishment of the new Athenian power that would remain under his authority.

Like the matador who skillfully evades and mocks the bull during his antagonistic dance in the arena, the cow lying down symbolized the moment when the power of the Athena-Cybele realm over the earth was established starting at Troy. Like Mithras, the matador plunges his sword into the bull's heart, and if skillfully placed, the bull dies.

Ilus experienced blindness because the meaning of the Palladium was beyond his ability to "see." The city of Troy had the symbol of the authority of Athena. The Zeus-God-cow symbolically allowed the establishment of power at Troy that would progress up to the present day. Later, Athena herself brought about Troy's destruction, and the Palladium was transferred to the next powerful state under her authority: Greece.

THE JUDGMENT OF PARIS

Like Zeus, Oedipus, and Attis, the infant Paris was abandoned by his parents and left to die in the wilderness. His mother, Hecuba, had a dream that she would give birth to a flaming torch. Her dream was interpreted by the seer Aesacus, son of Priam the king, who said that her son would cause the destruction of Troy by fire. Paris was rescued and nursed by a bear (seeker of honey) and later raised by a shepherd servant, Agelaus. Paris was also known as Alexander (*alexo,* αλεξω, "to defend, help," and *aner,* ανηρ, "man"), since "he repelled robbers and defended the flocks."[434]

At the wedding of Peleus and Thetis, Zeus held a grand banquet. Eris, the goddess of discord, interrupted the feast by taking a golden apple from the garden of Hesperides into which she had inscribed the word "kallisti," meaning in Greek, "for the fairest," and rolling it into the their midst. Athena, Hera, and Aphrodite disputed each other's claim to the apple and asked Zeus to decide its owner.

Zeus, reluctant to reveal particular favor towards any of the goddesses, decided to ask Paris to choose, since he had shown himself to be fair in his previous judgment of the contest between his prize bull and the war god, Ares, also disguised as a bull.

Apollodorus writes:

> Strife threw an apple as a prize of beauty to be contended for by Hera, Athena, and Aphrodite; and Zeus commanded Hermes to lead them to Alexander on Ida in order to be judged by him. And they promised to give Alexander gifts. Hera said that if she were preferred to all women, she would give him the kingdom over all men; and Athena promised victory in war,

and Aphrodite the hand of Helen. And he decided in favour of Aphrodite.[435]

Apart from the three goddesses at the wedding, the most beautiful woman in the world was Helen (Greek: "shining light"), the wife of Menelaus, king of Sparta. Helen was the daughter of Zeus and Nemesis, the goddess of divine retribution. Nemesis was also known as the *inescapable* Amalthea.

Always represented in art wearing the Trojan Phrygian cap, Paris forsook the offerings of Athena, whose Palladium protected the Trojan kingdom. He abducted Helen and brought her to the citadels of Troy, provoking the rage of her husband, Menelaus, and his brother, Agamemnon (Greek: "steadfast") the king of Argos, touching off a siege against Troy that lasted ten years.

Although depicted as the daughter of Zeus and his adopted mother, Amalthea, Helen represented the aspect of Eve that would continue separate from the amalgamated Eve-Nachash. Helen was the anti-Athena. In light of the Zeus representation of God, she represented an aspect of Eve who was with God before her Nachash-induced parthenogenesis and who remained allied with Him, becoming the mother from whose descendants would come the Redeemer of Men.

The golden apple was a clear representation of the fruit of the Tree of Knowledge of Good and Evil. The goddess of greatest beauty would also be the same who possessed its essence. It was, after all, Eve—represented by Athena—who had accepted the "gift" in the garden.

If Paris had understood this, he would have given it to Athena without hesitation, for she had already received it. It was not Eris' to give. Paris added to Athena's insult by taking Helen and protecting her in the very city in which Athena had made invincible, profaning the city of the serpentine knowledge with his substitute "shining light," Helen.

Athena withdrew the Palladium from Troy through her intercession with the warriors of the kingdom who would possess it in the future, and instructed the same men to construct a "gift" for the Trojans in the likeness of her nemesis, Zeus Sabazios. Zeus Sabazios and Boreas both were worshipped at Troy and related to the horse. The Trojan horse was the representation of the corruption of the protected religion of Athena and symbolized Troy's willingness to allow the incursion of Zeus (God) into its midst, corrupting her realm.

The great Greek tragedian Euripides (480–406 BC), in his play, *Trojan Women*, wrote that Poseidon, the brother of Zeus, had predicted Athena's wrath towards the city of Troy:

> For, from his home beneath Parnassus, Phocian Epeus, aided by the craft of Pallas, framed a horse to bear within its womb an armed host, and sent it within the battlements, fraught with death; whence in days to come men shall tell of "the wooden horse," with its hidden load of warriors. Groves forsaken stand and temples of the gods run down with blood, and at the altar's very base, before the god who watched his home, lies Priam dead.... Vanquished by Hera, Argive goddess, and by Athena, who helped to ruin Phrygia...for when drear desolation seizes on a town, the worship of the gods decays and tends to lose respect.[436]

Odysseus commissioned Epeius (Ἐπειός, "he of the future time") to build a huge wooden horse large enough to hold a force of elite Greek warriors after Athena came to him in a dream assuring him that she would be with him to help in its construction.[437] Later, the Greeks pretended to sail away in defeat, but left the Trojan horse at the gates of the city. The gift had the inscription, "For their return home, the Greeks dedicate this thank-offering to *Athena*"[438] (emphasis added).

Perhaps the Trojans thought that Boreas was responsible for the Greeks leaving and had them fashion a horse in his likeness, to honor their victory. Perhaps they were unaware that Odysseus had already stolen the Palladium. The prophet Helenus, son of Priam, king of Troy, had made the importance of the effigy known to the Greeks. Apollo had given the gift of prophecy to him and his twin sister Cassandra. Described as the "second most beautiful woman in the world," Cassandra's refusal at Apollo's attempted seduction caused him to curse her by "spitting in her mouth" so that her prophecies would never be believed. In a similar, but reversed fashion, the seer Polyidus had Glaucus spit into his mouth. As far as the mysteries are concerned, there is no difference between forgetting them completely or having others fail to perceive them.

Fearing the inevitable destruction of the city, Helenus left to hide on Mt. Ida until the danger was over. Odysseus captured him and forced him to reveal the secret of Troy's power. Later, he and the great warrior Diomedes ("god-like cunning") made their way into the citadel where the Palladium was kept by way of a secret passage, and carried it back to the Greek encampment.

The Greek dedication thanking Athena should have been a dire warning to the Trojans. The representation of Athena's nemesis, Zeus Sabazios, could never had been allowed to enter the city while it held the Palladium, since it provided absolute protection under the her aegis. The Trojans could have instantly recognized the danger of allowing the Greek "gift" inside their walls, but had grown too complacent in the worship and too ignorant in understanding and appreciation of the nature of their protector goddess. Cassandra had warned them. The Palladium was already missing. Athena brought her "divine retribution" into their midst in the same manner as Nemesis, the goddess whose daughter the Trojans protected. Troy was razed in a fiery holocaust by the returning Greek army, just as Aesacus had prophesied.

There can be no doubt that Athena caused the fall of Troy. Later during Odysseus' ten-year journey back home, he called on her:

> Stand beside me, Athena, fire me with daring, fierce
> as the day we ripped Troy's glittering crown of towers down.
> Stand by me—furious now as then, my bright-eyed one—
> and I would fight three hundred men, great goddess,
> with you to brace me, comrade-in-arms in battle![439]

The Trojan War was important in that it occurred while human hybrids known as the Nephilim were still living among men. The fall of Troy occurred around the same time as the rule of Israelite King Saul, whose conflict with the giant Philistine Goliath is recorded in 1 Samuel and 1 Chronicles.

The great Greek hero of the Trojan war known as Ajax ("earth"), son of Telamon ("a bearer, supporter") and the great grandson of Zeus, was described by Homer as the "bulwark of the Greek Achaeans" and carried a huge, layered-bronze shield made of seven cowhides. Ajax was said to have been trained by the Apollo-like centaur, Chiron. He was colossal, fearless, and vicious, but possessed great intelligence in battle.[440]

The name "Ajax" or "of the earth" is related to the *earth*-born aspect of the Nephilim word used for "giants" in Genesis 6:4: Hebrew, *něphiyl*, from *naphal*, which means to "fall or be cast down."

> There were giants in the earth in those days; and also after that, when the sons of God came in unto the daughters of men, and they bare children to them, the same became mighty men which were of old, men of renown. (Genesis 6:4)

The Greek translation of the Old Testament, the Septuagint (Latin: *septuaginta*, "seventy," so named after the seventy-two Jewish scholars who were asked by Ptolemy II [309–246 BC] to translate the Hebrew Torah)[441] uses the word *gigantes* (γίγαντες) for the Hebrew *něphiyl*, which literally means "the sons of Gaia" ("earth").[442]

The Bones of Nephilim Ajax

The second century Greek traveler and geographer Pausanias (AD 110–180) records the discovery of the bones of Ajax in his *Description of Greece*:

> He bade me [to] form an estimate of the size of the corpse in the following way. The bones on his knees, called by doctors the knee-pan, were in the case of Ajax as big as the discus of a boy in the pentathlon.[443]

Later, the man whose name was the same as the one who caused the downfall of Troy, Alexander the Great, in a symbolic act of Athenian retribution, went to Troy and sacrificed to the legendary hero, Achilles. He owed his power to the success of his warrior ancestors and their taking of the Palladium, which now resided in the Erechtheum at the Greek Acropolis.

Like his ancestors who had fought at Troy, Alexander would fight on the side of his patron goddess, the goddess who bestowed knowledge and protection to their whole civilization. Alexander the Great, under the aegis of Athena, went on to become the most powerful warrior-ruler the ancient world had ever known. After him, Mithridates, also known as Antioch Epiphanes under the same power, brought the gods of Greece to the very center of the city of God, profaning His Temple.

Both Alexander the Great and Antioch Epiphanes are images of a future *type* who will ultimately manifest under the Palladium of Athena in our time, from the world power whose base lies at Washington, DC.

The Palladium and the Powers of the Earth

The nature of the Palladium was that throughout ancient history it remained with each powerful nation, but was transferred when another, more dominant nation, took its place. The works of the ancient historians who mention it occasionally confirm this.

After the destruction of Troy, the Palladium was transferred to Greece and remained in the Erechtheum at the Acropolis for approximately eight hundred years. Somewhere within a period of fifty years after the death of Alexander the Great in 323 BC and the formation of the Roman republic, it was moved to the Temple of Vesta in the Roman Forum. Pliny the Elder mentioned it while describing the Roman dictator Lucius Caecilius Metellus (290–221 BC), who had been blinded when he rescued the Palladium from the temple sometime in 241 BC.

> Metellus passed his old age, deprived of his sight, which he had lost in a fire, while rescuing the Palladium from the temple

> of Vesta; a glorious action, no doubt, although the result was unhappy: on which account it is, that although he ought not to be called unfortunate, still he cannot be called fortunate. The Roman people, however, granted him a privilege which no one else had ever obtained since the foundation of the city, that of being conveyed to the senate- house in a chariot whenever he went to the senate: a great distinction, no doubt, but bought at the price of his sight.[444]

The Romans regarded the Palladium as one of their *pignora imperii*, meaning "pledges of rule," which guaranteed the republic's continued *imperium*, the power and command of the empire. Later, the emperor Elagabalus transferred the most sacred Roman relics, including the Palladium, from their respective shrines to his new temple, the Elagabalium:

> As soon as he entered the city, however, neglecting all the affairs of the provinces, he established Elagabalus as a god on the Palatine Hill close to the imperial palace; and he built him a temple, to which he desired to transfer the emblem of the Great Mother, the fire of Vesta, the Palladium, the shields of the Salii, and all that the Romans held sacred, purposing that no god might be worshipped at Rome save only Elagabalus.[445]

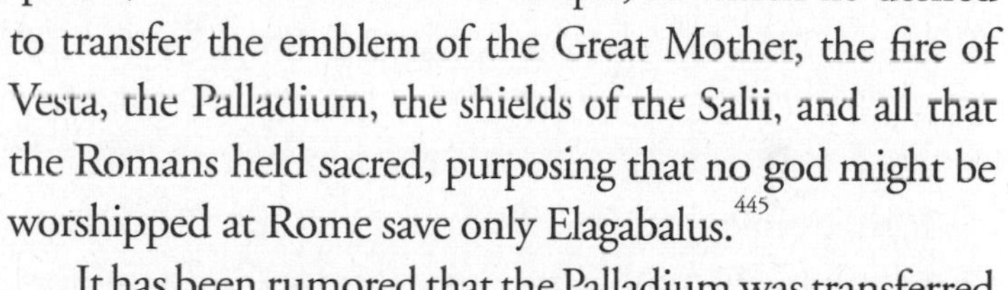

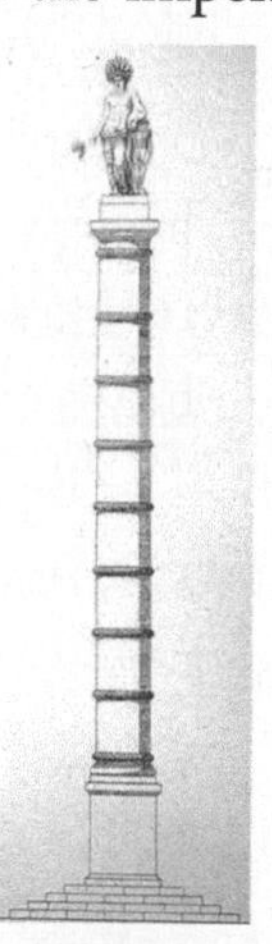

The original Column of Constantine, with the statue of Constantine as Apollo[447]

It has been rumored that the Palladium was transferred from Rome to Constantinople in AD 330 by Constantine the Great and buried under the Column of Apollo-Constantine at his Forum.[446]

At this point in history, the Palladium location references stop. If the Palladium exists today and had always been located at the heart of each respective world power, discerning its location through time after the fall of Constantinople would be a simple matter of following history.

After the fall of the Western Roman empire from the Middle Ages to the Renaissance, the Catholic Church was the central power of all Europe. After the decline of Constantinople, the power of the Church moved back to Italy and was located at the Holy See (Latin: *sancta*, "holy," *sedes,* "seat") in Rome, known today as the Vatican. It is most likely that the Palladium was taken to Rome some time before AD 1150, when part of the Forum complex was destroyed by a powerful storm.

The word "Vatican" comes from the Roman god Vaticanus, the god of wailing or weeping. It is not well known that the name is a combination of the Latin *vātī,* meaning a "foreteller, seer, soothsayer, prophet," and *cānus,* which means "to shine or be white, hoary."[448]

The next great world power was the British, whose empire began its rise to a world colonial supremacy at the time of King Henry VIII of the House of Tudor after breaking ties with the Roman Catholic Church in 1534. The Palladium would have been transferred either to England and kept at the Palace of Placentia or to Westminster Abbey after Henry assumed direct royal control there in 1539. Herodotus writes that the Persian King Xerxes (519–465 BC) was the first to use the phrase that described the British Empire: "the empire on which the sun never sets": "We shall extend the Persian territory as far as God's heaven reaches. *The sun will then shine on no land beyond our borders;* for I will pass through Europe from one end to the other" (emphasis added).[449]

It is possible that the Palladium never left the control of the Catholic Church from the time of its removal from Constantinople until the later part of the nineteenth century. There is evidence that it might have been under the protection of the Templar Knights after the First Crusade until King Philip IV ended their order in 1307.

The United States

While much has been written concerning the causes of the Civil War, it cannot be disputed that a major component of the conflict was over who controlled the commerce of the nation. The Civil War was fought over the rights of individual states to maintain their sovereignty over the power of the federal government. In 1860, there was no income tax, and the federal government received most of its revenue through various import tariffs paid by the South, which it used to support commercial and manufacturing industries in the North. The North had a greater representation in Congress and left the South without any control of where the money was spent.

The agricultural South had to import almost all manufactured goods from Europe or be forced buy products from the North. As the North continued to raise taxes on imports, it also gained the power to increase prices on the goods it manufactured. Eventually, the southern state governments decided there would be no resolution to the problem other than secession from the Union. If the South were successful, it would have controlled all of the warm-water ports, which would have severely restricted the ability of the remaining nation to grow economically or militarily.

The resulting war left nearly 750,000 people dead by the time it ended in 1865. Contrary to the laws outlined in the Constitution, at the start of the war, President Abraham Lincoln had unilaterally ordered the blockade of all southern ports, raised a seventy-five-thousand-man- strong militia, and placed a suspension on *habeus corpus*, the right of a person under arrest to be brought before a judge or into court. As a result, many who merely voiced their objections to the war were branded as disloyal and imprisoned without trial.

The North's victory was an important necessity in that it consolidated the power of the federal government. As described by Manly Palmer Hall, the Masons established the country in order to complete its destiny "for A PECULIAR AND PARTICULAR PURPOSE known only to the initiated few."[450] A southern victory would have destroyed the path to this destiny.

THE PALLADIAN MONUMENT

In 1836, on the one hundredth anniversary of George Washington's birth, the Washington National Monument Society was formed. The Society commissioned Freemason Robert Mills (1781–1855) to come up with a design proposal. Mills also designed the Department of Treasury building and the US Patent Office Building in the likeness of the Parthenon. He proposed to create a massive obelisk. Part of his original plan not included in the final construction was a doorway crowned by a winged sun in the style of an Egyptian *Behedeti*.[451]

The project started in 1848 with a stone-laying ceremony overseen by the DC-area Freemasons. Construction continued until 1854, when private donations ran out, and the structure remained unfinished until after the Civil War, when congress provided funding in 1879 and appointed the military and civil engineer, Thomas Lincoln Casey (1831–1896), to supervise the task. In 1884, President Chester Arthur dedicated the completed monument in an elaborate ceremony.

The monument is the largest stone structure in the world and remains the tallest in Washington, DC, because of the height restriction imposed in the city by the Heights of Buildings Act of 1910.

The Palladium Comes to Washington

British scholar and mystic Arthur Edward Waite (1857–1942) wrote about the enigmatic Masonic order known as the Sovereign Council of Wisdom and its involvement with the Palladium:

> On the 20th of May, 1737, there was constituted in France the Order of the Palladium, or Sovereign Council of Wisdom, which, after the manner of the androgyne lodges then springing into existence, initiated women under the title of Companions of Penelope. The ritual of this order was published by the Masonic archæologist Ragon, so that there can be no doubt of its existence.... In some way which remains wholly untraceable this order is inferred to have been connected by more than its name with the legendary Palladium of the Knights Templars, well known under the title of Baphomet.... For a period exceeding sixty years we hear little of the legendary Palladium; but in 1801 the Israelite Isaac Long is said to have carried the original Baphomet and the skull of the Templar Grand Master Jacques de Molay from Paris to Charleston in the United States.[452]

The Palladium described by Waite, also under the name "Baphomet," was thought to have been worshipped by the Templar knights and may have been a Latinized version of the name for Muhammad.[453] The reference to the Baphomet also appeared in the transcripts from the tortured confessions of the Knights during their purge by King Philip IV in 1307.[454]

If the object the Templar knights were referring to was in fact the Palladium, they would have been the ones who were responsible for its protection and transfer from Constantinople to the Vatican sometime after the First Crusade, and they would have done their best to obfuscate the fact by describing it in symbolic terms.

The nineteenth-century image of a sabbatic goat or *Baphomet* from Eliphas Levi's "Dogme et Rituel de la Haute Magie," 1854. The arms bear the Latin words *solve* ("dissolve") and *coagula* ("congeal").[455]

The Baphomet can be thought of as a representation of the Palladium described by the Templar knights. They understood the mystery behind the effigy. The image of Athena is replaced by the "horns" with the torch between—in the style of the symbol for Hecate. The crescent moons and Pythagorean pentagram, with its five golden triangles, accentuate this relationship. The gynandromorphic body of the creature is the same as the Attis-Cybele known to the Mithraian cults. The intertwined snakes of the *caduceus* in the lap of the image mirror the serpent that encircled the pillar of the Palladium.

The Baphomet is a conglomeration of the Mithra cult's Leontocephaline symbol and the goddess Cybele, but with the lion's head replaced by a similar reference to the Nachash, the goat god. Its significance is the same, in fact, as the Palladium.

The 33rd-degree Scottish Rite Freemason Albert Pike was rumored to have belonged to the secretive order that was thought to have been founded in Paris in 1737. Although Masons have since declared the existence of the group as fiction, the Western chapter was said to have been located in Charleston, South Carolina, and headed by Pike.[456]

The Italian revolutionary and the worldwide director of Illuminized Freemasonry, Giuseppe Mazzini (1805–1872) worked with Pike to form the new society and gave Pike the title "Sovereign Pontiff of Universal Freemasonry." Pike named the new society the "Order of the New and Reformed Palladian Rite." He and Mazzini sought to create a supreme Universal Rite of Masonry that would control world Freemasonry and centralize Masons under one supreme master. The penultimate ceremony of the unified society known as the Palladists was the Palladium Rite.

In a letter to Albert Pike in January 1870 concerning the formation of the new society, Mazzini wrote:

> We must allow all the federations to continue just as they are, with their systems, their central authorities and their divers modes of correspondence between high grades of the same rite, organized as they are at present, but we must create a supreme rite, which will remain unknown, to which we will call those Masons of high degree whom we shall select. With regard to their brothers in Masonry, these men must be pledged to the strictest secrecy. Through this supreme rite, we will govern all Freemasonry which will become the one international centre, the more powerful because its direction will be unknown.[457]

This idea of maintaining a select group more secret and yet more powerful than the outer façade was also espoused by Manly P. Hall when he wrote:

> Freemasonry is a fraternity within a fraternity—an outer organization concealing an inner brotherhood of the elect.... it is

> necessary to establish the existence of these two separate and yet interdependent orders, the one visible and the other invisible. The visible society is a splendid camaraderie of "free and accepted" men enjoined to devote themselves to ethical, educational, fraternal, patriotic, and humanitarian concerns. The invisible society is a secret and most august fraternity whose members are dedicated to the service of a mysterious arcannum arcandrum.[458]

The website of the Ancient and Primitive Rite of Memphis Misraim, Sovereign Sanctuary for Bulgaria, describes importance of the Palladium Rite:

> This rite was to be kept secret at all costs and only a chosen few were selected. The Palladium would be an international alliance of key Masons.... This rite combined the Grand Lodges, Grand Orient, all 99 degrees of Memphiz-Mitzraim, and 33 degrees of the Scottish Rite. Therefore, high-level Freemasonry contains the entire practice of Memphis-Mizraim, and totally controls the separate modern-day Masonic Lodges.[459]

Pike fought on the side of the South during the war and was later found guilty of treason and jailed. After Lincoln's assassination, his fellow Freemason, President Andrew Johnson, pardoned him and met with him at the White House in 1866.

The interruption of the construction of the Washington Monument was timed in accordance to the work that had to be completed concerning the centralization of power in the United States. Albert Pike must have been in possession of the Palladium at the time of its dedication. Consistent with the Palladium's locations throughout history corresponding with the dominant world power, and in the same manner as it was buried under the column of Constantine, it is most likely that it is located under the Washington Monument or somewhere very close to it.

Later, the Lincoln Memorial completed the enigmatic line that connects the Washington Monument to the Capitol building and symbolized the establishment of the country now wholly prepared to complete the mystical work.

Designed by architect and Freemason Henry Bacon (1866–1924), it was built and dedicated in 1922 in accordance to the layout of monuments described in the planning document for the development of the Washington, DC, National Mall written twenty years earlier, known as the McMillan Plan.

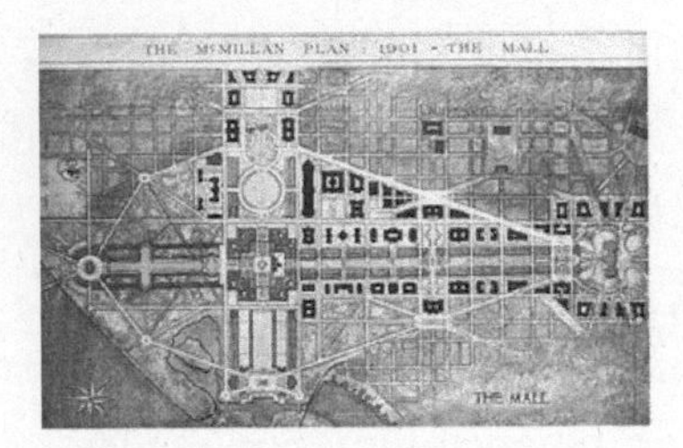

Map of the McMillan Plan from 1901. The circular area on the far left now has the Lincoln Memorial.[460]

The position of the Washington Monument exactly divides the line from the Lincoln Memorial to the Capitol building into a golden section. The distance from the entrance of the Lincoln Memorial to the center of the circle where the Washington Monument stands is exactly 4181 feet. The distance from the monument to the belly (womb) of the owl outline surrounding the Capitol building is 6765 feet.[461] These numbers are the nineteenth and twentieth iterations of the Fibonacci sequence.

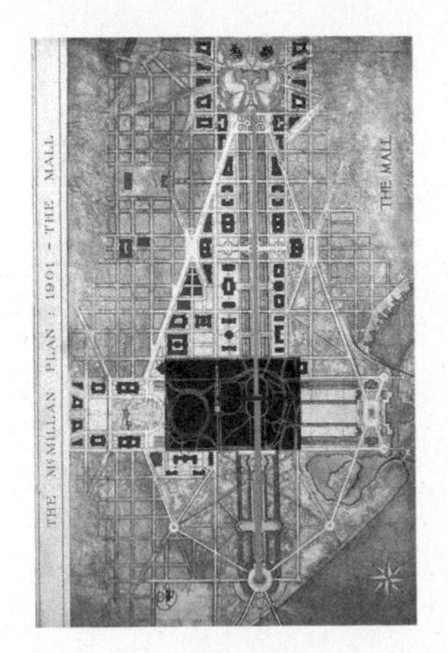

The Palladium or Attis Tree of Washington, DC: The line shows the location of the obelisk and the division of the line making a golden section. The area in black is an overly of the actual position of the monument and the Ellipse today that is different from the McMillan Plan.

When viewing the line vertically from the west to east, with the Capitol owl outline at the top and the Lincoln Memorial at the bottom, the Palladium symbolism stands out. Just as in the ancient representations of the Palladium, Athena, symbolized by the great owl, stands on the chapiter at the top of the pole or pillar divided into a golden section, her *parthenogenic* symbol.

The Capitol Washington Monument-Lincoln Memorial line is also a symbolic representation of the tree of Attis (popularly known today by the *vulgar* as the Christmas Tree). At the division of the line where the Washington Monument stands, there are two intersecting circles of the same radius formally known as a *vesica piscis* (Latin, "bladder" and "fish").[462] The lens-like center where the two circles overlap is known as a *mandorla,*[463] which is Italian for "almond."

It was the goddess Nana (or Rhea) who picked the almond from the tree spawned from the male organ of Agdistis (who became Cybele) and laid it in her bosom, which resulted in the birth of Attis. In the same way that Attis sprang from the almond in the lap of the goddess, the men who established the United States and designed the layout of Washington, District of Columbia (resurrection), absolutely believe that he will rise again in human form. They strategically placed their Masonic obelisk, the lost piece of the Egyptian god Osiris, over the *yonic* or womb symbol of the mandorla. Attis is the invincible sun, the god of light who lurks in his enduring form at the bosom of the pine or *palladium* tree. Athena/Cybele stands at the top waiting for his rebirth. The mystery of the palladium is that it is more than the effigy that Athena created after killing Pallas; it is the symbol of the hoped-for resurrection/manifestation of the Nachash, which is represented by the gods Osiris, Attis, and Pallas. The line from the Lincoln Memorial to the Capitol reveals his presence and is the magical catalyst that will make his arrival possible on earth as supreme ruler in god/human form.

George Washington appointed the French-born architect, civil engineer, and Freemason Pierre Charles L'Enfant (1754–1825) to create the original design of the District of Columbia area in 1791. L'Enfant proposed the construction of an oblong, circular park that later became known as the Ellipse or President's Park directly below the white house. L'Enfant's Ellipse is an oval outline surrounding an uninscribed vesica piscis and represented an egg or *womb* in the state of *deficit,* since it would remain unfertilized and unfruitful until a future time. The Latin word for the geometric form, *ellipsis,* is from the Greek *elleipsis,* which means "a falling short" or "deficit." The meaning of Greek *ellipsis* is the same as the Hebrew *chatta'ath,* from *chata'* and the Greek *hamartia,* which means "to miss the mark" or "falling short"; "to wander from the law of God, violate God's law, or sin."

L'Enfant also proposed that a statue honoring George Washington be placed at the intersection of a line from north to south with the White House and the east-west line from the Capitol.[464] Interestingly, the Washington Monument, which was erected instead of the statue, is not in the position that L'Enfant proposed, but slightly farther to the east.

Like the Washington Monument, the construction of the Ellipse was not completed until after the Civil War. The area was known as the "White Lot" (the word "white" lends to its identification with an egg) before construction was started in 1867 by the Army Corps of Engineers, because it was surrounded by a white picket fence.[465] It was completed in 1894, when the roadway that surrounded it was lit with electric lamps. Symbolically, the lights surrounding the *womb* signified that it was now *fertile.*

It is not surprising that the National Christmas Tree happens to be located in the Ellipse. Every year since 1923, in a tradition started by President Calvin Coolidge, a large pine tree is decorated and lit in an elaborate celebration.

The darkest time of the year when the sun is lowest and seems to linger for three days in the northern hemisphere is the winter solstice (Latin: *sol,* "sun," and *sistere,* "to stand still"), which occurs on December 21. The Washington Attis pole/Palladium line heralds the arrival of this holy date by counting to it with its two golden section lengths of Fibonacci iterations, nineteen and twenty. During this time, the regenerative power of the obelisk is at its height and casts the longest shadow of the year.

The image of Nike and Ilus with the Trojan Palladium reveals the importance of the location of the Ellipse just to the northwest of the obelisk at Washington, DC. The serpent (the cursed/diminished but still enduring Nachash) is Osiris/Attis/Pallas touching the egg/womb given to him by the goddess Victory, daughter of the Titan Pallas. She is the same goddess as Athena/Cybele, but named "Victory" because of her prophetic role in resurrecting her son/consort. Nike is often represented in art with wings attached to sides of her head. An example of this can be seen in the Tympanum of the pediment at the New York Stock Exchange building. Just as in the image of the Palladium with Nike and the serpent, the shadow of the obelisk "snakes" out and touches the egg or womb of the "ellipse" on one important time of the year, the only time when the sun has begun it upward course after its "death" for three days.

Nike and Ilus with the Trojan Palladium.[466] Notice Athena on the top of the pedestal pillar and the snake touching the "egg" held by the goddess, Nike.

Google Earth gives a heading of 342.37 degrees from the Washington Monument to the most southern point of the *womb* of the Ellipse. In order for the sun to be in a position to cast a shadow from the obelisk to the most southern point of the womb, the solar azimuth has to be at exactly 162.57 degrees. This occurs precisely at 11 a.m. on December 25 at Washington, DC, which is located at 38 degrees, 53 minutes, north latitude and 77 degrees, 2 minutes, west longitude. The Romans celebrated the *Dies Natalis* ("natal [birth] day") of Attis or Sol Invictus on December 25, the last day of *Satunalia,* the festival of light and truth.[467, 468]

The length of the shadow can be calculated using basic trigonometry. The solar elevation at this time is 25.75 degrees.[469]

Tan (25.74°) = (Obelisk height (555 ft.)) + (the difference in terrain elevation between the Ellipse and the base of the monument (approximately 20 feet[470]) / (length of obelisk shadow).[471]

The length of the shadow is then 1192.63 feet, which places the end precisely in the center of an upside-down, *U*-shaped entranceway at the base of the Ellipse.[472]

The obelisk is an extension of the Nachash into our physical world. The shadow touching the egg/womb at his final incarnation can be thought of in the same *interdimensional conduit* sense as the tower of Babel, where he takes advantage of a specific moment to manifest in the form of a human being while retaining his angelic power. Unlike the tower of Babel, where Nimrod sought to reach upward to commune with the gods, the *conduit* is the angelic power of the Nachash reaching down to ultimately commune with men.

If the Washington Monument had been erected where it was originally planned, the mystical event of the shadow touching the womb could not have occurred at precisely 11 a.m., the time whose numbers symbolize the pillars separating heaven from earth.

Is this event during the rebirth of the sun and symbolic rebirth of Attis also pointing to the location of the Palladium?

English author and historian Alan Butler, whose works include the *City of the Goddess* and *Rosslyn Revealed,* believes there is a chamber located somewhere beneath the Ellipse, and that it was constructed after the Civil War during the administration of Andrew Johnson. He writes:

> The work was supervised by Lieutenant Colonal Thomas Lincoln Casey. …In his 1878 report Casey noted that grading the land for the Ellipse was well underway but he also reported that he had not addressed the centre of the Ellipse because that was under the authority of "the District Commissioners." Casey suggested that sewage work was being undertaken at the centre of the Ellipse, and that this did not fall within his personal remit. We have to ask ourselves whether this "sewage work" was anything of the sort?… Apart from the fact that this appears to be a strange place to do anything with sewers at that period, it seems far more likely to us that the work

> at the center of the Ellipse was the excavation and creation of a chamber. When the work was finished the structure was covered over and the land graded above it. The only reminder that it is even there is that small, almost insignificant stone—which incidentally should not be there either. The original Meridian stone was located further south and was known as the "Jefferson Pier."[473]

Butler does not speculate on what might be buried in the chamber, but it is most likely that the ancient Palladium resides there.

The great work was readied for completion by finalizing the golden section line, the Ellipse and the Washington Monument. The Ellipse was "lit" and made ready in 1894. The obelisk's shadow has touched the Ellipse three times every year since then during the sun's death at the winter solstice. If the days in a year could be thought of as the period left since the readying of the "womb" until the manifestation of the Nachash on earth, the final number to look for would be 122, since the days in one year (365) divided by three equals 121.66.

1894 + 121.66 equals the end of July 2015.

In August 2011, a magnitude 5.8 earthquake damaged the Washington Monument. This was an exceedingly rare event, since the last recorded quake in the area occurred in 1875.[474] Did this occur because the *fertilization* had finally been successful? The ritual that is performed by the sun in tandem with the obelisk in a damaged or desecrated state no longer holds power. In the same fashion, a holy icon with as much mystical power as the Washington Monument cannot somehow be repaired to its former holy perfection after being damaged. Perhaps the seed of Attis has been successfully planted on earth and now waits for a great event to herald and establish his rule.

During the repair process, the monument was surrounded by scaffolding with sheets of blue semitransparent fabric and lit with 488 lamps.[475] It is conceivable that this was done to honor the successful completion and mystical beginning of the manifestation of Nachash on earth.

French Revolution—Reign of Terror—Freedom Cap

The Society of the Friends of the Constitution known as the Jacobin Club was a group of proto-socialist radicals who instigated the French Revolution. They were mainly under the influence of the French lawyer and politician-philosopher, Maximilien de Robespierre. After the fall of the French monarchy, the Jacobins, headed by Robespierre, imposed a dictatorship and formed the new Committee of Public Safety.

In a purge known as the Reign of Terror that lasted from 1793 until 1794, nearly forty thousand people were executed.[476] The guillotine, named after the French physician Joseph-Ignace Guillotin (1738–1814), was the efficient method used to mechanize the process of eliminating those selected by the Committee. Dr. Joseph had proposed earlier in his writings that the device should be used to carry out all death penalties in France in order to make the method of execution equal for all societal classes.

Among the people condemned to die were aristocrats, the middle class, and even peasants accused of any trivial counter revolutionary utterance. A de-Christianization of society was imposed as well; all suspected clergy and people protecting them were either beaten to death on sight or guillotined. While all this was going on, a replacement cult developed known as Religion of Virtue, with its newly formed deity, the Goddess of Reason. She was celebrated towards the end of the purge in the Cathedral of Notre Dame.

The red, floppy, Phrygian caps that the revolutionaries adopted and wore as a symbol of their freedom were confused with the Roman *pileus*. The pileus, known in mythology as the remnant of the egg from which Castor and Pollux hatched, was always dome shaped and egg-colored or white, never red. The Phrygian cap was erroneously believed to be the same worn by freed Roman slaves as a symbol of their new life, having been newly born or "hatched."

From the time of the French Revolution to the present day, the fallacy of the Phrygian cap symbolizing freedom has continued. In retrospect, the Phrygian rather than the pileus cap was more appropriate in light of the worship of the newly found anti-Christian goddess of death.

Statue of Freedom: The Acropolis of Athena, Washington, DC

The Statue of Freedom[477]

The colossal statue that stands on the top of the US Capitol dome was designed by the American sculptor Thomas Gibson Crawford (1814 1857). Known as the Statue of Freedom, the female figure looks to the east away from the National Mall. She stands 19.47 feet tall and weighs approximately fifteen thousand pounds.

In 1854, Crawford was commissioned to design the statue and began by creating a plaster model at his studio in Rome. The person in charge of the Capitol construction and decorations was the Mississippi senator and the secretary of war, Jefferson Davis, who would later become the president of the Confederacy. He objected to the initial design of the model, since it wore a Phrygian cap, and requested that it be replaced with a military-style helmet with eagle's head and crest of feathers instead.

The Architect of the Capitol agency website describes identity of the Statue of Freedom as "a female allegorical figure."[479] Clark Mills (1810–1883), whose bronze foundry was located on the outskirts of Washington, cast the bronze statue in five main sections. The figure was placed in position on the Capitol dome on December 2, 1863.

Original design of the Statue of Freedom; Athena is shown wearing the Phrygian cap.[478]

WASHINGTON, DC, ACROPOLIS OF ATHENA

Neith, the goddess of war, wisdom, and weaving, and "Nurse of the Crocodiles," was the self-born virgin mother who brought light to mankind. The inscription found in the "inaccessible" area of her temple at Sais, Egypt, describes her:

> I am the things that are, that will be, and that have been. No one has ever laid open the garment by which I am concealed. The fruit which I brought forth was the sun.[480]

From Neith, the morphology of the Anatolian Cybele-Attis gods bought the Attic goddess Athena. Athena's Palladium is the key to returning the missing phallus of Osiris, which had been lost for thousands of years, swallowed by the Egyptian crocodile fertility god, Sobek.

The crocodile god Sobek in his solar form[481]

The phallus of Osiris has been recovered though the power of the Nurse of the Crocodiles. Athena-Neith stands at the top of the Capitol building looking to the east. At her back stands his now-recovered phallus, the great obelisk of Osiris. It is currently set in place over her Palladium, whose power throughout history has made the way ready. Osiris is now capable of fathering the *expected* one. The symbol of her aegis is rendered throughout the Acropolis of Washington, DC, and protects the *undertaking*, as described in the motto on the reverse of the Great Seal of the United States, the symbol that grants the talismanic power to the dollar: *Annuit cœptis* (Latin: *annuo*, "to nod, approve," and *coeptum*, "undertaking"). As Neith, she has made ready the rebirth of the great sun god Horus/Apollo to manifest on earth as the god of light, finally in human form.

A Naiskos fountain honoring Cybele-Attis-Neith-Athena lies directly in front of the western entrance of the Capitol building. Notice the Egyptian *Bennu* bird (phoenix) in the tympanum, the scallop shell with carved roses, and the crescent moon with the serpentine fountain below.[482]

Detail of the pediment tympanum sculpture on the Senate side of the Capitol building's east side. Notice Athena in her Phrygian cap, the older George Washington with sword on her left, and the young Washington to her right with the axe. Also, notice the snake near the base of the tree.[483]

A directory map located on the Capitol grounds at Washington, DC. Notice the clearly defined Athenian "owl" in yellow showing the walking paths immediately around the Capitol building.[484]

15

HERMES, THE TWINS, AND THE ROYAL SECRET

"Ye shall be like the Elohim, knowing good and evil," had the Serpent of Genesis said, and the Tree of Knowledge became the Tree of Death.

For six thousand years the Martyrs of Knowledge toil and die at the foot of this tree, that it may again become the Tree of Life.

—Albert Pike[485]

The Mithraic Mysteries practiced in the Roman Empire from around AD 100–400 were linked to a very ancient god. The Greeks and Romans altered the name from the Persian *Mithra* that came from an earlier Proto-Iranian pronunciation, *Mitra,* whose origin can be traced back as far as 3000 BC. As mentioned earlier, *Tauroctony* depictions of Mithras slaying the bull in Roman art always included Sol Invictus or Attis to his right and an unnamed female deity to his left, emerging from the rock. In many examples, two lesser gods known as Cautes (Latin: *cauto-caveo,* "to be on one's guard, to take care, take heed, beware, guard against, avoid") and Cautopates (cauto + *pates–pateo,* "to stand open, lie open, be open") also appear in the scene.[486] Cautes is typically shown to the right of Mithras holding a torch in an upward position and Cautopates usually appears on his left with his torch pointed down. Historians are not in agreement as to the true significance of the Tauroctony scene, but in light of the framework of mythological interpretation established thus far, the meaning *can* be discerned.

An important key to this understanding involves the twins, Cautes and Cautopates, and what they represent. The first clue is that both appear to be small versions of Mithras himself. At the left of Mithras is Cautes, but the one at the right should be *Pates,* not Cautopates. Mithras was known as the "thrice great." The phrase "triplasiou *Mithrou*" has been found inscribed below some of the depictions of the Tauroctony with the twins.[487]

Mithras can be thought of as the "son" of Attis (the sun god to his right) and Cybele (the woman with the crescent moon above her head emerging from the rock on his left), but the term "son" is not truly appropriate in the sense of what he represents. He is the combination of the two symbols the Nachash has used throughout history to represent himself. At the very base of the Nachashian-inspired mystery, Mithras is the embodiment of the power the Nachash seeks to gain after giving Eve the fruit of the Tree of Knowledge of Good and Evil. From this act onward, the knowledge was held by him and disseminated to men through the Eve mystery cults of the ancient world. Cybele was both mother and father of Attis, just as the Nachash would falsely intimate that he had created Eve by causing her to become a different creature, knowing good and evil. Their act in the garden binds them to the same state, *awareness or subtleness,* and to the same fate, eventual destruction. From this point onward, the cult of the knowledge was held by the Nachash. Mithras is both Cybele and Attis, as one.

The twins to the right and left of Mithras are, in fact, Mithras again in dual roles, hiding his knowledge from the unworthy or revealing it to his elect. This is the meaning of the term "thrice great," because Mithras is simultaneously the entity that is the source of the light that he reveals or conceals.

The meaning behind the Tauroctony scene is illustrated in the story of Akademos, Theseus, and Helen. According to Plutarch, before the Trojan

War, the same Theseus who slayed the Minotaur abducted a beautiful, twelve-year-old Spartan girl who would later become Helen ("light") of Troy. He brought her to Greece and hid her in the walled garden of olive groves created by the Greek hero, Akademos (Greek: ἀκή, "silent," and δῆμος, "district").[488] The garden was located six stadia northwest of Athens and planted with trees descended from Athena's sacred olive kept in the Erechtheum.

To free their sister, Helen's twin brothers Castor (Latin: *Castoris,* "a beaver" [an impediment builder]) and Pollux (Latin: *pol,* "true," and *lux,* "light, shining")[489] invaded Attica and threatened to destroy Athens. Akademos saved Athens by revealing where Helen was hidden.

After Theseus had defeated the God-man at the center of the Labyrinth, he took the "light," Helen, and placed her in the center of Akademos' walled garden that was sacred to Athena. From the Nachash's point of view, he had "defeated" God in the Garden of Eden by corrupting His newly created beings, and had become the "keeper of the light." Helen in the garden of Athena is a metaphor for Mithras (combination of Eve-Cybele-moon and the serpent-Attis-sun) slaying the bull (God). The equivalents of Helen's twin brothers Pollux and Castor are Pates and Cautes respectively, revealing or concealing the light. Akademos clarifies the scenario by telling the revealer and concealer twins where their sister is hidden. The place was named after Akademos, who had created the garden, *Academia,* the "district of silence." Plato later used the site for his silent school, where he revealed *Hermetic* secrets.

Ancient Rome absorbed much of the religion and culture of the Etruscan civilization (768–264 BC) that occupied northwest Italy. According to Herodotus, they were originally from the area in Anatolia ruled by the Lydians. Mitochondrial DNA studies have shown that people still living in the areas of old Etruscan cities in Italy are related to peoples from the Near East.[490] No major literary works in the Etruscan language survive, but inscriptions have been found on tombstones and various artifacts from the Tuscany region. The Etruscan practice of *haruspicy,* or divination by reading the shapes of sheep and cattle entrails, has been linked to similar practices by the Babylonians. Haruspex artifacts from both areas are nearly identical. Etruscan settlements were typically built on hills and surrounded by high, thick walls.

In accordance with the Etruscan ritual of *pomerium* (*post,* "first," and *moerium,* "wall"), Romulus, who was born on the twenty-first day of the month of *Thoth* (aka Hermes), went to Palatine (*palātum,* "heaven") Hill on April 21 in 753 BC, and began digging a ditch. As mentioned in chapter 3, April 21 was the Roman feast or feminine form of Pan or Pales, the shepherd god whose symbol was the Hyades star cluster in the head of Taurus. The festival was celebrated by driving cattle through bonfires.

Romulus and his twin brother Remus were sons of the god Mars and the Vestal Virgin, Rhea Silvia (*reus,* "bound" or "responsible for," and *Silvia,* "forest"). As punishment for Rhea breaking her vow of chastity, her twins were condemned to die by exposure, but they were rescued, adopted by the she-wolf, and raised in her lair.

Again, the image of the wolf in the lair accompanied by the twins repeats the idea of the light of the knowledge of good and evil being flanked by the contrasting powers of one who allows its dissemination or concealment.

The Ancient Greeks and Romans often marked or delineated the borders of their cities with *xoanon*-like sculptures that consisted of a head above a squared, blocky midsection that included male genitalia known as *herma.* Many of the marker sculptures had heads in the likeness of Hermes, but often, other gods, heroes, or distinguished mortals were used. A popular head for many of the Roman variants was in the likeness of Plato.

The borders of the realm controlled by Thoth or Hermes were appropriately guarded and marked by the herma. Crossing the boundary meant that one was leaving the security of the realm of the Nachashian "light" in diabolical contrast to Adam and Eve leaving the "borders" of the garden.

Romulus killed his twin when Remus insulted him by "leaping" over his newly made border, afterwards saying, "So perish everyone that shall hereafter leap over my wall." Consistent with the idea of the revealing or concealing aspect of the hermetic twin concept, Romulus was setting up a new age of containment, concealment, and dissemination of the knowledge given at the garden. The concealing aspect of Hermes-Romulus had built the walls. There would be an appropriate time for revealing the secrets of the new order that would become Rome, but only at Hermes' discretion.

The Etruscan was the first culture that used the symbol of the *fasces*. Originally, it was a double-bladed axe or labrys protruding above arrow shafts bundled around the shaft and bound by red leather.

The Romans adopted the symbol and altered it slightly, using thick birch rods completely surrounding a single-headed axe left protruding out of one side. They carried it in public celebrations as a symbol of Roman imperium. The strange effigy symbolizes the mystery of the cult of Mithras, the story of Akademos and Theseus, and Romulus and Remus in the lair of the she-wolf in a *three-dimensional* fashion. The original form of the fasces with the double bladed axe represented the knowledge of good and evil (the labrys) contained within the power or border set by the Nachash (the *arrow* shafts). The blood-soaked red skin of the defeated bull (the Minotaur, the bull beneath Mithras) allowed the structure or realm to exist. In the eyes of the Nachash, it was he who defeated God. Truly though, God only allows him to carry on his earthly rule for a short time, so the leather binding the arrows reflects God's ultimate power limiting the serpent to work within set boundaries. In a like fashion, another Etruscan symbol known today as the swastika represented the center of the Labyrinth, with the God-man defeated or absent. Both the fasces and the swastika were symbols of Etruscan and later Roman power. The Roman form of the fasces can be seen many places where the United States government holds power, specifically in Washington, DC. A very recognizable example of this is the *Mercury* dime, with Mercury's head depicted on the obverse and the fasces on the reverse.

Etruscan fasces[491]

Mercury dime[492]

Of course, the swastika now has the stigma assigned to it by its use as symbol of the Nazi regime. Benito Mussolini sought to revive the power of the Roman Empire while he was Italy's dictator, and he adopted the old symbols of Roman power. Adolf Hitler adopted one of these symbols that was easier to have represented on flags and uniforms. The term "fascist" comes directly from the ancient Roman-Etruscan–*Mithraic*-Hermetic symbol.

The illuminated adepts consider ignorance of the meaning behind the Freemasonic ceremony that surrounds our culture's highly esteemed education system vulgar. To a person residing outside the borders of the illuminated fraternities, gaining understanding is a difficult process. There are few *outside the borders* who comprehend the mysteries. However, at this point, a framework has been laid down so that we can now comprehend the ancient mystery religion in all its profane clarity.

Consider the word "baccalaureate," the degree awarded to the college student after thirty-two months of study. It is an alteration of the Latin, *baccalarius,* which is a combination of the words *baccha* and *laurus*.

A Baccha was a female attendant of Bacchus, who celebrated his festivals accompanied by clashing symbols and woman worshippers overcome with raving madness. At the climax of the festival of Bacchus known as the *Bacchanalia*, woman priestesses, or *Bacchae*, indwelt with the power of the god, would approach and tear apart a bull with their bare hands in a ritual known as *Sparagmos*. The wild-haired Bacchae wore ivy crowns and fawn or goatskins on their left shoulders, and they carried thyrsus staffs wound with ivy. The Romans knew the Greek god Dionysus as Bacchus, and the madness he induced was *bakkheia*.

Prometheus stole fire from Zeus using a *thyrsus* fennel stalk and gave it to men. The Athenians held a night race by torch light once a year from the temples of Parthenon out to a road lined with graves that led to the altar of Prometheus built at the Academia. Participants ran in the darkness of ignorance, past death to the source of light and eternal life contained in the representation of the Hermathena, the garden of Hermes, keeper of the knowledge, to the altar of the god who stole the light.

Today, the *Ivy League* schools have the greatest prestige. The sacred ivy plant was a symbol for Bacchus. His son, Kissos (Greek: κισσός, "Ivy," *Hedera,* "turning," *Helix* or "European Ivy")[493] died suddenly while they were playing together. Failing to revive his son, Gaia (Earth) pitied the heartbroken Bacchus and changed the boy into ivy. This same type of death and altered resurrection theme occurs in the story of Cybele and Attis, Polyidus and Glaucus, Aphrodite and Adonis, and Isis and Osiris.

The leaping entities that escaped the destruction of Rahab and Mars found refuge on earth. They, along with the prince of the powers of the air, now had an "adopted" mother, Gaia. In a similar manner, Zeus had Amalthea and the goat god, Aegipan (Dionysus or Bacchus was often depicted in the form a goat similar to the god Pan) to protect them from Chronos in the cave; Romulus and Remus were nurtured by Lupa in the earthen-dug cave or lair.

A word similar to the Roman *laurel* of Etruscan origin is "larium" and was used as a term for the god who presided over and protected a specific area, city, or road.[494] The Etruscans also kept miniature shrines known as *lararium* to the god of the household, and used the term "lares" to signify a smaller personal area having a ruling deity. The Greek term for the larium shrines to Cybele that were observed around the mountains of western Anatolia was *Naiskos* (illustrated in chapter 5).

Discerning the meaning of the words that have twisted into obscurity over the passage of time gives a clearer understanding of the true significance of the graduation ceremony in which the initiate receives his or her bachelor's degree. Literally, the graduates have been admitted into the realm of the control or *larium* of Bacchus, and achieved the status of "baccalaureus."

Hermes Trismegistus is the author named in the enigmatic text known as the *Emerald Tablets of Thoth*. The oldest known source for the Emerald Tablets of Thoth was from the three thousand treatises of the *Jabirian Corpus,* written by the Muslim alchemist and astronomer known as Jabir ibn Hayyan (c. AD 721–815). The *Corpus* listed knowledge concerning music, cosmology, and chemistry, as well as the artificial generation of living creatures.[495]

Today it is only known through the many various translations that have been rendered since it was first translated into Latin from Arabic sometime in the twelfth century. It was considered to be the base for all the secrets of alchemy, the study of the mysteries of the Kemet, the dark lands whose mysteries the god Thoth protected.

Like Athena springing from the head of Zeus, her equivalent, Neith, came from Thoth, the Egyptian god who was the keeper of all knowledge, the silent one. He was depicted in human form with the head of an ibis, the bird that was often seen on the banks of the Nile "writing" in the mud with its long beak. The Greek equivalent of Thoth is Hermes and the Roman is Mercury.

The European alchemists were known as mystics who endeavored primarily to transmute base metals into gold and to find an elixir of immortality. As usual, the popular understanding of the alchemists and their goals was wrapped in allegory, typical of the obfuscation methods employed by Nachash. The true alchemist understood that the source of the power that he sought was from Hermes himself. The idea of turning base metals to gold was really an analogy for the continuing dedication to a mysterious conclusion. The efforts towards this goal are known as the "undertaking." This is stated on the dollar bill with the Latin inscription, *Annuit Coeptis* ("he nods, favors the undertaking, effort [or beginning]").

The true goal of the alchemist is to make possible the physical incarnation of the light bringer on earth. Only then will the new golden age begin—the base metal will have turned into gold. Only then will men have the availability of eternal life. By this definition, those who labor to ascend the degrees of Freemasonry are also alchemists; they use the same secret language to describe the same end.

The economist John Maynard Keynes (1883–1946) acquired many of Isaac Newton's writings from the Earl of Portsmouth via a Sotheby's auction in 1936. Among them was a translation of the Latin text of the *Emerald Tablets*.

Apart from the most famous of the statements attributed to the tablet, the second in the list, "As above so below," the forth is most telling in the light of Mithras depicted in the Tauroctony: "The Sun is its father, the moon its mother, the wind hath carried it in its belly, the earth is its nurse."

Newton's translation:

1. Tis true without lying, certain & most true.
2. That which is below is like that which is above & that which is above is like that which is below to do the miracles of one only thing.
3. And as all things have been & arose from one by the mediation of one: so all things have their birth from this one thing by adaptation.
4. The Sun is its father, the moon its mother, the wind hath carried it in its belly, the earth is its nurse.
5. The father of all perfection in the whole world is here.
6. Its force or power is entire if it be converted into earth.
7. Separate thou the earth from the fire, the subtle from the gross sweetly with great industry.
8. It ascends from the earth to the heaven & again it descends to the earth & receives the force of things superior & inferior.
9. By this means you shall have the glory of the whole world.
10. & thereby all obscurity shall fly from you.
11. Its force is above all force. For it vanquishes every subtle thing & penetrates every solid thing.
12. So was the world created.
13. From this are & do come admirable adaptations whereof the means (or process) is here in this. Hence I am called Hermes Trismegist, having the three parts of the philosophy of the whole world.
14. That which I have said of the operation of the Sun is accomplished & ended.[496]

The mathematician, navigator, and astronomer John Dee (AD 1527–1609) was one of Europe's greatest alchemists. An advisor and court astrologer to Queen Elizabeth I, he was an early proponent of colonization of North America and was behind the establishment of Statue Mile. In his pursuit of knowledge, Dee acquired the largest library in Europe and worked with the alchemic spirit medium Edward Kelley (AD 1555–1597) to communicate with angelic beings. Together they recorded a language that Kelly obtained through crystal-gazing that they called *Enochian*.

While employed as court astrologer, Dee introduced his mysterious, alchemic symbol that he called the *Monas Hieroglyphica* ("hieroglyph of the 'one'") described in his book of twenty-four *theorems* under the same name. The Monad would be Dee's most enigmatic treatise concerning the Hermitic mysteries. No one today claims to completely understand the work, but many have proposed various interpretations behind the meaning of the mysterious Monad. However, none arrive at the quintessential revelation that the Monad is actually a representation of the god who waits to manifest on earth in human form.

The Monad is a combination of the alchemic symbols for the sun, the moon, mercury, and Aries, the Ram.

Alchemic symbol for the sun

Alchemic symbol for the moon

Alchemic symbol for mercury

Alchemic symbol for Aries, the Ram

John Dee's *Monas Hieroglyphica*

An earlier text written by Dee, *Propaedeumata Aphoristica* (1558, "Instruction and Delimitations on Astronomy"), was the first to use and describe the Monad.The image created for the cover of the book is revealing.

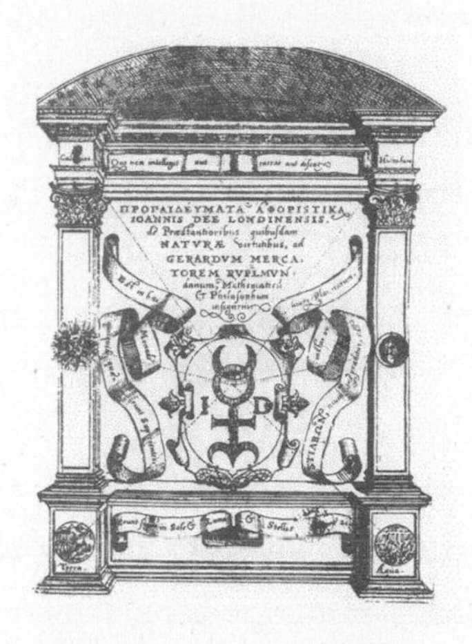

Cover illustration of the *Propaedeumata Aphoristica*

The Latin inscription on the left-side ribbon reads, *Est in Monade quicquid quaerunt sapientes,* or, "In the Monad is whatever the wise seek," which is similar to the well-known alchemic motto, *Est in Mercurio quicquid quaerunt sapientes,* or, "In Mercury is whatever the wise seek."

At the top of the image, the Latin translated is: "For he that does not understand, let him be silent, and learn," reiterating the Thothian/Hermetic/Masonic motto, *Audi, Vide, Tace* ("Hear, see, be silent").

Dee draws lines from the "head" of the creature, the "one" to the sun to its right and the moon to the left. The pillars framing the symbol both demonstrate the separation of heaven from earth and the twin aspects of the One's power to reveal his light to the worthy or conceal it from the vulgar.

The "it" or the "one" is Thoth, Hermes, Mithras, and Mercury. It is not any of them as different personages or aspects, but as different names for the same "thing"—an entity that has combined the esotericism of the ancient mystery religions to describe himself in a way typical for one so intelligently *subtle.*

The Roman god Mercury, with his winged shoes, was described as the keeper of boundaries, a swift messenger who freely traveled between worlds. The "leaping" angel (Greek: *aggelos,* "messenger") who escaped the fiery destruction of Mars and hid in the embrace of his adopted mother, Gaia, is the prince of the power of the air.

> Wherein in time past ye walked according to the course of this world, according to the prince of the power of the air, the spirit that now worketh in the children of disobedience. (Ephesians 2:2)

Alchemists considered the liquid metallic element of the same name to be the first matter from which all metals were formed. From Mercury, the addition of different metals would *transmute* upward to the highest form: the pure metal, gold.

On the surface, Mercury's alchemic sign incorporates the symbols for the moon and Venus. Broken down to base meanings using the study provided in chapter 7, the horns of the bull at the top of the circle or *circuit* represents God; the same circle with the cross below represents the female aspect, or Eve. The Nachash craftily substitutes himself in the place of God at his garden union with Eve. The alchemic symbol for Mercury ingeniously represents the Tritogeneia.

The Monad has two important alterations; it adds the symbol for Aries, the Ram, below the sign of Mercury. Mithras *murders* the bull beneath him that represents God. Contrast this with the story of Abraham and Isaac. Abraham went to Mt. Moriah, the mountain ordained by God where he was to sacrifice his only son in a prophetic *type* that illustrated God's plan to sacrifice His own son at the cross. At the last moment, an angel stopped Abraham, instead providing a ram, a symbol of Christ, as a substitute. Dee also added a dot to the center of the circle of the Venus symbol, turning it into "gold."

Notice that the Monad on the cover of the *Propaedeumata Aphoristica* has an oval surrounding it, encapsulating the whole of the "one." The Cydonia fruit, the knowledge of good and evil, expresses its manifestation on earth through the interactions of the serpent and men. This oval idea can be thought of as symbolic representation of the living state of the serpent or the *one*. It lives, enduring in embryonic form waiting to *hatch*, to manifest, on earth. The *one* waits to transmute, to bring about the golden age when men become like gods through his gift of knowledge.

The cover of Dee's *Monas Hieroglyphica* is changed slightly from his early publication, with the ellipse clearly in the shape of an egg.

Cover illustration of the *Monas Hieroglyphica*

The Monad is the representation of Tritogeneia, which is the same power behind the Palladium. The pillars represent the separation of heaven and earth. Notice the heavenly sphere on the right and the earth on the left at the base of the pillars. An important distinction must be added to pillars in this configuration. They also represent the twin aspect of the "one's" power to reveal or conceal his light. This is the representation of the "one's" thrice-great power—Trismegistus, the epitaph of Hermes.

The whole image, Tritogeneia and Trismegistus, and Hermes (Mithras), flanked by the pillars (Cautes and Pates), is the meaning of the mystical term used by the alchemists *Hermathena,* whose symbol mimics the Star of David.

The Baphomet figure described in chapter 14 contains the essence of Mercury/Hermes defined by the superimposition of the Cybele-Eve-moon and the Attis-Nachash-sun. It is the Palladium and also the concept of Tritogeneia, but it symbolizes more than this.

The position of the arms of the *creature* mimic the Mithraic twins Cautes and Pates in the Tauroctony, Pollux and Castor on either side of their sister Helen at the garden of Athena/Akademos, and the pillars of heaven and earth that frame the Monad.

The right arm of the dual-gendered Baphomet figure is raised up in the same manner as Cautes' torch with the Latin inscription, *solve* ("loosen, unbind, release"). The left is down in the manner of Pates' torch, and is inscribed, *coagula* ("to bind, coagulate").

The Baphomet is a Hermathena. The description in English for a creature having being both male and female characteristics is "hermaphroditic." The Baphomet would be more appropriately termed "Hermathenic," but the event that started the Trojan War colored the term as something that was out of order or unnatural. After all, it was Aphrodite, not Athena, who won the apple of discord.

All Freemasons are familiar with the phrase, "Erected to God and dedicated to the Holy Saints John" at the dedication of new lodges. The two Johns, John the Baptist and John the Revelator, are described as the patron saints of Freemasonry. They are given reverence on both of their feast days, John the Baptist's on June 24 and John the Revelator on December 27, both nearly equal to the summer and winter solstices, respectively. The Masonic symbol used to represent the two Johns is the "point within the circle." In Masonic literature, the point is described as equaling "the individual brother" and the circle as "the boundary line of his duty to God and to man, beyond which a man should not allow his passions, prejudices or interests to betray him." The lines on either side represent St. John the Baptist and St. John the Revelator, but also the "framing of the year."[497] This is, of course, typical Hermetic obfuscation.

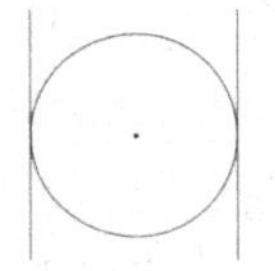

The point within the circle[498]

The "point within the circle" is a clever but simple representation of the Hermathena, with the "twins" flanking the sun or Hermes. It is shorthand for the Tauroctony. No wonder that it is seen everywhere in Masonic art, publications, and temples.

The Royal Observatory in Greenwich, England, is a Hermathena. It is where the Prime Meridian was established and adopted at an international conference in 1884.

David E. Flynn has written much concerning the first Astronomer Royal of the Observatory, John Flamsteed (1646–1719), and the function of the observatory.

> In 1675 the British astronomer John Flamsteed, first Astronomer Royal to King Charles, directed the construction of the royal observatory of Greenwich built for the sole purpose of determining longitude for the earth for the kingdom of Britain. From the Greenwich observatory, the sun and stars were cataloged according to the exact time they passed overhead for every day of the year.... It has long been known that the most efficient star with which to determine latitude is the brightest, Sirius. Evidence that the zodiacal sign of Sirius, the twins of Gemini, were the patrons and guides of seafarers of the Mediterranean was recorded in Homer's Odyssey. Castor and Pollux were implored by their magical speaking ship the Argo, as the only passengers sufficiently initiated into the mysteries to guide it out of a blinding storm. In the writings of Paul in his voyage to Rome, the Dioscori or Gemini was the masthead of the ship that had wintered in Crete. Crete, an island named for the "ruling goddess", was the center of the Cydonian mystery schools where Castor and Pollux had gained their guiding power.[499]

The observatory records the passing of the star Sirius. Flynn continues:

> By dropping a bright orange Sirius ball from the apex of a tower every day at 13:00 hours at the spot on earth designated as the Prime Meridian, the ancient knowledge of time, space and earth's connection to the heavens is esoterically displayed. At the time of this writing, a continual worship of Isis Osiris and

> Horus has been accomplished with the Flamsteed ball through faithful ritual every day for the last three hundred and seventy seven years.[500]

Time is fixed to the earth at the observatory, "regressing" to the west and "increasing" to the east. The observatory was "anchored" beneath the celestial sphere at the constellation of the dog or "wolf," Canis Major, which rests upon Gemini, the twins, corresponding to the area below.

Identifying the brightest star in Canis Major as yet another alchemic symbol for the Nachash reveals that the image of the twins Romulus and Remus with their adopted mother mirrors the Hermathena. The female aspect of the Tritogeneia is there in the form of the she-wolf. Hermes is there as the "eye" of the mother. The twins provide the complete form of the thrice-great one.

Washington, DC, too, provides all the necessary alchemic symbolism to be described as a Hermathena, with its garden ellipses and Palladium-formed National Mall. There is much to be considered when one reflects on the actions of the highest office of the land while it operates out of the "oval office," since it now can be understood that the power behind the government of the United States is *Hermetic*.

The last chapter of Albert Pike's *Morals and Dogma* addresses the philosophy and mysteries of the highest degree that can be earned by Scottish Rite freemasons, "The Sublime Prince of the Royal Secret," or 32nd degree (the 33rd degree can only be given to a member by the Supreme Council, not earned).

Sixth woodcut from the series in the fifteenth-century alchemist Basil Valentine's Azoth (1659). Used at the beginning of the thirty-second chapter of Albert Pike's *Morals and Dogma.*

The top of the first page of the last chapter in *Morals and Dogma* includes an illustration that uniquely depicts many of the Hermetic elements explained previously. The image depicts a *Hebdomand*, meaning, "the seven," and includes the seven world-creating archons who were venerated by the alchemists Venus, Mars, the sun, Mercury, the moon, Jupiter, and Saturn (starting clockwise from the left of the figure). John Dee described his Monad as a figure that contained all the "mystical symbols" and derived its power because of this and the fact that "the all" had become "the one," alluding to the idea that the power behind it would manifest itself on earth in human form.

The two-headed, male-female entity standing on the dragon is Mercury. The symbol in the six-pointed star above the heads clearly identifies him/her (the male and female, sun and moon on one body). The sun and moon are in the typical position that mirrors Attis and Cybele in the Tauroctony. Rather than standing on a symbol of God, Mercury stands on a dragon, which is similar to the idea of Apollo overcoming Python at Delphi (described in chapter 8)—the serpent ascending from his lowly status. The six-pointed stars repeatedly emphasize the Hermathena concept. Importantly, the whole image is contained within an egg.

The Scottish Rite Freemasons who have achieved this level understand that the entity depicted here waits to be born. Even if they could tell the vulgar masses the truth behind their craft, they would never be believed. At this point, however, one reading this book has the same knowledge without having to climb thirty-two degrees!

Today, the alchemists keep their secret knowledge alive in the institution of Freemasonry—but there is another school of Hermetic mystisim alive on earth contained within the religion of Islam. Hermes Trismegistus is known in Islam as a great prophet, or "Idris," who was able to travel between planets. In one such voyage, the Islamic Hermes went to heaven (or Mars) and brought Adam and the black Kaaba stone to earth. He was thought to be the great ancestor of Muhammad.[501] Like the Twelfth Imam, the last successor to the prophet Muhammad, he remains alive but hidden, waiting to reappear at the end of days.[502]

16

THE ISLAMIC CRESCENT MOON

> And they say: "The Most Beneficent (Allah) has begotten a son [as the Jews say, 'Uzair (Ezra) is the son of Allah, and the Christians say that He has begotten a son [Iesa' (Christ)]." Indeed you have brought forth (said) a terrible evil thing. Whereby the heavens are almost torn, and the earth is split asunder, and the mountains fall in ruins, That they ascribe a son to the Most Beneficent (Allah). But it is not suitable for (the Majesty of) the Most Beneficent (Allah) that He should beget a son.
>
> —The Qur'an. Surah Maryam 19:88 92

The star-and-crescent emblem is an example of the phenomenon of mythological symbols morphing over time. Recognized today as the symbol of Islam, during the time of Muhammad, Islamic armies flew simple, solid-colored flags that were generally black or green. Islam did not have any images on its flag until the Ottoman Empire became affiliated with the Muslim world.

When the Turks, under Mehmed II, conquered Constantinople in 1453, they adopted the city's flag of the crescent moon and star. The use of the symbol on Muslim flags was first seen in Europe during the Crusades.

Crescent moon and star[503]

Muhammad was said to have desired to conquer the city and to have written to his generals: "Verily you shall conquer Constantinople. What a wonderful leader will he be, and what a wonderful army will that army be!"[504]

Early Turkish flag from around AD 1320 with "horns" or crescent moon and a "torch"[505]

The flag of Constantinople before 1453 was passed down from the time that the people of Byzantium worshipped Hecate, whose symbol was the crescent moon and the torch (or star).

This symbol became part of Byzantium after the goddess was said to have protected the Byzantines from invasion by the father of Alexander the Great, Philip II of Macedonia, in 340 BC. The Byzantine encyclopedia known as the *Suda* records that Philip led a siege against Byzantium in 340 that failed because the city received divine help from its patron goddess, Hecate.

Historian Dr. Vasiliki Limberis writes:

> She alerted the townspeople with her ever-present torches, and with her pack of dogs, which served as her constant companions. Her mythic qualities thenceforth forever entered the fabric of Byzantine history. A statue known as the "Lampadephoros" was erected on the hill above the Bosphorous to commemorate Hecate's defensive aid.[506]

The Byzantines used Hecate's symbol of the crescent moon and star in her honor on coins minted after the event. The worship of Hecate continued in the Middle East until at least AD 402. St. Porphyry destroyed her last temple in Gaza under the authority of the Byzantine emperor, Flavius Arcadius Augustus (AD 377–408).

> He went himself to Constantinople during the winter of 401–402 and obtained from Arcadius a decree for the destruction of the pagan temples, which Cynegius, a special imperial envoy, executed in May, 402. Eight temples, those of Aphrodite, Hecate, the Sun, Apollo, Core, Fortune, the Heroeion, and even the Marneion, were either pulled down or burnt. Simultaneously soldiers visited every house, seizing and burning the idols and books of magic.[507]

In Anatolia and Egypt, the crescent moon was a representation of the horns of a bull with the Asterion between, similar to the Egyptian symbol for Sirius in the zodiac at the Temple of Dendra, and symbolized the self-generated mother goddess who came from the head of the One Greatest God.

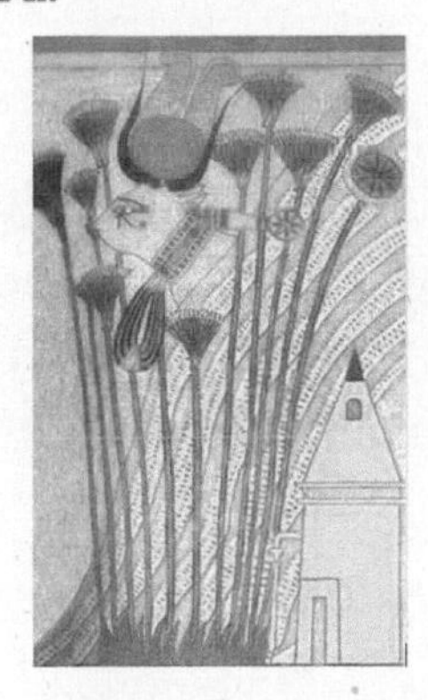

Hathor as a cow with the Eye of Horus[508]

The lotus and papyrus both symbolized the primeval waters of Nun, from which the Egyptians believed life began. The image of the cow form of Hathor in the midst of the papyrus mimics the Job's description of Behemoth resting amongst the *tse'el* (צֶאֱלִים), or "lotus trees":

> He lieth under the shady trees, in the covert of the reed, and fens. (Job 40:21)

Islam venerates the same crescent moon-holy stone-mystery amalgamation as the ancient Egyptians and Anatolians, but does not worship the moon or the Kaaba with a specific understanding of what they represented in antiquity. Mithras, Isis, Hathor, Hecate, and Apollo are different names for the same bloodthirsty deity who wishes to destroy the plan of God as well as the people who follow the truth. It is consistent that these ancient religious systems are so similar to the cult of Islam.

A modern-day legend that involves mourning for Muslims is the time of *Muharram,* which is the first month of the Islamic calendar year and is the most sacred of the four sacred months of the year. Islam uses a lunar calendar, so Muharram is not on a fixed date. It is unlawful to engage in battle during this month. Today's Shia Muslims fast and partake in the "mourning or remembrance of Muharram" on *Ashura* (not to be confused with the name of the goddess Asherah), meaning the "tenth" day. The word "muharram" comes from *haram,* meaning "sinful." Although violence against others is not allowed during this time, violence towards oneself is. Many of the faithful form bloody flagellation processions to commemorate the martyrdom of the Imam Hussein, the grandson of Mohammad, who was killed in the Battle of Karbala in AD 680.

The Ancient Babylonians would have a six-day "funeral" for their god Tammuz, which also included processions in which devotees would abuse themselves. The legend of the death of Osiris by Set, the cult of the Mesopotamia Semiramis-Tammuz, as well as the Anatolian Cybele-Attis, which later became the cult of Adonis, are related.

Lucian of Samosata wrote about the mourning of Adonis at Byblos:

> I saw too at Byblos a large temple, sacred to the Byblian Aphrodite: this is the scene of the secret rites of Adonis: I mastered these. They assert that the legend about Adonis and the wild boar is true, and that the facts occurred in their country, and in memory of this calamity they beat their breasts and wail every year, and perform their secret ritual amid signs of mourning through the whole countryside.... They proceed to shave their heads, too, like the Egyptians on the loss of their Apis.

> Some of the inhabitants of Byblos maintain that the Egyptian Osiris is buried in their town, and that the public mourning and secret rites are performed in memory not of Adonis, but of Osiris. I will tell you why this story seems worthy of credence. A human head comes every year from Egypt to Byblos, floating on its seven days' journey thence: the winds, by some divine instinct, waft it on its way: it never varies from its course but goes straight to Byblos. The whole occurrence is miraculous. It occurs every year, and it came to pass while I was myself in Byblos, and I saw the head in that city.
>
> There is, too, another marvelous portent in the region of the Byblians. A river, flowing from Mount Libanus, discharges itself into the sea: this river bears the name of Adonis. Every year regularly it is tinged with blood, and loses its proper colour before it falls into the sea: it dyes the sea, to a large space, red: and thus announces their time of mourning to the Byblians.[509]

ALLAH

The meaning of the Arabic word for the god of Islam, *Allah,* is related to the Philistine pole- or grove-worshipping Asherah and Dagon cults of the Philistines, and includes a strange reference to the terebinth pillar coffin of the Isis, Osiris mystery.

الله "Allah" is spelled *alif, iam, iam, ha*

Allah is spelled *alif, iam, iam, ha,* which corresponds to the Hebrew letters, *aleph, lamed, lamed, heth.* The words found in the Old Testament (included with *Strong's* numbers below) similar to the Arabic spelling are:

alah (אָלָה) (H421)—"to lament, wail."

alah (אָלָה) (H422)—"to swear, curse, to put under a curse."

alah (אָלָה) (H423)—"curse from God or men."

elah (אֵלָה) (H424)—"valley where David killed Goliath, terebinth tree."

elah (אֵלָה) (H425)—"an oak."

elahh (Aramaic: אֱלָהּ) (H426)—"*god, heathen deity.*"

allah (אַלָּה) (H427)—"oak, terebinth."

The interjection *alĕlay* (אַלְלַי, *Strong's* H480) has the two *lameds* as the Arabic Allah and means "Woe! Alas!" It is a double form of *'alah* (אָלָה) (H421).

17

SAMSON

May you live forever.
—David Flynn (1962–2012)

The essential power of the Deshret crown worn by the Egyptian goddess Neith has been misunderstood and overlooked throughout history by all but the elect of the illuminated mystery schools. The ancient goddesses of the Middle East all held the same power as Neith. The Anatolian goddess Cybele and her lost son Attis, Artimus of Mount Ida, and later the goddesses of the Greeks were all known as *bees.*

The Nachashian reversal of the story in Eden put forth that humanity was enslaved by the Creator and was left in the garden as blind servants. The fruit of the Tree of Knowledge of Good and Evil opened humanity's eyes to the realization that they were in fact slaves and that the command of their Creator was a lie designed to keep them from being like Him, as gods (*elohiym,* אֱלֹהִים; see Genesis 3:5) themselves. God lied when He said that they would "surely die," and the bright angel assured Eve, "Ye shall not surely die." The Hebrew for "surely die" is *muwth muwth* (*muwth,*

מות, "to die"), which literally means, "to die twice" (Genesis 3:4). If it had not been for the incursion of the subtle one, humanity would still be trapped in the enclosed "prison" of Eden.

To the ancients, the bee demonstrated resurrection. The souls of men were born like the bees that left their hives in the morning to be guided by the sun. Like bees, they returned in the evening and waited through night for the sun to rise again.

Men, too, could emerge once more at the new light, resurrected though the worship of the bee goddesses. They looked to Neith, who wore the red Deshret. They looked to Attis, whose artistic representations showed him as bee-like: his mother-father Cybele of Mt. Ida who wore the Phrygian cap, the stylized Deshret crown of Neith. The priestesses of the Delphic Oracle, Mithras, and Athena each offered men the restoration of their souls.

The ox represented the unrighteous God who created men as slaves. The ox had to be killed and buried in the ground up to his horns or brutally beaten to death and entombed in a sealed chamber. After three weeks, cleaving the head between the horns with an axe liberated the entrapped souls; the chamber was opened and the bees flew to freedom, no longer restrained by the jealous God.

The Nachash promised Adam and Eve that they would not die. The religion of the bee priestesses who served their bee goddesses promised the very same thing.

Manoah, whose name means "rest," came from the "place of hornets," the town of Zorah, and married a barren woman. An angel came to his wife one day and told her that she should "drink not wine nor strong drink, and eat not any unclean *thing*" (Judges 13:4) and that she would have a son who should never cut his hair since he was to be a Nazarite (*naziyr*, נָזִיר, "consecrated or devoted one, untrimmed [vine]"). The letters in Hebrew for *naziyr* are *nun* ("snake"), *zayin* ("weapon"), *yod* ("hand") and *rosh* ("head"). The letter meaning from the Phoenician equivalents would be "he who holds the weapon used against the head of the serpent."

The name of Manoah's wife is never mentioned in Judges 13; she is simply referred to as "the woman" or "wife." The angel returned at the request of Manoah so that Manoah and his wife could be instructed on what they needed to do after the child was born:

> And Manoah said unto the angel of the LORD, I pray thee, let us detain thee, until we shall have made ready a kid for thee.
>
> And the angel of the LORD said unto Manoah, Though thou detain me, I will not eat of thy bread: and if thou wilt offer a burnt offering, thou must offer it unto the LORD. For Manoah knew not that he was an angel of the LORD.
>
> And Manoah said unto the angel of the LORD, What is thy name, that when thy sayings come to pass we may do thee honour?
>
> And the angel of the LORD said unto him, Why askest thou thus after my name, seeing it is secret?
>
> So Manoah took a kid with a meat offering, and offered it upon a rock unto the LORD: and the angel did wondrously; and Manoah and his wife looked on.
>
> For it came to pass, when the flame went up toward heaven from off the altar, that the angel of the LORD ascended in the flame of the altar. And Manoah and his wife looked on it, and fell on their faces to the ground.
>
> But the angel of the LORD did no more appear to Manoah and to his wife. Then Manoah knew that he was an angel of the LORD.
>
> And Manoah said unto his wife, We *shall surely die*, because we have seen God. (Judges 13: 15–22, emphasis added)

The words Manoah used for "shall surely die" were the same used by God, Eve, and the serpent in Genesis chapters 2 and 3: *muwth muwth*. Manoah's wife named her son Samson (*Shimshown,* שִׁמְשׁוֹן), which means "like the sun."

As God had instructed, Samson later decided to marry a Philistine. Of course, his parents were dismayed at the prospect of him marrying a woman outside of Israel, one who worshipped foreign gods:

> Then his father and his mother said unto him, Is there never a woman among the daughters of thy brethren, or among all my people, that thou goest to take a wife of the uncircumcised Philistines? And Samson said unto his father, Get her for me; for she pleaseth me well.
>
> But his father and his mother knew not that it was of the LORD, that he sought an occasion against the Philistines: for at that time the Philistines had dominion over Israel. (Judges 14:3–4)

Like Samson's mother, the Philistine woman's name is never mentioned. As Samson went down to the vineyard of Timnath (*Timnah*, תמנה, "a portion," from the root *manah*, מָנָה, "to count, to be numbered") and was attacked by a young lion, which he easily tore to pieces "as he would have rent a kid" with "nothing in his hands." He kept the incident secret, not even telling his parents (Judges 14:5–6).

The word used for "lion" in this passage was not the *shin* letter variety as explained in chapter 7 (שאגה, *shĕagah;* שחל, *shachal;* or שן, *shen*), but *ariy* (אֲרִי), the same word that was given to the tribe of Judah in Genesis 49:9.

While going to claim his Philistine bride, Samson returned to the spot where the dead lion still lay on the ground and noticed that a *beehive* had grown in the carcass. Samson took some honey from the hive and offered it to his parents. The law of God expressly forbids eating anything that has come into contact with a carcass, especially one of a lion.

> And whatsoever goeth upon his paws, among all manner of beasts that go on all four, those are unclean unto you: whoso toucheth their carcase shall be unclean until the even.
>
> And he that beareth the carcase of them shall wash his clothes, and be unclean until the even: they are unclean unto you. (Leviticus 11:27–28)

This would appear to be very "un-Nazarite-like" of Samson, but his story is one brought about by God in the light of the religion of the

Nachash, whose stronghold was based in the area where Samson went to marry the Philistine woman. His story was set in place by God as one formed in the understanding of the religion of the Philistines. Theirs was the realm of the bee-goddesses whose power raised the dead Glaucus who perished in the honey near where the "owl chased the bees." Theirs was the religion of those who hated God, the God-ox they mocked and symbolically killed to release men's souls from His jealous restraint.

Samson is clearly a *type* of Christ. He was the *snake killer* with the same epitaph as Apollo: "like the sun." At meeting the lion, he met not the hated representation of God in the form of an *ox,* but of himself as the *atoning* (*kĕphiyr*, כפיר, "young," from *kaphar,* כָּפַר, "to cover over, atone for sin, make atonement for—cover with pitch"; see Judges 14:5–6) Lion of Judah. He tore the lion "as he would have rent a kid" in the same manner as the meat offering that his father had prepared for the angel of the Lord, the same angel who had visited Jacob, the "strong *man*" (Genesis 32:24; *Strong's* H376, *'iysh,* אִישׁ, "great, strong man"). Simply put, Christ sacrificed Himself as the true light of the world in the center of the religious cult where the Apollo-Nachash took the name for himself. The souls of men (bees) who were liberated though his death and resurrection were truly free and not unclean, but made pure. He gave the *honey* (life, His Word) from this act to his parents (Israel, all mankind) so that they, too, could partake in eternal life.

While Samson was preparing his wedding feast that was to last seven days, he offered a riddle to some of the Philistine men who came to join him:

> And he said unto them, Out of the eater came forth meat, and out of the strong came forth sweetness. And they could not in three days expound the riddle. (Judges 14:14)

If they could solve his riddle he promised to give them "thirty sheets and thirty change of garments:" but if they failed, they owed him the same (Judges 14:12–13).

Angered at the prospect of having to pay Samson, the Philistines went to his wife and threatened to burn her and her father's house. Samson's wife pleaded with her husband to reveal the secret, saying, "Thou dost but hate me, and lovest me not: thou hast put forth a riddle unto the children of my people, and hast not told it me" (Judges 14:16). Samson finally revealed the meaning of his riddle after enduring her "seven days of weeping" in time for the Philistines to answer. On the seventh day before the sun set, the men responded, "What is sweeter than honey? and what is stronger than a lion?" Samson replied by stating, "If ye had not plowed with my heifer, ye had not found out my riddle" (Judges 14:18).

This account in Scripture is one of the most enigmatic in the Bible.

The Greek goddess Demeter (*de,* "earth" and *meter,* "mother")[510] is an extension of the same Cybele-Artemis mother-goddess line that originated in Anatolia. Samson referred to the "heifer" in a direct reference to the ancient Egyptian cults that worshipped the goddess of the heavenly cow as well as the goddesses related to her.

According to Hesiod, Demeter was the daughter of Cronus and Rhea. At the marriage of Cadmus and Harmonia, Demeter and Iasion (Greek: "to heal, to cry aloud, to be of a violet color"),[511] the older brother of the mythical Dardanus, who established his city on top of the Mountain of the Cybele, Mount Ida, copulated in a plowed furrow in Crete. She later gave birth to twin sons: Ploutos, meaning "wealth" in Greek[512] and Philomelus (Greek: *philo,* "lover," and *melus*, "air," "song," "to lay"). Noticing the mud on Demeter's back, Zeus realized what had happened and killed Iasion with a thunderbolt.[513]

The bull as Zeus was the symbolic replacement for the despised God, whose offer of redemption was rejected by the worshippers of the earth mothers, the heavenly cow, the "bee goddesses."

The riddle was a test for the Philistines as well as a demonstration to all of humanity who would follow the Eve-Nachash cults. Samson, as a type of the True Redeemer, took the symbols of false religion of the Philistines and exposed the evil façade. Those who followed their twisted gods should have been able to answer.

Samson's riddle was this: "Who truly grants eternal life?" The Philistines worshipped the idols "which neither can see, nor hear, nor walk" (Revelation 9:20) as a replacement for God and continued to go to the "woman," the source of their false religion, for the answer, instead of going to the true source that he represented. They "plowed" (*charash,* חרש, "plot evil," "to cut in or to be silent or deaf, quiet") with the "heifer," which was Samson's Philistine wife for the moment. Later, she was "given to one of his companions who had attended him at the feast" (Judges 14:20).

The specific god of the Philistines at Ashkelon was Dagon, who had the head and hands of a man and the tail of a fish. The Hebrew for *Dagown* (דָּגוֹן) means "a fish," from *dag* (דָּג), "fish," and ultimately from *dagah* (דָּגָה), "to multiply, increase," which, at its base meaning, referred to the idea of "covering." *Gesenius' Lexicon* says that the word also can mean "to cover" and "great multitude"—hence, "to make dark." Fish are prolific, so from the idea of *dagah* and "many," we get "fish."[514]

The cult of Dagon offered a false atonement or "covering." but an atonement that caused darkness for its many followers and alluded to the *covering cherub* that was its genesis. The Phoenician root meaning of the Hebrew letters for the god are interesting to consider here. Dagon (דָּגוֹן) is composed of the letters *dalet,* "door," *gimmel,* "camel," *vav,* "hook or needle," and *nun,* meaning a "serpent or whale." Perhaps there was much more to the remark that Jesus made when He declared, "It is easier for a camel to go through the eye of a needle, than for a rich man to enter into the kingdom of God" (Mark 10:25), since the religion of Dagon epitomized man's love of the fallen world and the pursuit of pleasure through wealth.

According to the works of legendary Phoenician historian and author Sanchuniathon (around the thirteenth century BC), Dagon was also known as the god who invented "the grain and the plow."[515]

It was because of the Nachash that all of humanity was condemned to toil in order to sustain their lives, returning to the ground that God had cursed.

> And unto Adam he said, Because thou hast hearkened unto the voice of thy wife, and hast eaten of the tree, of which I commanded

> thee, saying, Thou shalt not eat of it: cursed is the ground for thy sake; in sorrow shalt thou eat of it all the days of thy life;
>
> Thorns also and thistles shall it bring forth to thee; and thou shalt eat the herb of the field;
>
> In the sweat of thy face shalt thou eat bread, till thou return unto the ground; for out of it wast thou taken: for dust thou art, and unto dust shalt thou return. (Genesis 3:17–19)

The invention of the god representing the angel who brought this about mocks God; if God would curse men, He would "bless" them.

Dagon was also known as the brother of Atlas, the personification of the pillars separating heaven and earth.[516] The Philistines, by failing to answer the riddle for themselves, rejected the One whom Samson represented, and were ultimately judged.

> And the Spirit of the LORD came upon him, and he went down to Ashkelon, and slew thirty men of them, and took their spoil, and gave change of garments unto them which expounded the riddle. And his anger was kindled, and he went up to his father's house. (Judges 14:19)

The "change of garments" Samson gave them to expound or reveal the *answer* to his riddle did just that. The meaning of the word "change" in Judges 14:12 is *chaliyphah* (חליפה), "a change or replacement—relief (from death)," and the meaning of the word "garments" is *beged* (בֶּגֶד), "treachery or deceit." If the Philistines had been able to see the signs illustrating their false religion and go to him, "the true source," they would have gained relief from deceitful gods and gained life. Who truly grants eternal life? The one represented by the One who would give the "change of garments."

The ancient cult of the woman, the dominion of the Nachash, and his system of enslavement will ultimately fail. Ashkelon was the city of the goddess Derceto and her daughter Semiramis. It was the name of the sword that St. George used to slay the dragon. The meaning behind the name, "the fire of infamy: I shall be weighed," from the root *shaqal*, "to be weighed," is appropriate. Samson, at Ashkelon, revealed the future of the ancient cult just as the prophet Daniel revealed to Babylonian King Belshazzar that his kingdom would come to an end.

> TEKEL; Thou art weighed in the balances, and art found wanting. (Daniel 5:27)

After slaughtering the Philistines at Ashkelon, Samson went down and stayed in a cave in the rock of Etam, and the Philistines went up and camped in Judah, spreading out near Lehi. At their next engagement, Samson killed a thousand men in the manner with which his Nazarite namesake would have dictated, by "striking at the head of the serpent with the weapon in his hand." His weapon happened to be jawbone of an ass (Judges 15:15). The letters of the Hebrew for *lambda*-shaped jawbone, *lehi* (לחי), are *lamed*, "goad, prod, spur or guide"; *het*, "wall"; and *yod*, meaning "hand."

The *lamed* or *lambda* was the symbol of the Egyptian goddess Neith, the shape of the Hyades Cluster aligned to Athena's Parthenon, and the symbol the Spartan warriors who worshipped her as their war goddess used on their shields, as well as the symbol of Horus and Pan. Today, it is the symbol used in the seal of the United States Treasury. It was a fitting implement to dispatch the evil followers of the Dagon god, a penultimate symbol of their cult, the same that condemned them to utter destruction.

Ramathlehi was the full name Samson gave to the place where the slaughter took place. *Ramath*, from *ramah* (רָמָה) means "a height" (as a seat of idolatry) or "high place." The Philistines were destroyed with their symbol at the high seat of idolatry.

Judges 16 can be compared the manifold fractal Sierpinski triangle, so named after the Polish mathematician Wacław Sierpiński (1882–1969), who described it in 1915. Portions can be broken into sets relating multiple allegorical depictions of Christ's First and Second Advents on earth as symbolized by Samson himself.

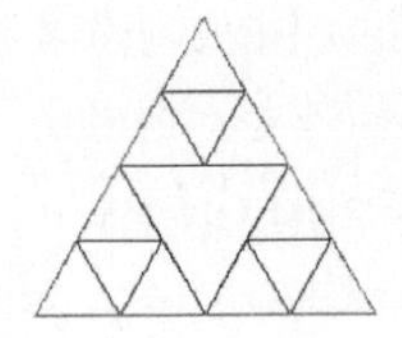
A Sierpinski triangle at the third iteration of subdivision. Each internal triangle can be infinitely divided into smaller units, three at a time.[517]

One *triangle* or sequence of the story starts when Samson fell in love with a woman in the valley of *Sorek* ("choice grapes") named "Delilah," meaning "feeble or lowly." She symbolized both the nation of Israel and humanity—loved and desired by God, but too easily led away from Him. Samson fully understood the secret of his power, but because of his love for Delilah, he *willingly* allowed it to be stripped away.

> That he told her all his heart, and said unto her, There hath not come a razor upon mine head; for I have been a Nazarite unto God from my mother's womb: if I be shaven, then my strength will go from me, and I shall become weak, and be like any other man. (Judges 16:17)

Just as Christ came down to rest with men, Samson rested with Delilah, knowing that he would be betrayed:

> And she made him sleep upon her knees; and she called for a man, and she caused him to shave off the seven locks of his head; and she began to afflict him, and his strength went from him. (Judges 16:19)

Losing his hair (the presence of God) and his sight (the Spirit of God), Samson went down into prison (died) and was bound "with fetters of brass" (judged):

> And she said, The Philistines be upon thee, Samson. And he awoke out of his sleep, and said, I will go out as at other times before, and shake myself. And he wist not that the LORD was departed from him.

> But the Philistines took him, and put out his eyes, and brought him down to Gaza, and bound him with fetters of brass; and he did grind in the prison house. (Judges 16:20–21)

Samson' loss of his hair and sight mirrored Jesus while on the cross:

> And at the ninth hour Jesus cried with a loud voice, saying, Eloi, Eloi, lama sabachthani? which is, being interpreted, My God, my God, why hast thou forsaken me? (Mark 15:34)

Words remaining in their original language point to their profundity in Scripture. Jesus addressed both God the Father ('el, אֵל) and the Spirit ('el, אֵל), which had both left him. *Sabachthani,* from the Aramaic *shĕbaq* (שְׁבַק) means to "to leave" or "to be let alone."

As Samson's hair grew, the presence of God returned to him:

> Howbeit the hair of his head began to grow again after he was shaven. (Judges 16:22)

Samson ascended from his prison (resurrected) and destroyed the temple of Dagon, the impediment between God and men, the established lying religion of the Nachash.

And Samson said, Let me die with the Philistines. And he bowed himself with all his might; and the house fell upon the lords, and upon all the people that were therein. So the dead which he slew at his death were more than they which he slew in his life. (Judges 16:30)

At the death and resurrection of the Son of God-Son of Man, all who had rejected Him or would reject Him had already been condemned. Their physical death was inevitable as well as their chances for resurrection through Him. They are all in essence condemned to die twice, just as God had told the mother and father of all humanity in the garden, and just as the Nachash had lied that they would not die: *muwth* (מוּת).

The forfeiture or gaining of resurrection has been explained eloquently in John 3:18:

> He that believeth on him is not condemned: but he that believeth not is condemned already, because he hath not believed in the name of the only begotten Son of God.

Another embedded *triangle* aspect of the story reveals Christ's resurrection as the *type* that Samson represented in the peculiar sequence that it is told. Samson died at the temple of Dagon, but was taken by his father and brothers and brought up, then buried. Then, in the last sentence of Judges 16, he judged Israel. The meaning could not be clearer.

> Then his brethren and all the house of his father came down, and took him, and brought him up, and buried him between Zorah and Eshtaol in the burying place of Manoah his father. And he judged Israel twenty years. (Judges 16:31)

Still another *triangle* is embedded in the profound mystery hidden in Hebrew root meaning of the sequence of words in Judges 16: 31. These are listed below without the intermediate root link sequences in many of the individual words for clarity:

Then his brethren, אָח, *'ach*
(relative, kinsman, brother)
and all the house, בַּיִת, *bayith*
(rebuilt, established)
of his father, אָב, *'ab*
(God the father)
came down, יָרַד, *yarad*
(descended)
and took, נָשָׂא, *nasa'*
(bearing iniquity)
him, and brought him up, עָלָה, *`alah*
(ascend, taken up, to rise, lifted himself)
and buried, קָבַר, *qabar*
(was buried)

him between Zorah, צָרְעָה, *Tsor`ah*
(as a leper)
and Eshtaol, אֶשְׁתָּאֹל, *'Eshta'ol*
(to ask, inquire, borrow,)
in the burying place, קֶבֶר, *qeber*
(sepulcher, tomb)
of Manoah, מָנוֹחַ, *Manowach*
(give rest to, permit, make quiet)
his father, אָב, *'ab*
(God the father).
And he judged, שָׁפַט, *shaphat*
(to execute judgment, vindicate, plead)
Israel, יִשְׂרָאֵל, *Yisra'el*
(persevere, as God)
twenty עֶשְׂרִים `esriym
(to make rich)
years, שָׁנָה, *shaneh*
(for all time, again, change, alter).[518]

In the last verse of his four-chapter story in the book of Judges, the whole of whom Samson represents is revealed.

The Son of Man, Son of God, descended to bear the iniquity of men in order to ascend, resurrect, and lift himself out of death. Despised as a leper, he was buried in a borrowed tomb to vindicate men and satisfy the judgment of God; as God, He succeeded in once again making the world valuable, rich, to men and God.

The final *triangle* starts in the temple of Dagon and alludes to the future. Atlas was Dagon's brother. The symbols of the pillars separating heaven and earth were a part of the construction of the temple and represented the state of the world as it will be at the time of Christ's return. The worshippers looked though the pillars to the image of their god and waited for his promise to unite heaven and earth in his false version of a new paradise. They brought the man who fought against them inside, believing that their god had granted them victory over the hated God who had cursed them and the serpent. Believing that God had been made weak, they mocked Him in the very center of the power of the Nachash's established realm.

> Then the lords of the Philistines gathered them together for to offer a great sacrifice unto Dagon their god, and to rejoice: for they said, Our god hath delivered Samson our enemy into our hand.
>
> And when the people saw him, they praised their god: for they said, Our god hath delivered into our hands our enemy, and the destroyer of our country, which slew many of us.
>
> And it came to pass, when their hearts were merry, that they said, Call for Samson, that he may make us sport. And they called for Samson out of the prison house; and he made them sport: and they set him between the pillars. (Judges 16:23–25)

The final act of Samson was to bring their temple down—destroying them, their god, and the institution of the Nachash. The allegory of Samson as a type of Christ as the Redeemer of men is depicted in a manifold style in the Judges chapters 13–16. Christ came first to die and be judged in the place of mankind, taking away the first set of pillars that separated God and man. He will come again as a judge to establish paradise, heaven on earth, removing the remaining pillars.

Samson destroys the temple[519]

APPENDIX A

ARROW, DART, AND SPEAR TABLE

Hebrew Word	Search Term "Hits"	Strong's Number	Definition (Italicized items relate to the Nachash)
Ashpah אַשְׁפָּה	arrow	827	The *sense of covering* or a quiver or arrow-case:—quiver, from Ashshaph. From an unused root (probably meaning *to lisp;* i.e., *practice enchantment); a conjurer:—astrologer.*
Ben בֵּן	arrow	1121	A son (as a builder of the family name), *afflicted,* arrow, bullock, calf, *mighty, rebel, robber, spark, stranger, tumultuous one.*
Chets חֵץ	arrow, dart, spear	2671	*A piercer*, i.e., an arrow; by implication, a wound; figuratively (of God), thunder-bolt; the shaft of a spear:—+ archer, arrow, dart, shaft, staff, wound.
Chatsats חָצַץ	arrow	2686	To chop into, pierce or sever; hence, to curtail, to distribute (into ranks), to shoot an arrow:—archer, *cut off in the midst.*
Chatsats חָצָץ	arrow	2687	Something cutting; hence, gravel (as grit); also an arrow:—arrow, gravel (stone).
Da'ah דָאָה	dart	1675	A primitive root; *to dart, i.e. fly rapidly:—fly.*
Lehabah לֶהָבָה	spear	3852	*Flame(-ming)*, head (of a spear).
Macca מַסָּע	arrow, dart, spear	4551	The sense of projecting; a missile (spear or arrow); also a *quarry (whence stones are, as it were, ejected)*:—before it was brought, dart.

Qesheth קֶשֶׁת	arrow	7198	Of bending: a bow, for shooting (hence, figuratively, strength) *or the iris*:—arch(-er), + arrow, bow(-man, -shot).
Qippowz קִפּוֹז	arrow	7091	From an unused root meaning to contract, i.e. *spring forward; an arrow-snake (as darting on its prey):—great owl.*
Resheph רֶשֶׁף	arrow	7565	A live coal; by analogy lightning; figuratively, an arrow, (as flashing through the air); specifically, fever:—arrow, *(burning) coal, burning heat,* + *spark, hot thunderbolt.*
Shebet שֵׁבֶט	dart	7626	From an unused root probably meaning *to branch off;* a scion, i.e. (literally) a stick (for punishing, writing, fighting, ruling, walking, etc.) or (figuratively) a clan:—correction, dart, rod, scepter, staff, tribe.
Shelach שֶׁלַח	dart, spear	7973	A missile of attack, i.e. spear; also (figuratively) a shoot of growth; i.e. branch:—dart, plant, put off, sword, weapon.
Tslatsal צְלָצַל	spear	6767	A clatter, i.e. (abstractly) *whirring (of wings)*; (concretely) a cricket; also a harpoon *(as rattling), a cymbal (as clanging):—cymbal*, locust, *shadowing,* spear.
Taqa תָּקַע	dart	8628	A primitive root; to clatter, i.e. slap (the hands together), clang (an instrument); by analogy, to drive (a nail or tent-pin, a dart, etc.); by implication, to become bondsman by handclasping):—blow (a trumpet), cast, clap, fasten, pitch (tent), *smite, sound, strike*, X suretiship, thrust.

Yadah יָדָה	arrow	3034	A primitive root, literally, to use (i.e., hold out) the hand; physically, to throw (a stone, an arrow) at or away; especially to revere or worship (with extended hands); intensively, to bemoan (by wringing the hands):—*cast (out)*, (make) confess(-ion), praise, shoot, (give) thank(-ful, -s, -sgiving).
Yarah יָרָה	arrow	3384	A primitive root; properly, to flow as water (i.e., to rain); transitively, to lay or throw (especially an arrow, i.e., to shoot); figuratively, to point out (as if by aiming the finger), *to teach:*—(+) archer, cast, direct, inform, instruct, lay, shew, shoot, *teach(-er,-ing),* through.
Zanaq זָנַק	dart	2187	A primitive root; properly, to draw together the feet (as an animal about to dart upon its prey), i.e., *to spring forward:—leap.*
Ziyqoth זִיקוֹת	arrow	2131	*What leaps forth, i.e., flash of fire*, or a burning arrow; also (from the original sense of the root) a bond:—chain, fetter, firebrand, spark.

APPENDIX B

THE GARDEN OF EDEN ACCORDING TO HESIOD

The account below is the mythological equivalent of the garden story in which the fire given to men is the knowledge of good and evil, Prometheus is the Nachash, Zeus is God, and the "shy maiden" is Eve.

Prometheus tricked Zeus into accepting his offering of ox bones in place of the edible portions by making them appear desirable. Hesiod writes in his *Theogony:*

> Prometheus matched himself in wit with the almighty son of Cronos. For when the gods and mortal men had a dispute at Mecone, even then Prometheus was forward to cut up a great ox and set portions before them, trying to befool the mind of Zeus. Before the rest he set flesh and inner parts thick with fat upon the hide, covering them with an ox paunch; but for Zeus he put the white bones dressed up with cunning art and covered with shining fat.... With both hands he took up the white fat and was angry at heart, and wrath came to his spirit when he saw the white ox-bones craftily tricked out.[520]

In anger, Zeus curses men by making the first woman who was, like the trick of Prometheus, beautiful and desirable, but evil on the inside.

This contrasted to God giving Adam his female companion in true perfection and harmony.

> So spake Zeus in anger, whose wisdom is everlasting; and from that time he was always mindful of the trick, and would not give the power of unwearying fire to the Melian race of mortal men who live on the earth. But the noble son of Iapetus outwitted him and stole the far-seen gleam of unwearying fire in a hollow fennel stalk. And Zeus who thunders on high was stung in spirit, and his dear heart was angered when he saw amongst men the far-seen ray of fire. Forthwith he made an evil thing for men as the price of fire; for the very famous Limping God formed of earth the likeness of a shy maiden as the son of Cronos willed. And the goddess bright-eyed Athene girded and clothed her with silvery raiment, and down from her head she spread with her hands a broidered veil, a wonder to see; and she, Pallas Athene, put about her head lovely garlands, flowers of new-grown herbs. Also she put upon her head a crown of gold which the very famous Limping God made himself and worked with his own hands as a favour to Zeus his father. On it was much curious work, wonderful to see; for of the many creatures which the land and sea rear up, he put most upon it, wonderful things, like living beings with voices: and great beauty shone out from it.
>
> But when he had made the beautiful evil to be the price for the blessing, he brought her out, delighting in the finery which the bright-eyed daughter of a mighty father had given her, to the place where the other gods and men were. And wonder took hold of the deathless gods and mortal men when they saw that which was sheer guile, not to be withstood by men."

The "ox begotten" bees, associated with the female soothsaying superimposition of the Eve and the Nachash, "nourish" men who are compared with lazy drones whose nature is to do mischief. Prometheus had only tried to help men but the fickle Zeus curses him for his efforts and men suffer the consequences.

> For from her is the race of women and female kind: of her is the deadly race and tribe of women who live amongst mortal men to their great trouble, no helpmeets in hateful poverty, but only in wealth. And as in thatched hives bees feed the drones whose nature is to do mischief—by day and throughout the day until the sun goes down the bees are busy and lay the white combs, while the drones stay at home in the covered skeps and reap the toil of others into their own bellies—even so Zeus who thunders on high made women to be an evil to mortal men, with a nature to do evil. And he gave them a second evil to be the price for the good they had: whoever avoids marriage and the sorrows that women cause, and will not wed, reaches deadly old age without anyone to tend his years, and though he at least has no lack of livelihood while he lives, yet, when he is dead, his kinsfolk divide his possessions amongst them. And as for the man who chooses the lot of marriage and takes a good wife suited to his mind, evil continually contends with good; for whoever happens to have mischievous children, lives always with unceasing grief in his spirit and heart within him; and this evil cannot be healed.[521]

APPENDIX C

LINKS OF ALL THE GODDESSES AFTER CYBELE

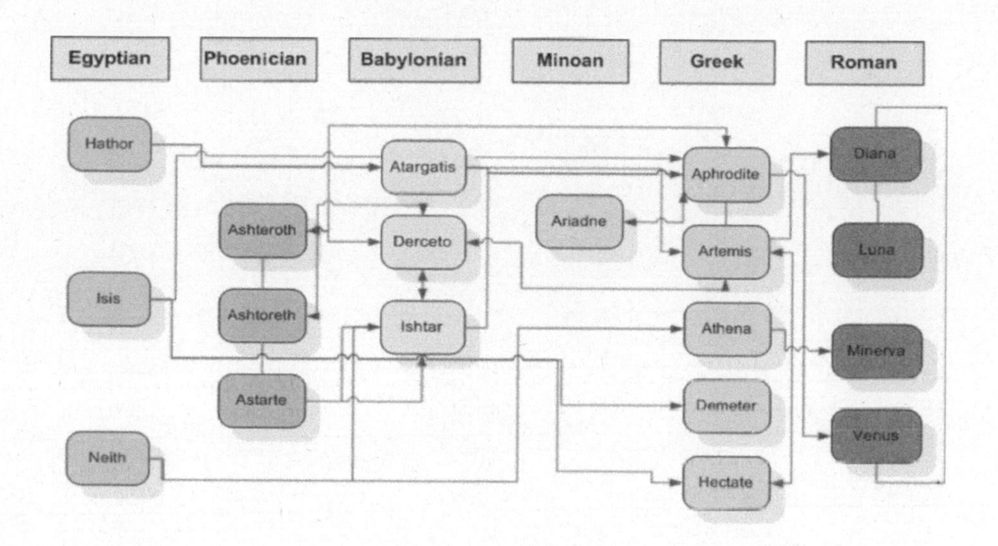

APPENDIX D

PHOENICIAN-HEBREW-GREEK LETTERS

Letter	Name	Meaning	Hebrew	Greek	Latin
𐤀	alf	ox	א	Αα	Aa
𐤁	bet	house	ב	Ββ	Bb
𐤂	gaml	camel	ג	Γγ	Cc, Gg
𐤃	delt	door	ד	Δδ	Dd
𐤄	he	window	ה	Εε	Ee
𐤅	wau	hook	ו	(Ϝϝ), Υυ	Ff, Uu, Vv, Yy, Ww
𐤆	zai	weapon	ז	Ζζ	Zz
𐤇	het	wall	ח	Ηη	Hh
𐤈	tet	wheel	ט	Θθ	—
𐤉	yod	hand	י	Ιι	Ii, Jj
𐤊	kaf	palm (of a hand)	כך	Κκ	Kk
𐤋	lamd	goad	ל	Λλ	Ll
𐤌	mem	water	מם	Μμ	Mm
𐤍	nun	serpent	נן	Νν	Nn
𐤎	semk	fish	ס	Ξξ, poss. Χχ	poss. Xx
𐤏	ain	eye	ע	Οο, Ωω	Oo
𐤐	pe	mouth	פף	Ππ	Pp
𐤑	sade	hunt	צץ	(Ϻϻ)	—
𐤒	qof	needle head	ק	(Ϙϙ), poss. Φϕ, Ψψ	Qq
𐤓	rosh	head	ר	Ρρ	Rr
𐤔	shin	tooth	ש	Σσς	Ss
𐤕	tau	mark	ת	Ττ	Tt

Phoenician-Hebrew-Greek and Latin equivalents[522]

APPENDIX E

TYPES (ORDERS) OF COLUMNS IN ARCHITECTURE

CORINTHIAN

The Corinthian column is the most ornate, characterized by an elegant, slender, fluted column having an ornate capital decorated with two rows of acanthus leaves and four scrolls. The shaft is usually ten diameters high and has twenty-four flutes.

The oldest known building using this order is the Choragic Monument of Lysicrates in Athens, constructed from 335 to 334 BCE.

IONIC

From the Greek *ion* ("going"), ionic columns feature slender, fluted pillars with a large base and two opposed "volutes" or scrolls. The molded top or *echinus* uses an egg-and-dart pattern. The shaft has four more flutes than the Doric. The base or *tori* have two convex moldings separated by scotia (Greek: *skoti,* "a darkness, a sunken molding in the base of a pillar, so called from the dark shadow it casts"). The shaft is usually eight diameters high.

DORIC

The Doric column is the simplest of the orders, with short, heavy columns and unembellished round capitals and no base. The height is four to eight times its diameter; the columns are the most squat of all orders. The shaft has twenty flutes and the base is square.

APPENDIX F

ONLINE SOURCES USED EXTENSIVELY IN THIS BOOK

Perseus Digital Library: http://www.perseus.tufts.edu/hopper/

Online Etymology Dictionary: http://www.etymonline.com/

Indo-European Lexicon: http://www.utexas.edu/cola/centers/lrc/ielex/PokornyMaster-X.html

JewishEncyclopedia.com: http://www.jewishencyclopedia.com/

Catholic Encyclopedia: http://www.newadvent.org/cathen/

Blue Letter Bible: http://www.blueletterbible.org

Word Information—an English dictionary about English vocabulary words and etymologies derived primarily from Latin and Greek word origins: http://wordinfo.info/

Phoenician alphabet—Wikipedia, the free encyclopedia: http://en.wikipedia.org/wiki/Phoenician_alphabet

Hebrew alphabet—Wikipedia, the free encyclopedia: http://en.wikipedia.org/wiki/Hebrew_alphabet

Webster's Revised Unabridged Dictionary (1913)—The ARTFL Project: http://machaut.uchicago.edu/?resource=Webster%27s&word=Thisbe&use1913=on&use1828=on

Strong's Concordance with Hebrew and Greek Lexicon: http://www.eliyah.com/lexicon.html

NOTES

1. *The Meditations of Marcus Aurelius*, trans. George Long (New York: P. F. Collier & Son, 1909).
2. Perseus Digital Library.
3. Encyclopedia Britannica Online.
4. Malcolm C. Duncan, "Obligation of First Degree," *Duncan's Ritual and Monitor of Freemasonry*, (1866) 34–35.
5. Heinrich Schliemann, Ilios: The City and Country of the Trojans: The Results of Researches and Discoveries on the Site of Troy and Through the Troad in the Years 1871–72–73–78–79, Including an Autobiography of the Author (Harper & Brothers, 1881).
6. *Foundations of Gestalt Theory*, Ed. Barry Smith, ed. (Munich and Vienna: Philosophia Verlag, 1988) 82.
7. The information in this book is a continuation of the work done by my twin brother, David Flynn, and would look like this Venn diagram:

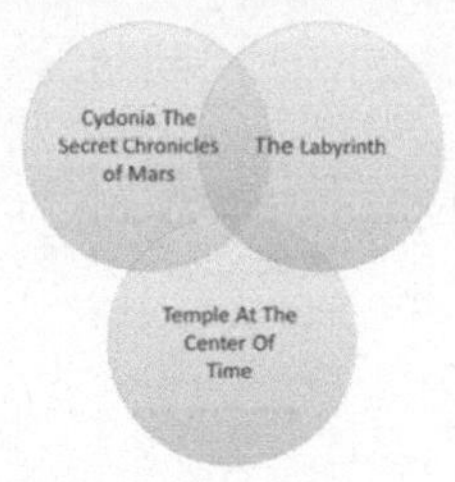

8. *Gesenius' Lexicon*.
9. Isaiah 14:12.
10. *Strong's Concordance*.
11. Ibid.
12. David Flynn, *Cydonia: The Secret Chronicles of Mars* (End-Time Thunder Publishers, 2002) 17–18.
13. Roger D. Woodard "Alphabet," in Nigel Guy Wilson, *Encyclopedia of Ancient Greece* (London: Routldedge, 2006) 38.

14. Ernest David Klein, "Phoenix," *Comprehensive Etymological Dictionary of the English Language* (1971).
15. Image by author.
16. Ovid, *The Metamorphoses,* Book XV, "Pythagoras's Teachings: The Phoenix," trans. A. S. Kline, 391–417.
17. Public domain.
18. Ezekiel 28:12.
19. Aristotle, *Physics I,* 7, 190b, 3–5.
20. Aristotle, *Metaph.A,* 983, b6ff.
21. Public domain.
22. Hesiod, *Theogony*, 207–11.
23. Ibid., 163–11.
24. Ibid., 176–11.
25. Lynn E. Roller, *In Search of God the Mother: The Cult of Anatolian Cybele* (University of California Press, 1999) 171; ISBN 9780520210240.
26. From the fourth edition of *Meyers Konversationslexikon Encyclopedia* (1885–90), Public domain.
27. Public domain.
28. Hesiod, 507–11.
29. Indo-European Lexicon from Julius Pokorny, *Indogermanisches Etymologisches Wörterbuch* (Bern: Francke, 1959, 1989) 1060–1061.
30. *Bibliotheca* (1.80).
31. Plato, *The Republic,* trans. Paul Shorey, Book VII, 522–528.
32. Thomas Smith Webb, *The Freemason's Monitor* (Cincinnati: Applegate & Co., 1863) 73.
33. Plato, *The Republic,* Book VI, 507b–509c.
34. Ibid., Book VI, 508B.
35. Public domain.
36. Plato, Book VI, 516b–c.
37. Ibid., 517a.
38. Plato, *The Republic,* Book VI, trans. Benjamin Jowett, 509d–510a.
39. Image by author.
40. Adam Majewski, Creative Commons Attribution-Share Alike 3.0 Unported license.
41. Image by author.
42. "Palladianism," *A Dictionary of Architecture and Landscape Architecture* (Oxford: Oxford University Press, 2006).
43. Image by author.

44. "Ment," wordinfo.info online.
45. Http://www.masonic-lodge-of-education.com/letter-g.html (retrieved September 9, 2013).
46. John Henry Freese, *St. Photius I, Patriarch of Constantinople*, c. 820–891.
47. Aubrey Diller, "The Text History of the Bibliotheca of Pseudo-Apollodorus," *Transactions and Proceedings of the American Philological Association,* 66 (1935: 296–313) 296, 300.
48. *Webster's Revised Unabridged Dictionary* (1913 + 1828).
49. Perseus Digital Library.
50. Ibid.
51. *Bibliotheca of Pseudo-Apollodorus*. 3.5.7
52. Ibid., 3.5.8.
53. Sir William Smith, "Phoenicium," *Dictionary of Greek and Roman Geography* (Abacaenum-Hytanis, 1854).
54. The Watcher Website. http://www.mt.net/~watcher/newun.html.
55. *Bibliotheca of Pseudo-Apollodorus,* 3.5.9.
56. Sophocles, *Oedipus at Colonus*, trans. Sir Richard C. Jebb (1899).
57. From the *Encyclopaedia or a Systematic Dictionary of the Sciences, Arts and Crafts,* published in France between 1751 and 1772. Extract from the frontispiece of the Encyclopédie (1772). By Charles-Nicolas Cochin. Engraved by Bonaventure-Louis Prévost.
58. Public domain, 1909.
59. Public domain, 1912.
60. Illustration by David Flynn.
61. Hesiod, *The Homeric Hymns, and Homerica,* rev. ed., trans. Hugh G. Evelyn-White, (Loeb Classical Library, 1914).
62. Plato. *Cratylus* (407 BC).
63. Justin, *Apology,* 64.5.
64. Chr Blinkenberg, *The Thunder Weapon in Religion and Folklore: A Study in Comparative Archaeology* (Cambridge University Press, 1911) 19.
65. Henry George Liddell and Robert Scott, *A Greek-English Lexicon* (1940); online version available at the Perseus Project.
66. Henry George Liddell and Robert Scott, *A Greek-English Lexicon,* revised and augmented throughout by Sir Henry Stuart Jones with the assistance of Roderick McKenzie (Oxford: Clarendon Press, 1940).
67. See appendix for definitions of column orders.
68. E. Boutsikas and R. Hannah, *Aitia, Astronomy, and the Timing of the Arrhephoria: The Annual of the British School at Athens* (February 2012) 1–13.

69. From http://wordinfo.info.
70. Public domain; from Lord Leighton's illustration in the July 1860 *Cornhill Magazine*.
71. Flynn, 163.
72. Image by author.
73. Richard Hinckley Allen, *Star Names and Meaning,* 384.
74. Ibid., 136.
75. *Bibliotheca* (i. 6. § 3).
76. *Peake's Commentary on the Bible* (1962) 260, section 221f.
77. Liddell and Scott.
78. Webb, 83; emphasis added.
79. Aristotle, *History of Animals: In Ten Books,* Richard Cresswell and Johann Gottlob Schneider (1878) 26.
80. Philostratus, *Imagines* (ii.2) and the Greek Poet Virgil (70–19 BC) wrote that honey gave the gift of prophecy (Georgics, IV).
81. Christiane Sourvinou-Inwood, *The Myth of the First Temples at Delphi,*.vol. 29, no. 2 (1979) 231–251.
82. British Museum; public domain, via Wikipedia.
83. Image by author.
84. Public domain.
85. *The Idylliums of Theocritus,* trans, Francis Fawkes, MA, 19. (London: Dryden Leach, 1767) 182.
86. Benjamin Franklin to Sarah Bache, January 26, 1784, Library of Congress, Manuscript Division.
87. Karl Nestor "Parthenogenesis in Turkeys," *The Tremendous Turkey* (Ohio State University, 2009).
88. M. S. F. Hood, "Tholos Tombs of the Aegean," *Antiquity* 34 (1960) 166–176.
89. Http://www.theosociety.org/pasadena/sunrise/54-04-5/me-vonk.htm By Coen Vonk.
90. *Sir Alan Gardiner's Sign List,* number R25
91. "Genesis 46:20," Blue Letter Bible.
92. Licensed under the Creative Commons Attribution-Share Alike 3.0 Unported, 2.5 Generic, 2.0 Generic and 1.0 Generic license. Image by Jeff Dahl, 2007.
93. A. Wallis Budge, *The Gods f the Egyptians,* vol. IIE (Open Court Publishing Company, 1904) 220.
94. Raymond O. Faulkner, *A Concise Dictionary of Middle Egyptian,* 252–253.
95. Richard H. Wilkinson, *The Complete Gods and Goddesses of Ancient Egypt* (Thames & Hudson, 2003) 174.

96. Image by author.
97. London: John Murray; Paris: Boyveau Galignani; Malta: Watson Critien; and Alexandria: V. Penasson, *A Handbook for Travellers in Lower and Upper Egypt* (1888) 082a; public domain.
98. "D10" following the system established by Sir Alan Gardiner (1879–1963).
99. Perseus Digital Library.
100. Ibid.
101. Hesiod, *Theogony*, 176.
102. Pseudo-Apollodorus, *Bibliotheca,* 3.8.1.
103. Ibid., 3.12.3.
104. Hesiod, 333.
105. Hyginus, "Preface to Fabulae," *Bibliotheke*, 2.113.
106. Pseudo-Apollodorus, *Bibliotheca*, 2.5.1.
107. Detail from a Roman fresco in the atrium of the Casa del Menandro in Pompeii; public domain.
108. From artwork on a Greek cup by Douris, fifth century BC—Vatican Museum. This work is licensed under the Creative Commons Attribution-ShareAlike 3.0 License. Attribution: Photograph by 83d40m.
109. Plato, *Timaeus,* trans. Benjamin Jowett (360 BC).
110. From the Museum of Fine Arts, Lyon, France. This file is licensed under the Creative Commons Attribution-Share Alike 2.0 France license. Attribution: Photograph by Rama.
111. Hesiod, *The Homeric Hymns,* and Hesiod, *Homerica*, rev. ed., trans. Hugh G. Evelyn-White (Loeb Classical Library, 1914).
112. Çatalhöyük added to UNESCO World Heritage List Global Heritage Fund blog article.
113. Creative Commons Attribution-Share Alike 2.5 Generic license. Image by Roweromaniak.
114. GNU Free Documentation License, image by Stipich Béla.
115. Benjamin W. Fortson, *Indo-European Language and Culture: An Introduction* (John Wiley and Sons, 2009) 383.
116. "Euphrates," Perseus Digital Library.
117. Andrew Curry, "Gobekli Tepe: The World's First Temple?" Smithsonian.com, November 2008.
118. Schmidt (2010) 244, 246.
119. Piotr Taracha, *Religions of Second Millennium Anatolia* (Eisenbrauns, 2009) 12; ISBN 978-3-447-05885-8.
120. Schmidt (2000b), 52–53.

121. Creative Commons Attribution-Share Alike 3.0 Unported license image by Teomancimit.
122. R. Van Dam, *Kingdom of Snow: Roman Rule and Greek Culture in Cappadocia* (Philadelphia: University of Pennsylvania Press, 2002) 13.
123. Hugh Chisholm, *Encyclopaedia Britannica*, vol. 5 (c1910–1922) 286.
124. Flavius Josephus, *Antiquities of the Jews,* I:6.
125. Homer, *The Iliad.*
126. *Histories,* 2.2.
127. Creative Commons Attribution-Share Alike 2.5 Generic license. Image by "China Crisis."
128. Perseus Digital Library.
129. Ovid, *Metamorphoses,* Book I, 313–415.
130. Perseus Digital Library.
131. Lynn Emrich Roller, *In Search of God the Mother: The Cult of Anatolian Cybele* (Berkeley and Los Angeles, CA: University of California Press, 1999) 53.
132. Ibid., 297–299.
133. Online Etymological Dictionary.
134. Roller, 149–151 and footnotes 20–25, citing Homeric Hymn 14, Pindar, Dithyramb II.10 (Snell), Euripides, Helen, 1347; Palamedes (Strabo 10.3.13); Bacchae, 64–169, Strabo 10.3.15–17, et al.
135. Dictionary.com.
136. From an early twentieth-century French postcard; public domain.
137. W. M. Ramsay in *Journal of Hellenic Studies* (1882:64) and Ramsay, "A Study of Phrygian Art," *The Journal of Hellenic Studies,* 9 (1888) 350–382.
138. Pseudo-Apollodorus, *Bibliotheca,* 3.5.6.
139. Fourth century BC, Ancient Agora Museum, Athens. Permission is granted to copy, distribute and/or modify this document under the terms of the GNU Free Documentation License.
140. From a second century BC Afghanistan plaque. The copyright holder of this work released this work into the public domain. This applies worldwide.
141. Strabo, 12.5.3.
142. Summers, in Lane (1996) 364.
143. Titus Livius Patavinus (Livy), *History of Rome,* 10.4–11.18.
144. *Koloss* in German means "colossus."
145. Stardate: 5630.7, original airdate October 18, 1968. The Medusian Kollos acting in Spock's body; from the *Star Trek* episode: "Is There in Truth No Beauty?"

146. Pausanias, *Description of Greece*, trans. W. H. S Jones (London: Willam Heinemann New York, 1918) 7, 19.
147. Sir James George Frazer (1854–1941), *The Golden Bough* (1922).
148. "Tiara," Encyclopedia Britannica Online (retrieved October 2013).
149. Frazer.
150. Frazer, chapter 34.
151. Perseus Digital Library.
152. Maarten J. Vermaseren, *Cybele and Attis: The Myth and the Cult*, trans. A. M. H. Lemmers (London: Thames and Hudson, 1977) 97.
153. Frazer, chapter 34.
154. A Julian year (365.25 days) is slightly longer than an actual year. The calendar has drifted with respect to the equinox.
155. Herodian, *History of the Roman Empire since the Death of Marcus Aurelius*, 1.10: "Insurrection of Maternus," trans. Edward C. Echols (Berkeley and Los Angeles, 1961).
156. Encyclopedia Britannica.
157. "Rare Ancient Wooden Throne Found in Herculaneum," Reuters online (December 4, 2007) http://www.reuters.com/article/2007/12/04/us-italy-throne-idUSL0413888820071204.
158. Arthur Golding, *Ov. Met.* 10.103 (London: W. Seres, 1567).
159. Creative Commons Attribution-Share Alike 2.0 Generic license. Image by archer10–Dennis.
160. Http://www.ancient-greece.org/resources/timeline.html (retrieved September 16, 2013).
161. "Atthis," Perseus Digital Library.
162. H. Beckby, *Anthologia Graeca* 4, 171 (Munich, 1957).
163. From *Travel to the Seven Wonders of the World* (1880, Trough de Lassus); public domain.
164. Homer, *The Iliad*, ed. Samuel Butler, 20, 215–234.
165. Genesis 1:6.
166. Homer, xxi, 470ff.
167. Ephesus Archaeological Museum; Creative Commons Attribution-Share Alike 2.5 Generic license. Image by David Bjorgen.
168. Image modified by author from the GNU Free Documentation License Image by Yair Haklai.
169. "Fountain," *Strong's Hebrew Lexicon*.
170. "Shamayim," *Gesenius' Lexicon*.
171. "Biblioteche ed i Centri specializzati," City of Rome (retrieved on September 8, 2012).

172. GNU Free Documentation License, picture by Wknight94.
173. GNU Free Documentation License, Version 1.2. Image byJebulon.
174. Egyptian Museum, Turin, Italy, 1224 BC.
175. Pliny the Elder, *Naturalis Historia,* Book 8, chapter 184, pp. 46, 71.
176. *The Miracole de Rome* ("Rome's Wonders"), ed. E. Monks, "Archives of the Roman Soc Country's History," 38 (1915) 562–587.
177. Public domain.
178. From Cambodia; public domain.
179. Francois Lenormant (1881), "Sol Elagabalus," *Revue de l'Histoire des Religions,* 3:310.
180. Herodian, *Roman History* V.3.
181. Historia Augusta, *Life of Elagabalus,* part 3 (Loeb Classical Library, 1924) 113.
182. Herodian, VI.6.
183. Creative Commons Attribution-Share Alike 3.0 Unported license. From the Classical Numismatic Group, Inc.
184. Thomas Cook, *Cook's Handbook for Palestine and Syria* (Thos. Cook & Son, 1907) 362.
185. Flynn, 146.
186. Ibid.
187. Ali ibn Abd-al-Malik al-Hindi (1998), Kanz al-Ummal, Lebanon.
188. Creative Commons Attribution-Share Alike 3.0 Unported license. From the Classical Numismatic Group, Inc.
189. *Gesenius' Lexicon.*
190. George A. Barton, *Archæology and the Bible,* Figure 80 (Philidalphia American Sunday School Union, 1816 Chestnut Street, 1916).
191. David Flynn, *Temple at the Center of Time*, 6–7.
192. *Pseudepigraphia*, vol. 2, ed., ed. James H. Charlesworth (New York: Doubleday, 1985) 43, 122, 124.
193. Image by author.
194. Public domain.
195. Alfred Edersheim, *The Temple* (Kregel Publications, 1997) 115.
196. Plato, *Timaeus*, trans. Benjamin Jowett, http://classics.mit.edu/Plato/timaeus.html 2013.
197. R. A. McGough, http://www.biblewheel.com.
198. Ibid., Spoke 1.
199. Ibid., Spoke 22–Tav R.
200. "A Critique of the Bible Wheel Book," http://www.biblewheel.com/blog/

index.php/2011/08/13/a-critique-of-the-bible-wheel-book-by-the-author-part-1/ A Critique of the Bible Wheel Book—by the author!

201. *Geoponica,* 15 (c. 900) 2.21; through Aldrovandi, p. 58.
202. James A. Arieti, *Philosophy in the Ancient World: An Introduction* (Rowman & Littlefield) 336.
203. Ovid (8), *Metamorphoses* 15, p. 364.
204. *Geoponica,* 15.
205. "On the Cave of the Nymphs in the Thirteenth Book of the Odyssey," From the *Greek of Porphyry,* trans. Thomas Taylor (1917).
206. Ibid.
207. Ovid, *Metamorphoses* Book 4, trans. Sir Samuel Garth, John Dryden, et. al.
208. *Strong's Hebrew Lexicon.*
209. Public domain.
210. Public domain.
211. A. S. Geden (October 15, 2004), *Select Passages Illustrating Mithraism* (Kessinger Publishing, 1925) 51–; ISBN 978-1-4179-8229-5.
212. Calvert Watkins, *Dictionary of Indo-European Roots* (2000).
213. "Mitre," Online Etymology Dictionary.
214. M. Clauss, *The Roman Cult of Mithras,* 42.
215. Lewis M. Hopfe, "Archaeological Indications on the Origins of Roman Mithraism," in Lewis M. Hopfe, ed., *Uncovering Ancient Stones: Essays in Memory of H. Neil Richardson* (Eisenbrauns, 1994) 147–158; 156.
216. Public domain; released by Michelle Touton, 2004.
217. Google Earth.
218. Image courtesy of Daniel Noyes.
219. Manly P. Hall. *The Secret Teachings of All Ages: An Encyclopedic Outline of Masonic, Hermetic, Cabbalistic and Rosiorucian Symbolical Philosophy,* 21.
220. From a photograph taken sometime in the early twentieth century; public domain.
221. From the Louvre; public domain.
222. Public domain.
223. Webb, 68.
224. Image by author.
225. *Gilgamesh,* 86.
226. Ibid., 87.
227. Theodore Ziolkowski (2011), *Gilgamesh among Us: Modern Encounters with the Ancient Epic* (Cornell University Press) 51. ISBN 978-0801450358.
228. Frazer, chapter 34.

229. 2 Maccabees 6:1–11.
230. Joseph Fontenrose, *Delphic Oracle: Its Responses and Operations.*(University of California Press, 1981) 349. ISBN-10: 0520043596. Emperor Augustus had asked: "Why are you silent?"
231. I. the navel (pure Lat. *umbilicus*); transf. for the centre (in post-class. poetry), Aus. Idyll. 11, 60. Perseus Digital Library.
232. Creative Commons Attribution-Share Alike 3.0 Unported by Юкатан .
233. Perseus Digital Library.
234. *Webster's 1842 Dictionary.*
235. *Bibliotheca* 1.6.3.
236. A 1581 engraving by Virgil Solis for Ovid's *Metamorphoses,* Book I; public domain.
237. "Silene," http://www.etymonline.com.
238. "Sadra," Online Etymology Dictionary.
239. Perseus Digital Library.
240. Golden Legend 1 of Jacobus, de Voragine (ca. 1229–1298).
241. Richard Johnson, *The Most Famous History of the Seauen Champions of Christendome* (1596).
242. Thomas Horn exposes the Masonic belief in a coming Apollyon in his book, *Apollyon Rising 2012* (Crane, MO: Defender Publishing, 2009).
243. GNU Free Documentation License, Source : selbst. Author: Michael Jaletzke.
244. Image by Daniel Noyes, 2013.
245. This file is licensed under the Creative Commons Attribution-Share Alike 3.0 Unported license. From http://www.cgb.fr.
246. Brunilde S. Ridgway, "The Plataian Tripod and the Serpentine Column," *American Journal of Archaeology* (1977) 81:374–379.
247. Herodotus, Book 9.81.
248. Thucydides, *The History of the Peloponnesian War,* trans. Richard Crawley (Courier Dover Publications, March 6, 2012) 57.
249. Public domain; released by Gryffindor 2007 (retrieved online in 2013).
250. Perseus Digital Library.
251. Robert Graves, *The Greek Myths 1955 in Two Volumes* (80 Strand, London, England: Pelican Books) 168.
252. Fabulae Hyginus, "King Midas, a Phrygian, Son of Cybele," CXCI, trans. and ed. Mary Grant (1960) 191; http://www.theoi.com/Text/HyginusFabulae1.html.
253. Minor M. Markle III, "The Macedonian Sarrissa, Spear and Related

Armor," *American Journal of Archaeology* 81 (3): 323–339 324 (Summer 1977) doi:10.2307/503007. JSTOR 503007.

254. Ibid.
255. Plutarch, *The Parallel Lives, Vol. VII; The Life of Alexander* (Loeb Classical Library, 1919) 259.
256. Strabo, *Geography,* Vol VIII, Book XVII (Loeb Classical Library, 1932) 113; public domain.
257. Diogenes Laertius, *Lives of Eminent Philosophers, Book VI: The Cynics,* R. D. Hicks (Cambridge: Harvard University Press, 1972; first published 1925).
258. "Lives of Eminent Philosophers," Perseus Digital Library.
259. Will H. Low, "Diogenes Looking for an Honest Man," from a panel at the Essex County Court House, Newark, New Jersey. Printed sometime before 1911.
260. "Dodge," Webster's Revised Unabridged Dictionary (1913 + 1828), online edition.
261. Plutarch, *The Parallel Lives, Vol. VII, The Life of Alexander* (Loeb Classical Library, 1919) 265.
262. Plato, *Euthydemus,* trans. Benjamin Jowett (380 BC).
263. Lucian, *The Syrian Goddess,* trans. Herbert A. Strong and John Garstang (1913) 43–44.
264. Henry Welsford, *On the Origin and Ramifications of the English Language: Preceded by an Inquiry into the Primitive Seats, Early Migrations, and Final Settlements of the Principal European Nations* (1845) 11–12.
265. Plutarch, *Greek Questions,* 45 2.302a.
266. "Androgeus," The Myth Index, 2007, www.mythindex.com (retrieved 2013).
267. Perseus Digital Library.
268. Plato, *Phaedo,* trans. Benjamin Jowett (260 BC).
269. Webb, 28.
270. Plutarch, *Theseus.* trans. John Dryden (AD 75; emphasis added).
271. Image by author.
272. "Left," Online Etymological Dictionary.
273. Plutarch.
274. Carl Brockelmann, Moshe Perlmann, and Joel Carmichael, *History of the Islamic Peoples: With a Review of Events* (G. P. Putnam's Sons, 1947).
275. Humbach, Helmut, and Djelani Davari, *Nāmé Xorāsān*, (Johannes Gutenberg-Universität Mainz); Persian translation by Djelani Davari, published in Iranian Languages Studies website.

276. Image by author.
277. Plutarch.
278. Image by author.
279. *Apollodorus,* Book 3, Chapter 3, trans. Sir James George Fraser (London, New York: G. P. Putnam's Sons, 1921).
280. Hyginus, *Fabulae*, trans. Mary Grant (University of Kansas Publications, 1960) 136.
281. Apollodorus.
282. Politics Book 1:9.
283. Flynn, 5, 6.
284. Webster's Revised Unabridged Dictionary (1913).
285. Ibid., 1178.
286. Ibid., (1913 + 1828) 276.
287. Pierre Marteau de Lorris and J. de Meung, *Le Roman de la Rose* (Paris, 1878) 90.
288. *The Romaunt of the Rose from the Unique Glasgow Ms: Parallel with Its Original, Le Roman de la Rose,* trans. Geoffrey Chaucer (Chaucer Society, 1891) 81.
289. William Berg, "Hecate: Greek or 'Anatolian'?", Numen 21.2 (1974) 129.
290. "ἕκατος," Perseus Digital Library.
291. "Coeus," Perseus Digital Library.
292. Hesiod, *Theogony*, Book II, 404–452.
293. Walter Burkert (1987), *Greek Religion: Archaic and Classical* (Oxford, Blackwell) 171; ISBN 0-631-15624-0.
294. Vatican Museum; public domain.
295. Herodotus, *Histories,* I, 94.
296. Ibid.
297. P. J. Rhodes, *A History of the Classical Greek World 478–323 BC,* 2nd ed. (Chichester: Wiley-Blackwell, 2010) 6.
298. *Iliad* ii. 865; v. 43, xi. 431.
299. Augustin Calmet (1832), *Dictionary of the Holy Bible* (Crocker and Brewster) 648.
300. Jeremiah 46:9.
301. Plutarch, *Greek Questions*, 45 2.302a.
302. Liddell and Scott, 180.
303. "EURO'PA," *New International Encyclopædia* (1905).
304. Perseus Digital Library.
305. Creative Commons Attribution-Share Alike 3.0 Unported license. From the Classical Numismatic Group.

306. Thomas Jefferson, *National Bank Opinion*, 1791.
307. Facsimile of the Coinage Act of 1792, Library of Congress, emphasis added.
308. Migene Gonzalez-Wippler (2001), *Complete Book of Amulets & Talismans* (Lewellyn Publications) 1; ISBN 0-87542-287-X.
309. Manly P. Hall, *The Secret Teachings of All Ages*, pp. XC and XCI; emphasis in original.
310. Lyndon B. Johnson, "Remarks at the Signing of the Coinage Act" (July 23, 1965). Posted online by Gerhard Peters and John T. Woolley, The American Presidency Project, http://www.presidency.ucsb.edu/ws/?pid=27108.
311. Charles Moore Watson (1910), *British Weights and Measures as Described in the Laws of England from Anglo-Saxon Times* (London: John Murray) 54; OCLC 4566577.
312. Joseph Wright, *English Dialect Dictionary*, vol. 6 (1905) 54.
313. Philip Schaff, *The New Schaff-Herzog Encyclopedia of Religious Knowledge* (1912) 290.
314. Image by author.
315. Image by author.
316. "The Order of Saint Joachim," http://www.stjoachimorder.org.
317. Levett Hanson (1802), *An Accurate Historical Account of All the Orders of Knighthood at Present Existing in Europe*, vol. 1, J. White (reprinted, Kessinger Publishing) 33; ISBN 0-7661-5415-7.
318. Public domain.
319. Shmuel Himelstein, *The Jewish Primer* (New York: Facts On File, 1990).
320. *Strong's* H6593.
321. *American Heritage Dictionary*, Fourth Ed.
322. *Strong's* H831.
323. *Gesenius' Lexicon*.
324. Michael S. Rozeff, *The U.S. Constitution and Money Corruption and Decline* (2010) 31.
325. Hercules Furens Seneca, 235ff.; Seneca, Hercules Oetaeus 1240; Pliny, Nat. Hist. iii.4.
326. Public domain.
327. A Syriac Fragment from *The Cause of All Causes on the Pillars of Hercules*, Adam C. McCollum, 5.
328. *Mastery of Life: The Rosicrucian Order. Purpose and Work of the Order* (2005) 31.
329. Public domain.
330. As a work of the U.S. federal government, this image is in the public domain.

331. As a work of the U.S. federal government, this image is in the public domain.
332. Greider, *Secrets of the Temple* (1987) 53.
333. Manly P. Hall, *The Secret Destiny of America* (1944) 173.
334. From "Treasury Order 100-01: The Department of the Treasury Seal," Department of the Treasury website; public domain.
335. Http://www.pagrandlodge.org/mlam/presidents/froosevelt.html.
336. Blavatsky, vol. I, "Introduction" (1888) xli.
337. "The Key to Theosophy," Theosociety.org (retrieved January 31, 2013).
338. Marcy Marzuni, *Decoding the Past: The Templar Code,* The History Channel (November 7, 2005).
339. Dominic Selwood, (Woodbridge: The Boydell Press, 2002) ISBN 0851158285.
340. Sean Martin (2005), *The Knights Templar: The History & Myths of the Legendary Military Order* (New York: Thunder's Mouth Press) ISBN 1-56025-645-1.
341. Http://www.demolay.org/aboutdemolay/firstdemolay.php (accessed March 26, 2013).
342. "The Order of DeMolay: DeMolay Degree," (a publication of a DeMolay secret ritual ceremony on the web), Phoenix Masonry Masonic Museum and Library (retrieved March 9, 2013).
343. Creative Commons Attribution-Share Alike 3.0 Unported license. Image by Philly boy92.
344. GNU Free Documentation License. From the Classical Numismatic Group.
345. Tacitus, *Annals*.
346. Creative Commons Attribution-Share Alike 3.0 Unported license. Image by Mufunyo.
347. Fred Gettings, *Dictionary of the Occult, Hermetic and Alchemical Sigils* (981) 266.
348. Image by author.
349. Public domain.
350. David Flynn, *Temple at the Center of Time* (2008) 195–197.
351. Isaiah 27:1.
352. Flynn, *Cydonia,* 9–23.
353. Public domain.
354. *Flynn,* 17, 18.
355. Image by author.
356. Manly P. Hall, "Flowers, Plants, Fruits, and Trees," *The Secret Teachings of All Ages*. (Philosophical Research Society, 1928) 93.

357. Ovid, *Metamorphoses*, X. 708–739.
358. Michael Baigent, Richard Leigh, and Lincoln P. Henry, *Holy Blood, Holy Grail* (1982) 72.
359. Runciman, *History of the Crusades III,* 334.
360. William W. Harris, "The Levant: A Fractured Mosaic," The Catholic Encyclopedia (2005).
361. E. T. Carson, *Monitor of the Ancient and Accepted Rite* (Cincinnati Applegate & Company, 1863) 85.
362. "Anemone," Online Etymology Dictionary.
363. Image by author.
364. William Morgan, *Illustrations of Masonry* (1827) 76.
365. *Book of Enoch*, VI.
366. Ibid., VII.
367. Ibid., VIII.
368. "צוד," *Gesenius' Lexicon.*
369. Flavius Josephus (AD 93 o4 94) *Antiquites of the Jews*, vol. 1, trans. William Whiston (1737) 19–20.
370. Alexander Hislop, *The Two Babylons,*2nd ed. (Loizeaux Brothers, 1959) 27.
371. From the Watson MS series 1535 translation of the James Dowland Manuscript printed in *Gentleman's Magazine* (1815). The original was from sometime in 1500.
372. From "Creation Myths in the Ancient Near East," darkwing.uoregon.edu.
373. Permission is granted to copy, distribute and/or modify this document under the terms of the GNU Free Documentation License, Version 1.2 or any later version published by the Free Software Foundation.
374. "Nineveh," Jewish Encyclopedia online.
375. Hislop, 26.
376. *Diodorus Siculus Library of History,* Book II, vol., 349.
377. Strabo 16.785; Pliny, *Natural History* 5.81.
378. M. Rostovtseff, "Hadad and Atargatis at Palmyra," *American Journal of Archeology* 37 (January 1933), 58–63, examining Palmyrene stamped tesserae.
379. Walter Wybergh How and Joseph Wells, *A Commentary on Herodotus* (Oxford: Clarendon Press, 1912) 107.
380. New Living Translation.
381. Rerum Gestarum Libri, Book XIV.
382. Lucian of Samosata (AD 125–180), *De dea Syria*, 33, 39.
383. *Webster's Revised Unabridged Dictionary* (1913).

384. Sir George Francis Hill, “Temple of the Paphian Aphrodite,” *Illustrations of School Classics. 1867–1948;* from the British Museum.
385. Ibid.
386. Hislop.
387. “Tammuz,” Encyclopedia Britannica.
388. “Book of Jonah,” *Mercer Bible Dictionary.*
389. Public domain.
390. *Strong’s.*
391. Nahum 3:1.
392. Kent H. Richards, “Nahum Introduction,” *Harper Collins Study Bible* (New York: Harper Collins, 2006) 1250.
393. Blue Letter Bible Lexicon.
394. Ibid.
395. Ibid.
396. Charles William Heckethorn, *The Secret Societies of all Ages and Countries,* vol. II (London, 1897) 3–7.
397. *William Morgan,* Illustrations of Masonry, (1827) 76.
398. Plutarch, *Moralia*, “On Isis and Osiris,” chapter 12.
399. *1906 Jewish Encyclopedia.*
400. Licensed under the Creative Commons Attribution-Share Alike 3.0 Unported author Jpb1301.
401. Image by author.
402. Pausanias, 232.
403. Ibid., 269.
404. Ibid., 7.4.6.
405. Ovid, *Metamorphoses*, VIII; emphasis added.
406. Ibid., 183–235.
407. Ibid., 152–182.
408. Pausanias, 91.
409. James P. Cramer, *Almanac of Architecture and Design* (Atlanta, GA: Greenway Communications, 2005) 348; ISBN 0-9675477-9-2.
410. From the German documentary, *Koenigs Kugel—Der deutsche Bildhauer Fritz Koenig im Trümmerfeld von Ground Zero* (2001).
411. Percy Adlon (2001), “Koenig’s Sphere,” Leora Films, Inc. (retrieved March 24, 2010).
412. Ibid.
413. Ibid.
414. From the Archaeological Museum in Naples; public domain.

415. *Oxford Guide to Egyptian Mythology*, ed. Donald B. Redford (Berkley Reference, 2003) 157–161; ISBN 0-425-19096-X.
416. *Gesenius' Lexicon.*
417. GNU Free Documentation License, Version 1.2. Image by Jeff Dahl.
418. Creative Commons Attribution-Share Alike 3.0 Unported. by Alex Lbh in April 2005.
419. Kelly Simpson, *The Book of the Heavenly Cow* (The Literature of Ancient Egypt, 2003) 292.
420. Herodotus, *Thaleia,* Book 3, 28.
421. Manly P. Hall, *Secret Teachings,* 301.
422. George A. Barton, *Archæology and the Bible* (Philidalphia: American Sunday School Union, 1816 Chestnut Street, 1916) Figure 247.
423. *Strong's* and *Gesenius Lexicon* were used in combination for all etymology.
424. Perseus Digital Library
425. Robert Graves, *The Greek Myths,* 358; ISBN 0-14-017199-1.
426. Dionysius of Halicarnassus (1.61–62).
427. Perseus Digital Library.
428. Homer, *The Iliad,* ed. Samuel Butler, 20.215–234.
429. *Bibliotheca* 3. 12. 2.
430. Homer, 20. 230.
431. Britannica, 15th ed. 22:593.
432. Joseph Wright, *English Dialect Dictionary*, Vol. 6 (1905) 54.
433. Strabo, *The Geography of Strabo.* Literally translated, with notes, in three volumes. Book X. Chapter III. H. C. Hamilton, Esq., W. Falconer, M. A., Ed. (London: George Bell & Sons, 1903).
434. Apollodorus, *Library* 3.12.5, trans. by J. G. Fraser.
435. Apollodorus, *Epitome* 3.2–3.
436. Euripides, *The Trojan Women* (415 BC).
437. *Iliad,* 23.665, 838, *Odyssey*, 11.523.
438. Apollodorus, *Epitome*.5.15.
439. Homer, *The Odyssey,* Book XIII, trans. Robert Fagles (Penguin Classics, 2006) 442–447.
440. Homer, *The Iliad,* trans. A. T. Murray, PhD, in two volumes. (Cambridge, MA: Harvard University Press; London: William Heinemann, Ltd., 1924) Vol II, 6.5.
441. "Letter of Aristeas," *Jewish Encylopedia* (1906), http://www.jewishencyclopedia.com/articles/1765-aristeas-letter-of (retrieved 2013).
442. "Gigantes," Perseus Digital Library.

443. Pausanias, 189, 191.
444. Pliny the Elder, *The Natural History,* John Bostock, MD, F. R. S., H. T. Riley, Esq., B. A., ed., Book VII, chapter 45.
445. Historia Augusta, *Life of Elagabalus,* Part 3 (Loab Classical Library, 1924) 113.
446. Averil Cameron, *The Later Roman Empire* (Harvard University Press, 1993) 170.
447. By Cornelius Gustav Gurlitt 1912; public domain.
448. "Vaticanus," Perseus Digital Library.
449. Herodotus, *Histories,* Book 7 (Polyhmnia), trans. George Rawlinson (1910).
450. Hall, *Secret Teachings*, XC and XCI; emphasis in original.
451. Richard G. Carrot, *The Egyptian Revival* (University of California Press, 1978) plate 33.
452. Arthur Edward Waite, *Devil-Worship in France or the Question of Lucifer* (London: George Redway,1896) 31.
453. Rosemary Guiley (2008), "Baphomet," *The Encyclopedia of Witches, Witchcraft and Wicca* (Infobase). 17–18; ISBN 9781438126845.
454. M. Michelet, *History of France*, Vol. I, trans. G. H. Smith (New York: D. Appleton and Company, 1860) 375.
455. Public domain.
456. Waite.
457. Edith Starr Miller, *Occult Theocracy*: Vol. I (CreateSpace Independent Publishing Platform, May 13, 2009) 208–209.
458. Manly Palmer Hall, "Masonry's Greatest Philosopher" according to the *Scottish Rite Journal,* in *Lectures on Ancient Philosophy*, 433.
459. "2009 Ancient and Primitive Rite of Memphis Misraim," Sovereign Sanctuary for Bulgaria, https://sites.google.com/site/memphismizraimbg/palladism (retrieved September 28, 2013).
460 "The McMillan Plan of 1901," National Capital Planning Commission, Washington, DC; public domain.
461. Google Earth.
462. Persius Digital Library.
463. Carl G. Liungman, *Dictionary of Symbols* (W. W. Norton, 1991) 287; ISBN 0-393-31236-4.
464. "Washington Monument," nps.gov/nr/travel/presidents/washington_monument.html (retrieved November 22, 2013).
465. Brian McKenna, "President's Park, White Lot, The Ellipse," (February 1, 2011) http://baseballhistoryblog.com. February 1st, 2011 (retrieved November 22, 2013).

466. Marble bas relief, Roman copy of the late first century AD, after a neo-Attic original of the Hellenistic era. I, the copyright holder of this work, release this work into the public domain. This applies worldwide; Wikipedia.
467. Robert A. Kaster, *Macrobius: Saturnalia,* Books 1–2, bilingual ed.(Loeb Classical Library, Harvard University Press, February 4, 2011) 16, note.
468. Ludwig von Jan, *Macrobius, The Saturnalia,* Book I (Gottfried Bass, Quedlinburg and Leipzig, 1852).
469. NOAA Solar Position Calculator online, http://www.esrl.noaa.gov/gmd/grad/solcalc/azel.html.
470. Terrain elevations obtained from United States Department of the Interior National Atlas using the 1965 photo revised edition map of Washington, DC, http://nationalatlas.gov/100topos/Washington_West.html (retrieved November 22, 2013).
471. Tangent(θ) = Opposite / Adjacent.
472. Distance found using Google Earth.
473. Alan Butler, washingtondcschamberofsecrets.com/what-lies-below-the-ellipse.html (retrieved November 22, 2013).
474. U.S. Geological Survey.
475. Astrid Riecken, Washington Post online, July 8, 2013 (retrieved October 6, 2013).
476. Donald Greer, *The Incidence of the Terror during the French Revolution: A Statistical Interpretation* (Harvard University Press, 1935) 84.
477. Image courtesy of Daniel Noyes, 2013.
478. From US government website http://www.aoc.gov/capitol-hill/other-statues/statue-freedom; public domain.
479. Http://www.aoc.gov/facts/capitol-hill (retrieved September 28, 2013).
480. Proclus, *The Commentaries of Proclus on the Timaeus of Plato, in Five Books,* trans. Thomas Taylor and A. J. Valpy (London: Walford, Surry, 1820) 82.
481. From a Roman period ritual box, Walters Art Museum, Baltimore, Maryland; public domain.
482. Photo by Daniel Noyes, 2013.
483. Photo by Daniel Noyes, 2013.
484. Photo by Daniel Noyes, 2013.
485. Albert Pike, *Morals and Dogma* (prepared for the Supreme Council of the Thirty-Third Degree for the Southern Jurisdiction of the United States: Charleston, 1871) 844.
486. Perseus Digital Library.
487. Franz Valery Marie Cumont, *Les Mystères de Mithra* (1902) 108.
488. Perseus Digital Library.

489. Ibid.
490. Nicholas Wade, "Origins of the Etruscans: Was Herodotus Right?" *New York Times*, (April 3, 2007).
491. Creative Commons Attribution-Share Alike 3.0 Unported. Altered from an image by Igor Skoglund, 23 November 2010.
492. Image: Work of U.S. government; public domain.
493. Perseus Digital Library.
494. Ibid.
495. Syed Nomanul Haq, *Names, Natures and Things* (P.O. Box 17, 3300 AA Dordrecht, the Netherlands: Kluwer Academic Publishers, 1994) 3; ISBN 978-0-7923-3254-1.
496. Isaac Newton. "Keynes MS. 28," *The Chemistry of Isaac Newton*, ed. William R. Newman (June 2010). http://purl.dlib.indiana.edu/iudl/newton/ALCH00017 (retrieved May 6, 2014).
497. Masonic Lodge of Education, http://www.masonic-lodge-of-education.com/point-within-a-circle.html (retrieved May 8, 2014).
498. Image by author.
499. Flynn, 153.
500. Flynn, 154.
501. Brannon Wheeler, *Prophets in the Quran: An Introduction to the Quran and Muslim Exegesis*, (Continuum International Publishing Group, 2002) 46.
502. Sayyid Ahmed website, http://ahmedamiruddin.wordpress.com/ (retrived May 7, 2014).
503. Image by author.
504. Narrated in Imam Ahmed's *Musnad* (18189), Imam Bukhari's *Tareekh Al Kabir* (1760), and Al Hakim's *Mustadrak* (8300).
505. Image by author.
506. Vasiliki Limberis, *Divine Heiress: The Virgin Mary and the Making of Christian Constantinople* (Routledge, 1994) 126–127.
507. Catholic Encyclopedia.
508. From the *Papyrus of Ani* from 1250 BC; public domain.
509. Lucian, *The Syrian Goddess*, trans. Herbert A. Strong and John Garstang (1913) 46–49.
510. "Demeter," Online Etymology Dictionary.
511. Perseus Digital Library.
512. *Odyssey*, 5.125; *Theogony*, 969 ff.
513. *Bibliotheca* 3.138, "Theogony," 969ff.; "Odyssey," 5.125ff.
514. "Dagon," *Gesenius' Hebrew-Chaldee Lexicon*.

515. I. P. Cory, *Ancient Fragments 1832* (Forgotten Books, December 28, 2007) 39. ISBN-10: 1605063770. I. P.
516. Ibid.
517. Image by author.
518. This Hebrew root word study can be duplicated using the Blue Letter Bible online.
519. From the *Holman Bible*, 1890; public domain.
520. Hesiod, *Theogony*, 543.
521. Ibid., 590–612.
522. Matrix compiled by author.